Debt, Innovations, and Deflation

This book is dedicated to all of the students whose lives have touched ours. Having you in the classes we taught has kept our spirits alive and minds engaged. Your thirst for knowledge has inspired us through the years.

Debt, Innovations, and Deflation

The Theories of Veblen, Fisher, Schumpeter, and Minsky

J. Patrick Raines

Dean, College of Business Administration, and Professor of Economics
Belmont University, USA

Charles G. Leathers

Professor of Economics
University of Alabama, USA

Edward Elgar
Cheltenham, UK • Northampton, MA, USA

Published by
Edward Elgar Publishing Limited
The Lypiatts
15 Lansdown Road
Cheltenham
Glos GL50 2JA
UK

Edward Elgar Publishing, Inc.
William Pratt House
9 Dewey Court
Northampton
Massachusetts 01060
USA

A catalogue record for this book
is available from the British Library

Library of Congress Control Number: 2008930895

ISBN 978 1 84542 785 6

Printed and bound in Great Britain by MPG Books Ltd, Bodmin, Cornwall

Contents

Preface

An appropriate title for this book might well have been *Deflation: Whence It Came, How It Went*. Japan had experienced mild deflation in the 1990s, but in late 2002 Federal Reserve officials acknowledged a concern that deflationary forces posed a potentially greater threat than inflation to economic growth in the U.S. At about the same time, the International Monetary Fund commissioned a task force to study the deflation risks internationally, with particular emphasis on the U.S., Japan, Germany, and China. The report of the task force, which included considerations of policy options, was released on the Internet in May 2003. After decades of a primary concern about inflation, the emergence of deflation as a policy issue was somewhat similar to scientists suddenly announcing after years of warning about global warming that a new ice age might possibly be looming.

Because the Federal Reserve officials were characteristically vague about the economic theories that guided their concepts and analyses of deflationary forces, we perceived a need for a critical re-examination of the theories of deflation that have appeared in the economic literature. Of particular interest was whether any of those theories suggest that post-World War II capitalist economies may have an inherent tendency toward deflation that had been held in check by institutional reforms and economic policies. If so, did the possibility of a new episode of deflation indicate that those reforms and policies had been rendered ineffective by institutional and technological developments, particularly financial deregulation, innovations in the real and financial sectors of the economy, and economic globalization? Or did the prospect of new deflation point to evolutionary structural changes that allowed deflationary forces to manifest in more complex ways in the modern capitalist economy?

While our research into the economic theories of deflation was well underway, current events took another curious change. In the spring of 2004, the Federal Reserve's perception of the current conditions had been revised. Approximately 18 months after the first official revelation that deflation was a concern for the U.S. economy, it disappeared from the Federal Reserve's economic radar screen. That development, which apparently transpired within only a few weeks in early 2004, only added interest into an examination of deflation theories. Could any of these theories explain how deflation could appear and disappear so quickly?

As we note in the chapters to follow, Thorstein Veblen, Irving Fisher, Joseph A. Schumpeter, and Hyman Minsky had theories of deflation that merit critical attention. Of particular importance are the evolutionary theories of Veblen, Schumpeter, and Minsky. Together the four theories explain how technological, organizational, and financial innovations combined with developments in business finance and the financial system related to the creation and use of debt give rise to conditions in which both deflation and inflation can be present in the modern economy. Hence, the title *Debt, Innovations, and Deflation* seemed most descriptive of what we do in this book.

1. Introduction

Even if deflation is not considered a significant near-term risk for the economy, the increasing discussion of it could be clearer in defining the circumstances. (Alan Greenspan in an address to the American Economic Association, January 1998)

[W]ith the global economy yet to fully emerge from the widespread slowdown that began in 2001, it is important to ask just how vulnerable the world is now to deflation. (International Monetary Fund Report, May 2003)

After a long period in which the desired direction for inflation was always downward, we are now in a situation in which risks to the inflation rate can be either upward, toward excessive inflation, or downward, toward too-low inflation or deflation. (Federal Reserve Governor Ben S. Bernanke, July 23, 2003)

[S]ince the (FOMC's) May 6 statement, the concept of deflation has commanded wide public attention for the first time in many decades. (Federal Reserve Governor Ben S. Bernanke, July 23, 2003)

[R]ecent data suggest that the worrisome trend of disinflation presumably has come to an end. (Alan Greenspan, April 21, 2004)

As the year 2002 was drawing to a close, Federal Reserve Board Chairman Alan Greenspan (2002f) and Governor Ben S. Bernanke (2002) publicly acknowledged that a fundamental shift had occurred in the Federal Reserve's assessment of the state of the U.S. economy. The new perception was that deflation posed a potentially greater risk to economic growth than did inflation. The Japanese economy had experienced mild deflation in the 1990s, and the International Monetary Fund (IMF) was concerned about global deflationary pressures in other Asian countries and in Germany. But for the first time since the Great Depression of the 1930s, *deflation* was being seriously treated as a monetary policy issue in the United States. The report of an IMF task force issued in May 2003 concluded that with the exception of Germany, the risks of deflation were low in the euro-area countries. But it also stated that sustained deflation in Germany could 'spill-over' in the other euro countries through the financial system (Kumar, et al. 2003, p. 16).

In the post-World War II period, episodes of macroeconomic weakness had manifested in recessions characterized by unemployment, reduced

Debt, Innovations, and Deflation

output, and sluggish growth. Rates of inflation sometimes fell but, except for a few months in 1948-1949, there was no deflation in the nominal price levels of goods and services. Chronically worried about inflation, monetary authorities were reluctant to ease the monetary strings when the economy was weakening, and they were usually quick to return to an anti-inflation stance when the economy appeared to be gaining strength. Ironically, Greenspan described the possibility of deflation as an unexpected development arising from the Federal Reserve's success in achieving and maintaining price stability in the 1990s, which was an abrupt reversal in Greenspan's take on the U.S. economy. Only three years earlier, he had initiated a 'pre-emptive strike' against perceived inflationary forces stemming from the 'wealth effects' of rising stock prices on aggregate demand in the booming 'new economy.' From June 1999 through May 2000, the Federal Open Market Committee (FOMC) increased the targeted federal funds rate five times, raising it from 4.75 to 6.5 percent, with the May 2000 increase being 50 basis points. Just seven months later, the FOMC sharply reversed course, lowering the federal funds rate twice in January 2001. (In a telephone conference meeting, the FOMC members voted to cut the rate a half-percentage point on January 3, then reduced it another half-percentage point at their regularly scheduled meeting on January 31.) The reductions continued until the fed funds rate was down to 1.75 percent by the end of 2001. In November 2002 the rate was reduced to 1.25 and in May 2003 it was set at a 40-year low of 1.0 percent.

In early 2001, Greenspan attributed the economic slowdown to a temporary problem of excess inventories and expressed guarded optimism for a strong and lasting recovery based on expectations of a strong resurgence of capital investment spending. But that optimism dwindled as the economy continued to weaken and stock prices continued to fall. By the fall of 2002, Federal Reserve policymakers had recognized that a set of economic factors had emerged, and were potentially gaining strength, that was making this different from the other post-World War II recessions. While insisting that there was only a remote possibility that deflationary forces would become a real threat, Greenspan and Bernanke repeatedly assured that the Federal Reserve was being vigilant in monitoring the situation and would promptly implement appropriate policies if the need should arise.

The acknowledgements that deflation was being treated seriously as a monetary policy issue provoked several lines of questions. The first had to do with the Federal Reserve's analyses of deflationary pressures. Conventional indicators of inflation had provided little support of a need for the 1999-2000 increases in the federal fund rate as a 'pre-emptive strike' against inflationary pressures. With the exception of falling prices in the stock market, those same indicators provided little real support for the possibility of a general deflation. Indeed, a number of 'inflation hawks' were warning that currently weak inflationary pressures might be re-ignited by the exceptionally low interest rates, especially in combination with the rapid shift from projected federal budget surpluses to large and growing deficits.

Some of the sustained deflationary periods in the past had followed periods of inflation that usually had occurred during wartime. The prime examples were in Britain after the Napoleonic War and in the U.S. after the Civil War. But the deflation of 1930-1932 came abruptly after a period of relative price stability for goods and services. Although a substantial inflation in stock prices had occurred that ended in a crash, the inflation during the Viet Nam war was followed not by deflation, but rather by 'stagflation' in the 1970s, as inflation accompanied recession and slow economic growth. Thus, the serious perception of the economy in 2002 as teetering between inflation and deflation was a new phenomenon. Had this been made possible by fundamental structural changes in the economy? Had new forces of deflation emerged that were different from those experienced in the 19th century and in the 1930s, more complex such that they co-mingled on almost equal terms with forces of inflation? Or is it possible that the Federal Reserve officials simply misread the economy? Were there really no deflationary forces of any consequence?

The second line of questions had to do with possible policy measures that monetary authorities could implement if deflation did occur. While monetary policies aimed at containing inflationary forces can drive interest rates upward, the nominal overnight interest rates that the Federal Reserve controls (the discount rate and the federal funds rate that banks pay to borrow reserves) could only be driven down to zero. If nominal interest rates should reach zero levels and prices continue to fall, real interest rates could become positive and rising, and real debt burdens could continue to increase as the monetary unit gains purchasing power. Questions about the ability of monetary policy to effectively counter deflationary pressures in the modern economy stemmed, in part, from the failure of monetary policy to prevent the deflation of the 1930s. Indeed, some economists, such as Milton Friedman, have assigned a substantial degree of blame for that deflation to the Federal Reserve's policies. At the January 2004 meeting of the American Economic Association, a session was devoted to the topic 'Policies to Deal with Deflation.' Although the references in the papers that were presented were to the Japanese deflation, the impetus for the session was clearly a concern about the possibility of deflation in the U.S. economy.

A convergence of the two lines of questions came in response to the FOMC's statement in December 2003 that 'The probability of an unwelcome fall in inflation has diminished in recent months and now

appears almost equal to that of a rise in inflation' (FOMC, 2003d). In April
2004, Greenspan told the U.S. Senate's Banking Committee that the Federal
Reserve no longer regarded threats of deflation as a monetary policy issue.
The cover of the June 19, 2004 issue of *The Economist* announced that
inflation had returned, worldwide. The general interpretation by Wall Street
and others in the financial sector was that the Federal Reserve was shifting
its focus back to containing the threat of inflation. Was it possible that there
were never any real deflationary tendencies? Had Greenspan, Bernanke,
and the FOMC erred in their analyses of the economy? If that was not the
case, had the deflationary forces grown weaker from natural causes? Had
the relative balance changed, with deflationary forces remaining present
while the forces of inflation gained strength? Or had the combination of
expansionary monetary policies that put the federal funds rate down to its
lowest level in 40 years and fiscal policy actions of tax cuts that turned
projected large budget surpluses into large deficits effectively countered the
deflationary forces?

STATEMENT OF PURPOSE

An understanding of what Greenspan (1998a) called the 'circumstance' of
deflation requires both empirical and theoretical approaches. Policy issues
about the actual direction of price trends, i.e., whether deflation or inflation
should be the concern, call for empirical analyses that accurately measure
what is happening. As Greenspan acknowledged, there have been questions
about the ability of indices to accurately measure price trends. The political
controversy over whether currently used indices, such as the popular
consumer price index, over-estimated the rate of inflation in the early
1990s, thus leading to excessive cost-of-living adjustments in entitlement
programs that are indexed, is a case in point.

But more fundamentally, the need is for theoretical analyses that explain
the nature and sources of deflationary pressures and identify policies that
will counter those pressures. In one of several Levy Institute Public Policy
Briefs on deflation, Wray and Papadimitriou (2003) noted that little was
being said about the causes of deflationary pressures in today's economy in
the statements about deflation by policymakers. Since the end of the Great
Depression of the 1930s, inflation has commanded the bulk of attention
from economists. The traditional quantity theory of money links the general
price level to the money supply, given the levels of national output and the
velocity of money. But in the economic literature, there are four theories of
deflation that differ substantially from the quantity theory. Those appear in
the writings of Thorstein Veblen, Irving Fisher, Joseph A. Schumpeter, and
Hyman Minsky. Our purpose in this book is a critical examination of the

four deflation theories and their relevance to deflation in modern capitalist economies.

With respect to the theories, we seek to answer essentially three questions. First, how are the nature and causes of deflation explained and how do those explanations relate to perceptions of the economic processes of the particular historical periods? In several cases, the authors of the theories later switched their focus to inflation in their interpretations of the institutional changes that had occurred. Second, to what extent do the theories involve common or complementary elements? Do differences reflect observations of different economic processes in different historical periods or do they stem from methodological differences between the economists involved or both? Are the differences complementary, making for a more robust theory of deflation, or are they contradictory, offering differing explanations of deflation? Third, and ultimately the most important, what analytical and policy insights do these theories provide, individually or collectively, into the concerns about deflation in 2002-2003?

The title of the book, *Debt, Innovations, and Deflation*, is indicative of the complexity of the major theories of deflation. In some form or other, developments in the financial sector and in the real economy through investment in new technologies are explained as interactive elements in the processes that give rise to deflationary tendencies. And, with Fisher's theory as the one prominent exception, the fundamental economic processes at work are evolutionary and dynamic in nature, generating both growth and fluctuations over time. Again, with that one exception, economic changes and financial instability are generated endogenously rather than being the consequence of external shocks in an economic system that works itself back to equilibrium.

Debt-Deflation

A prominent common element in the theories is that deflationary forces are closely linked to an accumulation of debt during periods of prosperity. As Dimand (1998) has noted, the modern theory of debt-deflation is most closely associated with Minsky, whose financial instability hypothesis is being expanded and applied by a growing number of talented economists. But debt also figured prominently in the three earlier deflation theories. Among those, that which Fisher presented in *Booms and Depressions* (1933a) and an article in *Econometrica* entitled 'The Debt-Deflation Theory of Great Depressions' (1933b) have received the most attention. For example, Dimand (1994) has provided analytical clarification of Fisher's theory and Wolfson (1996) has shown that modifications explain how debt-deflation was prevented after the 1987 stock market crash. In contrast, the debt-deflation theories in Veblen's *The Theory of Business Enterprise*

(1904) and in Schumpeter's *The Theory of Economic Development* (1934) and *Business Cycles* (1939) have received less attention.

In indirect fashion, Fisher and Schumpeter linked the three earlier theories. Fisher claimed that he had presented an original theory but acknowledged in the endnotes to his *Econometrica* article that Wesley Claire Mitchell had informed him that Veblen's theory had come 'nearest to the debt-deflation theory' (Fisher, 1933b, p. 350). In *Business Cycles*, Schumpeter discussed the phenomena that occur in the 'secondary wave' of a phase of prosperity in terms of Fisher's 'Debt-Deflation Theory.' But he emphasized that he was accepting only the account of what happens while criticizing Fisher for not understanding the underlying cause (1939, p. 146).

In describing his financial instability hypothesis as having both empirical and theoretical aspects, Minsky (1992) cited not only Keynes, but also Fisher and Schumpeter. The empirical aspect of the hypothesis was linked to Fisher's debt-deflation theory as 'the classic description of a debt deflation.' The word 'description' is important because, like Schumpeter, Minsky acknowledged acceptance of only Fisher's depiction of events. He explicitly stated that Fisher lacked a theoretical explanation of the financial crisis that precipitates a debt-deflation. On the theoretical side, the financial instability hypothesis rested on Minsky's interpretation of Keynes' *The General Theory*, but also drew from Schumpeter's treatment of money and finance. Minsky stated that the validity of his own 'prior positions on economic theory' had been reinforced by Schumpeter's analytical framework and vision of the process of economic development in which financial evolution through financial entrepreneurship plays a central role (Minsky, 1990, p. 51).

Curiously, Veblen never mentioned Schumpeter's theory of economic development, although he was obviously familiar with the works of the leading European economists on business cycles of that period. Nor did Schumpeter ever acknowledge Veblen's analyses of financial crises, deflation, and chronic depression. Even more curious is that Minsky, who was recognized as providing an important link between Post Keynesians and institutionalism (see Papadimitriou and Wray, 1998), never acknowledged Veblen's earlier work. Mehrling (1999, p. 129) stated that, from a historical perspective, Minsky's work 'represents a continuation of the American institutionalist tradition of monetary thought'. Published comparisons of Veblen's and Keynes' theories of business cycles (e.g., Brockie, 1958) seemingly would have drawn Minsky's attention to Veblen. The relationship between Veblen's theory of financial crises and Minsky's financial instability hypothesis has been the subject of several insightful papers (Dimand, 2004, in particular; see also Kelso and Duman, 1992).

Technological and Financial Innovations

Fisher's (1933b) succinct presentation of his 'debt-deflation theory of great depressions' in the *Econometrica* article might give the impression that deflation theories primarily focus on the changes in nominal and real debt burdens that occur during periods of prosperity and the subsequent periods of deflation. The extent of cause and effect may appear to be in the role of nominal debt loads contributing to a speculative prosperity and how deflation turns manageable nominal debts into unbearable real debt burdens that reinforce the deflationary pressures. But Fisher dealt with a relatively static institutional structure in which, on rare occasions, abnormal developments manifest to knock the economy far off its normal pendulum movement to an unstable equilibrium. In contrast, the theories of debt-deflation developed by Veblen, Schumpeter, and Minsky gave special attention to technological and financial innovations that produce evolutionary institutional changes in the real economy and in the financial system.

Both Veblen and Schumpeter explained the debt-deflation phenomena within the context of their unique theories of the dynamics of evolutionary structural change in which technological progress plays a key role. Veblen's analysis of the deflationary tendencies was an integral part of a general theory of chronic depression that results from the combination of cost-reducing advances in industrial technology and the nature of capital and corporate finance in the modern business enterprise system. Schumpeter's debt-deflation theory was part of his general theory of business cycles and economic development driven by clusters of innovations financed by credit created by bankers. Minsky's financial instability hypothesis, in which debt-deflation either occurs or is countered by policies, stresses the importance of evolutionary changes in the financial environment that result from financial innovations in the private sector and policies implemented by government. Indeed, the role of government, expressed in terms of 'small government' economies versus 'large government' economies, is an important factor governing the tendency for financial instability to have large or small consequences.

Prices

Deflation is generally defined as a period of falling prices just as inflation is generally defined as a period of rising prices. But in a highly complex economy, there are different sets of prices, e.g., prices of consumer goods and services, producers' prices, commodity prices, and prices of financial assets. Inflation is usually thought of as rising consumer prices or prices of output in general, while rising stock prices are treated as either based on rational expectations of increasing corporate profits or irrationally-driven by speculative trading. Of particular interest is the attention given to the relationship between stock prices, prices of capital goods, and prices of consumer goods and services in several of the deflation theories. A critical point of interest is the manner in which the different theories explain the relationship between falling prices in the real economy (goods and services) and falling prices in the financial sectors.

From Deflation to Inflation

Three of the theories have particular relevance to the curious shift in the Federal Reserve's concern about inflation to deflation in 2002-2003 and back to inflation in 2004. In 1904, Veblen presented his debt-deflation/chronic depression thesis in *The Theory of Business Enterprise*. But in 1923 that was replaced with a credit-inflation thesis in *Absentee Ownership*. Similarly, a build-up of unproductive debt followed by deflation was an integral part of Schumpeter's theory of economic development and business cycles in 1912 and 1939. But in *Capitalism, Socialism, and Democracy*, first published in 1950, and in several articles published in the 1940s, Schumpeter focused on inflation rather than deflation. While there is an inherent tendency for debt-deflation to occur in Minsky's financial instability hypothesis, his evolutionary institutional analyses explained how monetary and fiscal policy actions have countered that tendency but, in the process, have produced tendencies toward inflation.

OVERVIEW OF CHAPTERS

In the first part of Chapter 2, 'How Deflation Became a Monetary Policy Issue,' we review the predominant focus of policymakers on inflation from 1940 through 2000. The rest of the chapter develops a rather detailed chronological review of how deflation had become a monetary policy issue in 2002. As early as 1998, Greenspan was speaking about deflation in the manner of an academic exercise. From 1998 through 2002, expressions of concern about deflation on a worldwide basis came from meetings of economists and the financial publications. The chapter ends with a comparative summary of the major points in the Federal Reserve officials' statements in 2002-2004 related to their perceptions of the nature, causes, and consequences of deflation; what was indicated about the role of innovations and debt; policies that might be implemented to prevent or ameliorate deflationary forces; and how they explained the disappearance of deflation as a policy concern so soon after it appeared.

In Chapter 3, 'Monetary Theories of Deflation,' we briefly review the explanations of deflation provided by the traditional classical/neo-classical quantity theory of money for the purpose of separating the traditional theory from Veblen's, Fisher's, Schumpeter's, and Minsky's theories. That is particularly important in the case of Fisher's debt-deflation theory of great depressions, since he was so closely connected to the modern quantity theory. In addition, we briefly review the monetary theories of business cycles. This is appropriate because, at times, several of the deflation theories might appear to be simply another version of the monetary theories of business cycles and price trends.

In Chapter 4, 'Debt, Innovations, and Deflation in Veblen's Theory of Business Enterprise,' we examine Veblen's theory of deflation and chronic depression that was presented in *The Theory of Business Enterprise* (1904) and also his replacement of deflation/chronic depression with 'habitual credit-inflation' in *Absentee Ownership* (1923). In each case, we begin with a review of the historical setting. *The Theory of Business Enterprise* was written against the backdrop of the long period of deflation and recurring depression between 1867 and the 1890s. In writing *Absentee Ownership*, Veblen was interpreting developments in the period between 1904 and 1923 during which the Panic of 1907 had led to the establishment of the Federal Reserve System and the U.S. experienced the economic and financial changes associated with its participation in World War I and the immediate aftermath.

In Chapter 5, 'Fisher's Debt-Deflation Theory of Great Depressions,' we examine Fisher's debt-deflation theory of great depressions which tried to explain the aftermath of the 1929 stock market crash and the crises of the early 1930s. In reviewing the historical setting of the boom period of the 1920s, the stock market crash of 1929, and the deepening depression of the early 1930s, we note that developments from the mid-1920s onward appeared to invalidate Veblen's 1923 credit-inflation thesis and re-validate his 1904 debt-deflation theory. Our review of Fisher's debt-deflation theory begins with his attempt to explain the 1929 stock market crash in his book *The Stock Market Crash – And After*, written in December 1929 and published in early 1930. There he attributed the crash to stock market excesses funded by excessive reliance on brokers' debt. We then examine Fisher's 'debt-deflation theory of great depressions' as it was presented in the book *Booms and Depressions* (1933a) and in the *Econometrica* (1933b) article, and how that theory differed from his earlier writings on cyclical fluctuations. The chapter concludes with selective review of recent interpretations and modifications of Fisher's debt-deflation theory.

In Chapter 6, 'Innovations, Debt, and Deflation in Schumpeter's Theory of Business Cycles,' we examine deflation as an integral part of Schumpeter's theory of economic development and business cycles driven by successful technological and organizational innovations. That theory was introduced in *The Theory of Economic Development* in 1912, and was reiterated and somewhat expanded in Volume I of *Business Cycles* (1939). The relationship between innovations, debt, and prices was further developed within the context of his historical analyses of business cycles in *Business Cycles*. Particularly revealing are his analyses of the role of debt in the prosperity of the 1920s and the depression through 1937, and his interpretations of the policy-induced institutional changes in the 1930s. Attention is paid to how his theory of deflation stands in relation to Veblen's and Fisher's theories.

As did Veblen, Schumpeter subsequently turned his attention to conditions that he interpreted as inducing inflation in his book, *Capitalism, Socialism, and Democracy*, first published in 1942, and in various articles and papers published in the 1940s. As a prelude to our examination of that analysis, we review the historical context, which focuses attention on evolutionary institutional changes that Schumpeter perceived within the capitalist system, particularly the institutional and policy changes associated with the New Deal of the 1930s and the early post-World War II era.

In Chapter 7, 'Minsky's Financial Instability Hypothesis and Debt-Deflation,' we move forward to the post-World War II era through the mid-1990s, in which the economic and financial system was shaped by the institutional and policy reforms of the 1930s as well as by continuing innovations in both the real economy and the financial sector. Unlike the periods observed first-hand by Veblen, Fisher, and Schumpeter, a serious deflation never occurred in the post-World War II period and was never even considered to be a remote possibility. (Perhaps the one exception was during the mild deflation in 1948-1949 when the memory of the 1930s was still very fresh.) Rather, inflation intermittently contained by recession was the primary concern of policymakers.

Minsky's financial instability hypothesis and his analyses of the institutional and policy changes since the 1930s explained why there is an inherent tendency for the modern capitalist economy to experience financial crises that lead into debt-deflation. Equally important, or perhaps even more so, his analyses of the institutional and policy changes since the 1930s explained that financial crises and debt-deflation, such as described by Fisher, did not occur in the post-World War II era largely because of the role of 'big government.' But together, Minsky's financial instability hypothesis and his analyses explain that the successful use of monetary and fiscal policy to prevent major financial crises and debt-deflation produced a chronic tendency toward inflation and financial instability on the upside.

In Chapter 8, 'Deflation Theories and the Recent Deflation Concerns,' we begin by developing a comparative summation of the four theories that identifies the common elements and differences. Some of the differences reflect the different institutional situations in the different historical periods in which the theories were developed. While certain aspects of their theories dealt with institutional situations that have changed, the fundamental elements continue to be relevant. That is particularly the case for Veblen's and Schumpeter's evolutionary theories, and Minsky's concepts of 'small government' economies and 'large government' economies account for much of the differences on that basis. Of special interest are the differences in the theories that reflect different methodological approaches and personal normative values. Again, that is particularly the case for Veblen and Schumpeter. But we find the key differences to be, on the whole, rather complementary, such that the four theories provide the basis for an informal general model that explains the possibility of both deflationary forces and inflationary forces existing simultaneously in modern complex economies.

In the rest of the chapter, we consider the insights the four theories provide into the recent concerns about deflation, starting with a recognition that developments in 2002-2003 can be explained largely as a phase in the Schumpeterian business cycle of the 'new economy' that began in the 1990s. On the one hand, the insights do provide theoretical clarity of some of the Federal Reserve officials' assessments of the potential for deflation forces to become a threat in 2002-2003. But the more penetrating analyses by Schumpeter, Veblen, and Minsky reveal just how limited those assessments were in theoretical depth and scope. The ultimate conclusion is that the threat of deflation, in terms of a trend of falling output prices, was never as great as seemed to be suggested but the threat of a financial breakdown was genuine and could be avoided only by policies that continued to support a massive debt structure.

2. How Deflation Became a Monetary Policy Issue

Except for a brief interval in 1948-1949, when memories of the Great Depression were still fresh, the U.S. economy had not experienced an episode of deflation since the 1930s. For six decades, from 1940 through 2001, the Federal Reserve regarded inflation as the primary threat to the economy, with a secondary concern for unemployment and sluggish growth. For five decades, dating from the Accord of 1951 which freed the Federal Reserve from the subordinated role of supporting the U.S. Treasury's management of the public debt, the monetary authorities maintained vigilance against the forces of inflation. Even when price indices fell in 1948-1949, evoking fears of a return to the 1930s in the public's mind, the Federal Reserve was focused on inflation, using its selective credit control powers to raise the minimal down payment on consumer installment loans.

At times, the Federal Reserve's anti-inflation monetary policies were viewed as being unnecessary or excessive. Vice-President Richard Nixon blamed his defeat in the 1960 Presidential election and President George Bush blamed his failure to win re-election in 1992 on sluggish economic conditions caused by overly tight monetary policies. During the 1970s, some critics argued that the monetary authorities had misinterpreted the nature of the inflation. A restrictive monetary policy is appropriate to counter inflation if it is due to excess demand. But a supply-side inflation caused by rising energy costs and the exercise of pricing power by large corporations in oligopolistic markets would only be intensified by higher interest costs under a tighter monetary policy. 'Stagflation' occurs as the economy experiences a recession while inflation persists. At the same time, so-called 'inflation hawks' argued that the monetary policies were insufficiently and inconsistently anti-inflation in nature, and in some cases contributed to inflationary expectations. At various times throughout the post-World War II era, monetary policymakers did implement expansionary policies to cope with recession. But their concern was with rising unemployment, falling national output, and slow economic growth, not with falling prices.

A chronological account of how deflation suddenly emerged to rival inflation as a monetary policy issue in 2002 is the subject of this chapter. We begin with a brief review of the experience with inflation during World War II and the wartime policies that were implemented to contain inflationary forces. That is followed by a quick review of the post-World War II policies through the 1990s. With that backdrop in place, we then critically examine the expressions of concerns about deflationary forces by Federal Reserve officials and others that began as early as 1998. The chapter concludes with a topical summary of the Federal Reserve officials' perceptions on the nature, causes, and consequences of the deflationary forces and the types of monetary policy actions that they proposed to implement if deflation should occur.

CONTROLLING WORLD WAR II INFLATION

With the coming of World War II, the U.S. economy experienced an abrupt transition from the lingering depression of the 1930s to severe inflationary conditions created by the combination of a shrinking aggregate supply of civilian goods and greatly increased aggregate demand made possible huge increases in government spending and conditions of full employment that generated higher incomes. Even as the total national output was greatly increased, the production of civilian goods was drastically reduced as economic resources were diverted to meeting the military needs of waging wars on two major fronts — against Germany in Europe and against Japan in the Pacific. Even before the Japanese attacked Pearl Harbor and Germany declared war on the U.S. in December 1941, Congress and President Roosevelt had begun preparing for a wartime economy. Planning for the mobilization of resources for military needs began in 1940 with the establishment of the Office for Emergency Management, the revival of the Advisory Commission to the Council of National Defense. Preparation for meeting military manpower needs on a broad basis began in September 1940 with the Selective Service Act. In 1941, the Office of Production Management was established and the Office of Emergency Management essentially became a holding company charged with the responsibility of creating new defense or war agencies as the need arose. That was followed by creation of the Supplies, Priorities, and Allocation Board, empowered to determine the necessary production requirements and establish policies or programs to meet those needs.

Once the U.S. was attacked and war began against both Japan and Germany, numerous new governmental agencies were created to quickly achieve full mobilization of available manpower and resources to support the defense program and sustain the civilian population during the duration of the war. The Reconstruction Finance Corporation, established in 1932 under the Hoover Administration to provide emergency loans to banks, insurance companies, and railroads, essentially became the source of capital for both war-related business investments and government enterprises.

The U.S. economy still had unemployed labor and excess industrial capacity in 1941. But the wartime demands for manpower and materials far exceeded what could be produced simply by absorbing the unemployed workers and industrial plants without reducing outputs of civilian goods. At the same time, aggregate demand was greatly increased by deficit financing of huge government expenditures and by the needs of businesses to invest in new capital equipment to meet government orders. The substantial rise in household incomes as the civilian labor force became fully employed would have resulted in an increase in aggregate consumption spending if not held in check. Attempts to contain the inflationary pressures included increases in income tax rates to reduce disposable incomes of consumers and firms and the imposition of general price and wage controls. Monetary policy could not restrain growth in the money supply and raise interest rates to curb aggregate demand because the Federal Reserve was subordinated to the U.S. Treasury's need to float huge loans and to keep the interest cost on the rapidly growing debt as low as possible. The discount rate was kept at 1 percent throughout the war and patriotic purchases of government bonds helped to postpone consumption spending out of after-tax incomes. The savings rate rose from 4.1 percent of income in 1939 to 16.7 percent in 1945 (Galbraith 1994, p. 119).

In May 1940, President Roosevelt established a Price Stabilization Division of the National Defense Advisory Council, with compliance being voluntary. The Office of Price Administration (OPA), established in April 1941, was given the power to make its price guidelines mandatory after the attack on Pearl Harbor. John Kenneth Galbraith was put in charge and remained in that post until forced out by political pressure during the summer of 1943. In April 1942, OPA issued general price regulations, freezing prices at their highest level in the previous month. A year later, President Roosevelt issued an order that stopped any further price increases. A full-fledged set of wage and price controls, combined with rationing, were imposed and in effect until Japan surrendered in August 1945. From that date until June 1946 the controls were reduced. After the controls were lifted in June 1946, complaints about rising prices led to the imposition of selective price controls which were removed in October 1946.

The overall effectiveness of price and wage controls during World War II remains an issue of some controversy. Galbraith described the controls as being 'economically successful, popular with the public but, in their administration, politically offensive' (1994, p. 118). The retail price index rose by only about 30 percent between 1939 and 1945 due to the price controls. But Galbraith also noted that while the controls were designed for, and largely accomplished, a prevention of 'the social discomforts and discontents of inflation,' they had an additional and perhaps more important effect. Corporate profits could not be increased by raising prices. The recourse was to expand production as demand increased (p. 117).

POST-WAR 'PENT-UP DEMAND' INFLATION GIVES WAY TO MILD DEFLATION

When controls were lifted in 1946, prices surged upward in what has been called an episode of 'pent-up demand' inflation. From June to December 1946, consumer prices rose 15 percent and wholesale prices rose 25 percent (Williams 1994, p. 251). The spending of savings accumulated during wartime and back-pay of military personnel, combined with the conversion of industrial processes from production of military goods to civilian goods and housing, resulted in aggregate demand temporarily exceeding aggregate supply. According to one view, a 'wage-price spiral' form of inflation that lasted through the 1950s began with the repeal of the wartime excess-profits tax in late 1945. Labor unions had agreed not to strike or raise wages during the war if corporate profits would be limited by an excess profits tax. While workers were facing lower incomes with the elimination of overtime work in many industries, after-tax corporate profits were expected to rise with the repeal of that tax. Labor unions responded by staging a number of strikes for higher wages in the winter of 1945-1946 (Williams 1994, pp. 248-249).

Fiscal policy was decidedly anti-inflationary as federal spending fell from $93 billion in 1945 to $30 billion in 1948, and the budget went from deficit to surplus (with the surplus being used to pay down the public debt). While the subordination of monetary policy to the Treasury's debt management prevented the Federal Reserve from raising interest rates, limited selective credit controls could be exercised. In early 1948, regulation of consumer credit was temporarily reinstated. It allowed the Federal Reserve to set the minimum down-payment on auto loans at 33 percent. While not specifically intended to counter inflation, the Federal Reserve raised the margin requirement on stocks to 100 percent in early 1946 but then lowered it to 75 percent in 1947 and, ultimately, to 50 percent in 1949.

By 1948, the pool of savings that had fueled the pent-up demand had largely been spent, and, with the economy being fully converted back to the production of civilian goods, aggregate supply had more than caught up with aggregate demand. In 1948-1949, the economy entered its first post-war recession and deflation briefly replaced inflation. By the end of 1949, whole prices were down 11 percent from the peaks in August 1948, and the cost of living had fallen by 5 percent. Although the general public and some political leaders feared a return to the 1930s, economists generally continued to focus on inflation. (An exception was Kenneth Boulding, who was one of ten leading economists participating in a symposium on inflation in late 1947. While the other nine focused on various aspects of the current inflation, Boulding (1948) argued that a 'sharp deflation' was likely to follow the current inflation. He proposed the novel approach of re-imposing wage-price controls to force nominal prices and wages overall to fall as fast as the either the money supply or the velocity of money.)

THE KOREAN WAR INFLATION: 1950-1952

The recession and deflation were short-lived. A rise in exports, stemming from the Marshall Plan to rebuild Europe, and a budget deficit, resulting from tax cuts that Congress enacted over President Truman's veto, stimulated the economy. With the Cold War intensifying and the Korean War beginning in summer of 1950, federal military spending rose. The public initially reacted to the war by increasing purchases of consumer durable goods, fearing a return of the shortages and rationing of World War II. The result was a sharp increase in the inflation rate, with the cost of living rising between May 1950 and March 1951 by 8 percent and wholesale prices by 19 percent (Williams 1994, p. 272).

That brought to a head the Federal Reserve's concern that the subordination of monetary policy to the Treasury's management of the public debt had made the Federal Reserve the engine of inflation. The monetary authorities wanted to abandon the bond-pegging program in order to combat inflation with a tighter monetary policy. With the Accord of 1951, the Federal Reserve gained the independence to raise or lower the discount rate and required reserve ratio, and to sell or buy Treasury securities in the open market based on its own reading of economic conditions and trends. While emergency selective credit control powers over consumer and real estate credit were reinstated during the Korean War, they were lightly used and were suspended in 1952.

During the 1950s, the Eisenhower administration generally worried about recession and unemployment while the Federal Reserve focused more on inflation. The Korean War inflation subsided in 1953, but Eisenhower's Chairman of the Council of Economic Advisors, Arthur Burns, expressed concern that an excessively tight monetary policy was weakening the economy. After shifting to an easier policy, the Federal Reserve tightened again when prices and wages began rising in 1955, a move which critics charged made the recession of 1957 more severe than the 1953-1954 recession. Monetary policy was eased in late 1957 and early 1958 but was tightened again when the economy began to recover in 1959, which critics charged resulted in the recession in 1960. As we noted earlier, Nixon believed that the Federal Reserve's policies were largely responsible for his defeat in the Presidential election.

VIET NAM WAR INFLATION

While inflation was not a major problem during the brief Kennedy administration, the perception that inflation was of the 'wage-spiral' variety resulted in the implementation of voluntary wage-price guidelines. Prices remained relatively stable in 1964-1965 as tax cuts fueled a substantial economic expansion. But inflation surged again in 1966 with the expansion of the Viet Nam war, rising from a rate of 1.9 percent in 1965 to 6.1 percent in 1969. Significantly, this was the last inflation that could objectively be viewed as caused by excess demand. The economy was as close to full employment as could be realistically expected and the increase in aggregate demand from government expenditures for the war was not offset by higher taxes or reductions in other federal expenditures. In 1966, the Federal Reserve tightened monetary policy but some sectors of the economy were affected more than others in a 'monetary crunch.' In 1968 and 1969, a combination of restrictive monetary and fiscal policy failed to contain the inflationary pressures. Higher interest rates contributed to, rather than checked, higher rates of inflation.

WAGE-PRICE CONTROLS AND 'SUPPLY-SIDE' INFLATION IN THE 1970S

In 1970 the economy went into recession and the Fed eased monetary policy. But, as inflation continued, the Nixon administration moved to the view that it was of the cost-push variety and, in 1971, imposed a temporary wage-price freeze that was followed by a system of price controls. While the controls held inflation in check, monetary and fiscal policies became more expansionary. But the price controls were ended in spring of 1973, in response to gasoline shortages at the regulated price. The inflation rate, which was held to 3.4 percent in 1972, rose to 8.8 percent in 1973, to 12.2 percent in 1974, and to 14 percent in 1975. While inflation surged, the economy went into a recession that did not bottom out until early 1975. While the immediate cause of the 'stagflation' was, in large part, the shocks of OPEC oil price increases, proponents of the monetarist doctrine put much of the blame on the Federal Reserve allowing the money supply to grow too rapidly in 1970-1973.

As the rate of inflation began to accelerate, the voluntary wage-price guidelines implemented by the Carter administration proved to be ineffective. Inflationary expectations became incorporated in nominal interest rates and depository financial institutions with interest-rate sensitive assets suffered growing losses. In 1979 Paul Volcker was appointed Chairman of the Federal Reserve Board. Until 1982, he pursued a monetarist-oriented policy of restricting the growth rate in the money supply. The result was extremely high interest rates, a collapse of bond prices in 1980, and recession that lasted until the end of 1982. Despite large federal budget deficits resulting from increased government spending and substantial reductions in income tax rates (Reagan's 'supply-side economics' policies), the rate of inflation fell from 13.5 percent in 1980 to 3.5 percent in 1983 and averaged 3.6 percent through the rest of the 1980s. The weakening of inflation was largely due to the 'rolling recessions' that marked the Reagan years and an expansion in cheaper imports as the U.S. began to run up large trade deficits (Williams 1994, p. 447).

GREENSPAN'S 'PRE-EMPTIVE STRIKES' AGAINST INCIPIENT INFLATION

When Greenspan was appointed as Chairman of the Federal Reserve in August 1987, he was expected to continue Volker's emphasis on anti-inflation monetary policies. Greenspan acted quickly to establish his credentials as an inflation-fighter by raising the discount rate by ½ percentage point in September. He has recently attributed that action to a perception that inflationary pressures had begun building due, in part, to the rapidly rising stock prices (Greenspan, 2004a). The Federal Reserve responded to the October 1987 stock market crash 'with an immediate and massive injection of liquidity to help stabilize highly volatile financial markets' (ibid.). Once the stock market crisis had past, Greenspan resumed a policy of 'preemptive tightening' in early 1989, but reversed course in the summer of 1989 as the economy weakened.

Greenspan credited his 'preemptive policies' for the mild 1990 recession. But the economic recovery remained weak and the banks were constricting credit in response to major losses on real estate and foreign loans. The Federal Reserve responded by reducing the federal fund and discount rates to their lowest level since 1962, which enabled banks to restore their profitability by borrowing reserves at a discount rate of 3.0 percent and investing in Treasury notes that paid 6.0 percent. In 1994, a perception of increasing inflationary pressures led to another round of 'preemptive strikes' which raised the federal funds rate by 300 basis points over a twelve month period. Greenspan (2004a) credited that action with achieving a 'soft landing' for the economy in 1995, which 'set up two powerful expectations that were to influence developments over the subsequent decade.' The first expectation was that the Federal Reserve could control inflation over the business cycle with rate changes, thus making price stability an achievable objective. The second was that contained inflation would reduce the economic volatility so that the swings in the past would not be part of the 'New Economy.'

MONETARY POLICY AND THE 'NEW ECONOMY'

In the latter half of the decade, there was increasing speculation that a 'new economy' was emerging in which innovations in information technology would allow a much faster rate of growth and a much lower rate of unemployment without igniting inflation. While the 'new classical' macro-economists viewed the 'non-accelerating inflation rate of unemployment' as around 5 percent, Greenspan began suggesting that it had been reduced to the neighborhood of 4 percent because labor productivity had been increased while wages remain relatively constant, thus keeping costs stable or declining. In his speeches and testimonies, Greenspan repeatedly cited Schumpeter's concept of the 'creative destruction' effects of innovations and argued that both technological and financial innovations, such as financial derivatives, together with financial deregulation and globalization had produced a dynamic and flexible new economy in which expectations of future profits assured a sustainable strong stream of investment spending and justified the higher stock prices (for a more detailed discussion, see Leathers and Raines, 2004).

In 1998, Greenspan reversed his earlier concern about 'irrational exuberance' in the stock market and suggested rising stock prices were playing a positive role in a 'virtuous cycle.' Future profits were being increased by cost-reducing investments in information technologies. The higher future profits were being capitalized in higher stock prices which, in turn, stimulated aggregate demand through the wealth effect on consumption spending and the lower cost of capital on the level of investment spending. Other than the possibility of negative impacts from the Asian financial crisis, the only threat to this 'virtuous cycle' was that inflationary pressures could be unleashed if wages should suddenly increase. While the forecast indicated a slower rate of economic growth, the Federal Reserve would remain vigilant against inflation caused by rising wages and rising aggregate demand from the wealth effect of the boom in stock prices on consumption spending (Greenspan, 1998b).

The Final 'Pre-emptive Strikes' in 1999-2000

Against the fear that the East Asian financial crisis in 1997 might spread to the U.S., the federal funds rate was held constant despite the Federal Reserve moving to a higher alert against inflation. When the Russian financial crisis in 1998 resulted in the collapse of the Long Term Capital Management Hedge Fund, the fed funds rate was cut three times in less than three months. In 1999, however, Greenspan believed that the wealth effect on consumption from booming stock prices was threatening to cause aggregate demand to grow faster than the aggregate supply. To check that potential surge in aggregate demand, the FOMC initiated a series of federal funds rate increases that raised it from 4.75 percent in June 1999 to 6.5 percent in May 2000.

THE EMERGENCE OF DEFLATIONARY CONCERNS

A sharp reversal in monetary policy was initiated in January 2001. Greenspan had been optimistically forecasting a continuation of strong capital investment spending in new information technologies for years to come. (His forecasts were based in large part of the reports of the top 1000 securities analysts who were supposed to be well informed about the investment plans of the corporations they monitored. Subsequent events revealed that many of those analysts were fraudulent in their reporting.) But, during 2000, capital investment spending declined substantially and stock prices began to fall. Belatedly recognizing the growing weakness of the economy, Greenspan reduced the federal funds rate to 6.0 percent in an unscheduled meeting of members of the FOMC in early January 2001. At its scheduled meeting several weeks later, the FOMC reduced the federal funds rate to 5½ percent. As the economy continued to weaken, the rate reductions continued. In November 2002, the federal funds rate was reduced to 1¼ percent and Federal Reserve officials began publicly acknowledging that deflation had become a monetary policy issue.

Indications that Federal Reserve officials were beginning to worry about developing deflationary forces were actually given months before the federal funds rate hikes were initiated in 1999 as a 'pre-emptive strike' against inflation. In a talk delivered in January 1998 to the annual meeting of the American Economics Association, Greenspan raised the issue of deflation under the topical heading of 'Problems of Price Measurement.' He began by stating that in the new environment of low inflation a new set of issues were emerging on the policy agenda because of the mounting importance of having a deeper understanding of the economic characteristics of sustained price stability. The issue at hand was the critical need for central bankers to have accurate measures of prices.

> For most purposes, biases of a few tenths in annual inflation rates do not matter when inflation is high. They do matter when, as now, inflation has become so low that the policymakers need to consider at what point effective price stability has been reached. Indeed, some observers have begun to question whether deflation is now a possibility, and to assess the potential difficulties such a development might pose for the economy. (Greenspan, 1998a)

Given that deflation was now being discussed, Greenspan posed three questions. What does deflation mean? What are the economic effects? Was deflation a real possibility for the U.S. economy? With respect to the latter, Greenspan stated that: 'Even if deflation is not considered a significant near-term risk for the economy, the increasing discussion of it could be clearer in defining the circumstances' (1998a).

The complexity and ambiguity of the meaning of 'deflation' was recognized, as the term was used 'to describe several different states that are not necessarily depicting similar economic conditions' (ibid.). But, with stock prices soaring in 1997, Greenspan was concerned about the possibility of 'an ongoing fall in the prices of existing assets' (ibid.). Deflation in stock prices could affect the real economy through reduced consumption and investment spending and also possibly by negatively affecting financial intermediaries. He argued that the economy can usually withstand slowly deflating stock prices but historical experiences show that rapid declines in stock prices tend to result in serious economic disruptions. The severe economic contraction of the early 1930s and the associated persistent declines in product prices would probably not have happened if the stock market had not crashed in 1929. Greenspan only briefly commented on deflation of prices of goods and services. While stock prices can fall for a variety of reasons, persistent deflation in the prices of currently produced goods is necessarily rooted in changes in monetary conditions that lead to a flight from goods to money.

Like inflation, even moderate rates of deflation can hamper the economy by leading to a state of fear and uncertainty that results in significant increases in risk premiums and contraction of economic activity. But Greenspan noted that deflation presented special problems for monetary policymakers. Nominal interest rates can only be decreased to zero but real interest rates can increase as prices continue to fall. If nominal wages are sticky, deflation can result in increases in real wages that lead to higher unemployment levels. Consistent with his optimistic statements about the 'new economy,' however, Greenspan suggested that increases in real interest rates and real wages might be countered if rapid productivity growth ensures high rates of return on investment. In his words:

If such high-tech, high-productivity-growth firms produce an increasing share of output in the decades ahead, then, one could readily imagine the economy experiencing an overall product price deflation in which the problems associated with a zero constraint on nominal interest rates or nominal wage changes would seldom be binding. (Greenspan, 1998a)

International Concerns About Deflation

Greenspan concluded that speech by returning to the issue of the importance of more exact measurement to the pursuit of the goal of price stability and would say no more about deflation until December 2002. But deflation on an international basis became a topic of growing interest for financial journalists, macroeconomists, and central bankers after the East Asia financial crises in 1997. In early November 1997, *Business Week* had a special report on 'The Threat of Deflation.' The authors, Mandel and Engardio (1997), reported that consumption was lagging behind the growth in productive capacity throughout the world and the excess capacity would probably grow worse as the Asian economies tried to cope with their financial difficulties by exporting more. The global economy might be headed for 'an era of deflation' as prices were either falling or stagnant around the world. The prospect of 'devastating deflation' would be increased if economic growth in the U.S. economy were to weaken.

The growing concern about deflation in the international business and financial press was revealed in a series of articles in *The Economist*. In November 1997, under the title 'Deflation and all that,' readers were informed that 'some economists' were becoming concerned that the worldwide capacity to produce had grown to extent that excess supply, combined with the economic problems of East Asia, threatened to unleash downward pressures on prices which would depress profits and force many firms into bankruptcy. But *The Economist* regarded those fears as being exaggerated, noting that prices were falling in some sectors but rising in other sectors. Monetary policy, not excess capacity or East Asian countries dumping products on the world markets, determines whether inflation or deflation will occur. Lower interest rates could take care of any problems with deficiency in aggregate demand. But rate reductions were not needed since aggregate demand and the money supply in the U.S. were far from contributing to deflationary tendencies. Inflation, not deflation, was still more likely to occur.

In October 1998, under the title 'Singing the deflationary blues,' *The Economist* reported on a growing and widening concern about deflation, but noted that what many seemed to be calling deflation (falling general price levels) was actually recession, which is quite different and with different consequences. Two forms of deflation were identified, one of which was harmless. 'Technological deflation' occurs when productivity gains are passed on to the consumers in the form of lower prices based on lower costs. Profit margins and real incomes can increase substantially, as illustrated by the real growth rate of 4.3 percent in the latter part of the 19th century when wholesale prices fell by approximately one-half. The dangerous form of deflation, 'monetary deflation,' was caused by contracting money supply. But there was little likelihood of that happening as the money supply in the G7 nations was increasing at the fastest rate since 1991. Even in Japan, which was 'certainly teetering on the brink of deflation,' *The Economist* (1998, p. 78) asserted that real deflation had not occurred. The article ended with the statement that 'in a modern economy, it is quite difficult to create deflation.'

In February 1999, *The Economist* addressed deflation in an article entitled 'Could it happen again?' Changes in the sub-headings of the 1997, 1998, and 1999 articles revealed a growing acceptance of the possibility of deflation. The sub-heading of the 1997 article assured readers that fears of deflation were exaggerated. The sub-heading of the 1998 article stated that for good reasons deflation rarely occurs but left out any assurance that such a rare event was unlikely. The sub-heading of the 1999 article stated that deflation could pose a greater danger than inflation in most of the world. *The Economist* now accepted as being 'conceivable' that a deflation of falling consumer prices could occur on a global basis. Again, a distinction was made between the 'friendlier form' of lower prices due to cost-reducing productivity gains and the type that leads to financial crisis and economic depression. But the current situation was worrisome and difficult to assess because both forms of deflation now seemed to be at work, and were mixed together in cases. At the moment, only a few economies were experiencing true deflation and Japan's deflation was far milder than the early 1930s deflation. Among the reasons for concern were a worldwide excess supply ('output gap'), slow nominal GDP growth, and lower commodity prices. But the 'biggest risk' was a failure of all parties involved in the economy to adjust from expectations of inflation to expectations of deflation. The ultimate message was that deflation is caused by monetary policy. With the world economy being 'precariously balanced on the edge of a deflationary precipice,' monetary and fiscal policy should be used to pull it back, not to continue fighting non-existent inflationary pressures.

In November 2001, *The Economist* again addressed deflation concerns under the heading 'The new bogeyman,' with the sub-heading 'Falling inflation is a worldwide worry.' Falling consumer and producer prices in the U.S. and other countries were cited. While the distinction between 'friendly' and 'dangerous' deflation was continued, the term 'disinflation' was to describe what was happening in most developed countries other than Japan. An expository transition was made to a concern as to whether low inflation could make a recession worse. Was there an optimal rate of inflation that exceeded zero? Had monetary authorities succeeded in pushing the rates of inflation too low? In November 2002, *The Economist* was asking whether lowering interest rates could 'prevent the spread of debt-deflation to America and Europe.'

By 1999, highly respected academic economists were also addressing the possibility and consequences of deflation. J. Bradford DeLong (1999) considered the economic consequences of deflation in a paper, 'Should We Fear Deflation?,' published in the *Brookings Papers on Economic Activities*. He opened with the statement that 'Deflation is back. In the six months from October 1998 to March 1999, some 438 articles about deflation appeared in major U.S. newspapers, compared with only 36 in the first half of 1997 and 10 in the first half of 1990' (ibid., p. 225). The low rate of inflation was invoking fears of deflation because economic institutions had changed their expectations from inflation expectations to something approaching price stability. Although the probability of serious deflation was low, the fact that it was greater than zero meant that the economic consequences of deflation should be feared more than those of inflation (ibid., p. 227). Because the nominal interest rate could only drop to zero, deflation could result in real interest rates becoming very high, which would cause large transfers of wealth from debtors to creditors, depress investment spending, lower aggregate demand, increase unemployment, and disrupt the functioning of the financial system, which would exacerbate the negative effects on investment. Since monetary policy works with time lags, the effects of deflation could be experienced well before the remedies start to have effect.

As an eminent economic historian, DeLong could cite historical experiences of the economic evils of deflation. Entrepreneurs with long positions in real assets and short positions in nominal assets were forced into bankruptcy and the fear of falling prices caused them to curb their operations and unwind their positions. Beyond the reduced output and employment, the harmful consequences of deflation stem from nominal debts increasing in real terms while revenues are falling due to sales at lower prices. The impairment of borrowers' balance sheets result in the failure of debt contracts to work. Losses of net worth mean that stockholders and managers have little incentive to act in the interest of their creditors.

DeLong noted there was no reliable evidence about the vulnerability of the U.S. economy to deflation in 1999. But because the danger of deflation stems from falling net worth and depends on the degree of financial fragility of the economy, falling stock prices could have led to bankruptcies of businesses and curtailment of credit by financial institutions. Delong warned that long lags in the effects of monetary policy meant that deflation in the prices of currently produced goods and services might be more likely than expected. If the expectations of deflation rise ahead of expansionary monetary policies, the zero-limit on nominal interest rates would significantly limit the stimulating effects of those policies on output. But there was also a recognition that deflationary forces could result largely in reduced unemployment rather than falling prices because of wages being 'sticky' on the downside. Given that deflation is not much more difficult to cause than a reduction in the rate of inflation when that rate is already low, the appropriate monetary policy goal should be a consistent rate of change in prices above zero.

Federal Reserve Officials Acknowledge Deflation Concerns

In his January 2002 testimony to Congress on the state of the U.S. economy, Greenspan (2002a) remained focused on containment of inflationary forces. Although energy prices had recently declined, a rise in prices of energy futures contracts suggested that would not continue. As usual, Greenspan was worried about the possibility of wage-inflation, claiming that gains in labor pay had exceeded gains in labor productivity in the corporate sector. While he stated that most American businesses were experiencing a 'virtual absence of pricing power,' there was no suggestion of declining output prices. On the contrary, corporations were handling the pressure on corporate profit margins by moving 'aggressively' to stabilize cash flows by reducing employment. Moreover, he continued to accept projections of budget surpluses, which if used to pay down the federal debt would free up private saving to be channeled into capital investment.

In his July 2002 semi-annual testimony to Congress on monetary policy, Greenspan (2002b) reported that inflation was 'currently contained,' but said nothing to suggest a concern about deflation. Aggregate demand was still being stimulated by household spending financed, in large part, by refinancing home mortgages but pent-up demand had been spent. The real weakness was in capital investment spending. The 'loss of pricing power' had led businesses to protect profit margins by employing cost-reducing technologies and, even though the economy remained weak, profits were actually experiencing a sharp increase. The problem was that corporate scandals had left investors doubting the profit data. Clearly, fiscal policy was not contributing to deflationary pressures as Greenspan concluded by warning Congress about the return of federal budget deficits. Reductions in income tax rates were acceptable but the spending binge by Congress indicated a diminishing of fiscal discipline.

In his November Congressional testimony on 'the economic outlook,' Greenspan (2002d) noted further declines in stock prices and that many businesses, particularly automobile manufacturers, were offering 'deep discounts.' But real estate prices remained buoyant as home sales and housing starts continued to be very strong. Inflation in housing prices had resulted in capital gains for home owners than partially offset the negative wealth effect of fall in stock prices. It should be noted that in early 1997, Greenspan (1997) had indicated some concern about near record-high consumer debt burdens and sharp increases in credit card delinquencies and personal bankruptcies. In contrast, he hailed the increase in net debt of households in 2002 as a positive development for the economy. While businesses continued to experience zero pricing power, Greenspan appeared to be describing competitive markets rather than a trend of falling prices. Alternatives now existed for most products, and buyers were able to utilize new information technologies to seek out the low-price sellers.

The first real public acknowledgement of the Federal Reserve's concern about deflation came in November 2002 in a speech entitled 'Making Sure "It" Doesn't Happen Here' made by Bernanke to the National Economists Club in Washington, D.C. (Despite the fact that in the economic literature, the term "It" is associated with Minsky's financial instability hypothesis, Bernanke did not mention him.) Bernanke's general theme was that while experiences with deflation have been rare, Japan's 'relatively moderate deflation' proved that it could happen unexpectedly and, thus, it was only prudent for policymakers to consider the cause, economic effects, and preventive policy measures. It was unlikely that the U.S. economy would experience 'significant deflation' because of the 'resilience and structural stability' of the economy and financial system. The banking system was healthy and well-regulated and neither firms nor households had any particular debt problems. Moreover, the Federal Reserve was committed to avoiding deflation as well as inflation, and possessed sufficient policy instruments to ensure that any deflation that might occur would be mild and short-lived.

With respect to the cause of deflation, Bernanke (2002) differentiated between price declines in particular sectors of the economy and general price declines as measured by broad-based indices such as the consumer price index. By implication, a 'mild and brief' deflation meant a general trend of falling prices of consumer goods and services caused by a collapse in aggregate demand so severe that producers are forced to reduce prices to find buyers. The economic effects are similar to those associated with any drop in aggregate demand — recession, unemployment, and financial stress. In a footnote, Bernanke stated that while there were no 'unambiguous' examples of a 'supply-side deflation,' he acknowledged that aggregate supply factors could contribute to deflation if there were rapid gains in productivity and broadly decreasing costs. But that would be associated with an economic boom rather than with a weakening economy.

With respect to the economic consequences, Bernanke (2002) addressed the problems of rising real interest rates and real debt burdens when nominal interest rates reach zero and prices continue to fall. As the real cost of borrowing becomes prohibitive, capital investment, purchase of new homes, and other types of spending decline, thus worsening the economic downturn. The financial stress placed on households and firms as their real debt burdens increases the fragility of the financial system — defaults on loans, bankruptcies, and bank failures as described in Fisher's 'debt-deflation' theory.

With respect to preventive policy measures, Bernanke (2002) assured his audience that even though monetary policy is constrained by the zero level of overnight rates, the Federal Reserve can prevent deflation in three ways. Those were maintaining an 'inflation buffer zone' by not reducing the inflation rate to zero; assuring a stable well-capitalized banking system and smoothly functioning capital markets as the first line of defense against deflationary shocks, and acting as a lender of last resort to protect the financial system (as it did after the 1987 stock market crash and the September 11, 2001 terrorist attacks.) Even if deflation suddenly did occur, the Federal Reserve could always 'reinflate' by purchasing longer-term securities to bring down longer-term rates and create expectations that it would keep those rates pegged, and by making low-interest loans to banks. Cooperative action by monetary and fiscal policymakers was also a possibility. Fiscal policies of broad-based tax cuts supported by open market purchases would be particularly effective.

In a speech to the Economic Club of New York in December 2002, Greenspan (2002f) began by lamenting that monetary policy had 'allowed a persistent overissuance of money' since the end of the gold standard, which resulted in 50 years of 'chronic inflation.' Since Volcker's appointment as Chairman of the Federal Reserve Board, monetary policy had resolutely choked off inflation. During that time, concerns about deflation had seldom surfaced. But Japan's recent experience with deflation had 'refocused attention on the possibility that an unanticipated fall in the general price level would convert the otherwise relatively manageable level of nominal debt held by households and businesses into a corrosive rising level of real debt and real debt service costs' (ibid.).

Greenspan's statement that 'It now appears that we have learned that deflation, as well as inflation, are in the long run monetary phenomena, to extend Milton Friedman's famous dictum' (ibid.) implied that tight monetary policies were the cause of potential deflationary forces. But Greenspan immediately noted that the linkage between money and prices in the medium run is less clear because of globalization and a more rapid pace of technological innovations in the U.S. economy were increasing aggregate supply more rapidly than aggregate demand.

While reiterating that the U.S. economy was 'nowhere close to sliding into a pernicious deflation,' Greenspan (2002f) then explained the reasons why deflation could be presumed to be more of a threat to economic growth than inflation, prefacing that explanation with emphasis on central bankers' view that price stability is 'conducive to maximum sustainable economic growth' (ibid.). The first reason was that real interest rates could continue to rise when the nominal rate hits zero. Even if debtors refinanced at zero nominal rates, they could face high and rising real rates that cause their balance sheets to deteriorate. A second reason was that nominal wages tend to be sticky, so that real wage rates rise with deflation, resulting in higher rates of unemployment. At the same time, the significance of those negative effects might be reduced by more rapid advances in productivity growth that would stimulate aggregate demand by buoying expectations of higher wages and earnings, thus enabling real interest rates to be higher without slowing economic growth.

While there was little chance of the U.S. experiencing 'a pernicious deflation,' the flexibility of the economy would enable it to with the potentially destabilizing effects of substantial negative shocks. That flexibility was due to globalization, de-regulation in energy, transportation, communication, and financial markets, as well as the dramatic gains in information technology that allow businesses to address imbalances before they inflict significant damage. Greenspan also cited an increasing general willingness of workers to embrace innovation.

The title of Greenspan's speech might well have been 'Bubbles and Deflations,' because of the statement that 'lurking in the background of any evaluation of deflation risks is the concern that those forces could be unleashed by a bursting bubble in asset prices' (ibid.). That led to a discussion of how price stability could lead to a stock market bubble by raising investors' feeling of confidence, with Greenspan repeating his earlier denials that such bubbles could be prevented by monetary policy or even detected by monetary authorities before they burst. There was no explanation of how falling stock prices would unleash deflationary forces, only that a 'renewed weakening in equity prices' during the summer of 2002 had been a factor that hindered the recovery.

Greenspan rejected any possibility that debt could be a factor in unleashing deflationary forces. On the contrary, he stated that the 'often-cited concerns about the levels of debt and debt-servicing costs of households and firms appear a bit stretched.' Consumer and mortgage debts as a share of disposable income had reach a historical high. But that was due, in part, to financial innovations that increased the access of many households to credit markets, enabled loan officers and credit card companies to identify good credit risks, and allowed home owners to spend part of the appreciation in equity in their houses. Greenspan insisted that household debt was 'not a significant cause for concern.' His only negative comment on debt was that 'Some strain from corporate debt burdens became evident as rates of return on capital projects financed with debt fell short of expectations' (2002f).

Greenspan only returned to the subject of deflation in the opening sentence of his summary statement: 'as we focus on the dangers of bubbles, deflation, and excess capacity, the marked improvement in the degree of flexibility and resilience exhibited by our economy in recent years should afford us considerable comfort for now' (ibid.). Greenspan was vague about the causes of deflation; offering only that firms lacked 'pricing power' because of excess supply. Greenspan's assertion that traditional monetary and fiscal policies were no longer sufficient, that structural policies aimed at increasing the flexibility of the economy were an important complement to traditional monetary and fiscal policies, offered an opening for explaining how structural changes had created the potential for deflation. But Greenspan did not take that opening.

In 2003, Federal Reserve officials began to change their terminology from deflation to 'disinflation' or 'an unwelcome fall in inflation,' but the concern was the same. In his February monetary policy report to Congress, Greenspan (2003a) described lower federal funds rates as 'worthwhile insurance' against 'unwelcome substantial declines in inflation from already low levels.' In the April follow-up to his monetary policy report to Congress, Greenspan (2003b) mentioned only that with price inflation already at a low level, substantial further 'disinflation' would be unwelcome because it would put pressure on profit margins and impede the revival of business investment spending.

The minutes of the FOMC's meetings revealed the extent to which the monetary policymakers perceived the presence of both inflationary and deflationary forces in the economy in the spring of 2003. The minutes of the March 18 meeting (FOMC, 2003a) noted that overall price inflation had been boosted by steep increases in energy prices, but there had been a deceleration of the core Consumer Price Index over the past year. Further disinflation was judged to be a 'distinct possibility' over the next several quarters due to 'persisting slack in resource utilization.' In the minutes of the May 6 meeting (2003b), the assessment was that high levels of excess capacity made the probability of further disinflation higher than a pickup in inflation. Any adverse development that restrained the economic expansion would increase the probability of further disinflation. If that happened, economic activity and the functioning of financial markets and institutions would be negatively affected and it would increase difficulty of an effective monetary policy. In the statement released after the May 2003 meeting, the FOMC (2003c) reported that 'the probability of an unwelcome substantial fall in inflation, though minor, exceeds that of a pickup of inflation from its already low level.'

Greenspan (2003c) reiterated the FOMC assessment of the deflationary forces in his May testimony on the economic outlook before the Joint Economic Committee. In a teleconference speech to Berlin in June 2003, Greenspan stated that the Federal Reserve was worried about 'corrosive deflation,' defined as a broad-based decline in prices that feeds on itself and brings down the stock market and the whole economy (Miller 2003). In July, Greenspan reported to the House of Representatives' Committee on Financial Services that:

> The FOMC stands prepared to maintain a highly accommodative stance of policy for as long as needed to promote satisfactory economic performance. In the judgement of the Committee, policy accommodation aimed at raising the growth of output, boosting the utilization of resources, and warding off unwelcome *disinflation* can be maintained for a considerable period without ultimately stoking inflationary pressures. (Greenspan 2003d, emphasis added)

In the conclusion section of that testimony, Greenspan seemingly sought to avoid using the term 'deflation,' speaking of the remote possibility of inflation 'falling too low' and 'too little inflation.' But he acknowledged 'there is an especially pernicious, albeit remote, scenario in which inflation turns negative against a backdrop of weak aggregate demand, engendering a corrosive deflationary spiral.' Greenspan assured once again that the Federal Reserve was studying how to respond with 'potentially feasible policy alternatives' to the conventional primary tool of targeting the fed funds rate, although for now conventional policy was still viable.

In July, Bernanke (2003b) discussed the meaning and implications of the FOMC's May 2003 statement in a speech entitled 'An Unwelcome Fall in Inflation?' While the achievement of price stability is 'the bedrock principle of a sound monetary policy,' it had produced 'a situation in which risks to the inflation rate can be either upward, toward excessive inflation, or downward, toward too-low inflation or deflation.' In making that the official position of the Federal Reserve, the FOMC statement had been the first 'to assess the risks to economic activity and inflation separately, recognizing explicitly that upside and downside risks to inflation could exist under varying conditions of the real economy.' Because the media and financial markets had responded so strongly to the FOMC's expressed concern that inflation might actually fall low, Bernanke sought to clarify the Federal Reserve's position. There was no reason to think that a drastic change in the inflation rate was imminent, but a more gradual downward drift of that rate over one or two years was a possibility. Hence, the May FOMC statement did not refer specifically to deflation, but rather to a substantial fall in inflation. Bernanke (2003b) argued that the terminology was important. In the current circumstances, disinflation (a decline in the rate of inflation) and deflation (a falling price level) were not necessarily the same. But if price indices tend to overstate inflation, inflation at the low end of the 'implicit preferred range' may fail to provide a buffer against 'accidental deflation.'

While the economic problems posed by low inflation and deflation are 'qualitatively similar,' the associated costs can be expected to rise sharply as deflationary pressures intensify. What actually happens depends upon the state of the economy. If the financial system is fragile, with banks holding non-performing loans and balance sheets in poor condition, real debts increasing may exacerbate financial distress. Bernanke (2002) insisted that currently was not the case for the U.S. economy. A more relevant set of circumstances in which disinflation/deflation could pose significant problems is if aggregate demand is too weak to support strong growth even if the real interest rate is zero or negative. In the worst case scenario, a destabilizing dynamic could conceivably be touched off by the interaction of deflation, short-term nominal interest rates, and aggregate demand. With prices falling and aggregate demand weak, deflation may grow worse as economic slack leads to more aggressive cuts in wages and prices, causing rises in the real interest rate that further curtail aggregate demand.

Bernanke (2002) conceded that it might seem odd that the Federal Reserve was worrying about further disinflation when financial markets and forecasters seemed to be moderately optimistic about economic recovery. The problem was that forecasting inflation over the intermediate term is fraught with difficulties. Models used by the Federal Reserve see inflation affected primarily by four factors: economic slack, inflation expectations, supply shocks, and inflation persistence. Money growth is not included, although ultimately inflation is a monetary phenomenon, but instabilities in money demand, financial innovation, and many special factors affecting the monetary aggregates make them relatively poor predictors of medium-term inflation. The factor most likely to exert downward pressure on inflation in the U.S. was the degree of economic slack. Even if pace of real activity picks up considerably, as financial markets and forecasters appeared to be expecting, persistent slack might result in continuing disinflation.

In November 2003, Greenspan (2003e) noted that the low rate of inflation was the critical factor that distinguished the current economic environment from previous recessions in which the underlying inflation rate at economic troughs remained above levels that could be associated with price stability. The current situation was unique in that the core consumer price inflation, as measured in the national income and product accounts, was running at only a little more than 1 percent and firms were not gaining 'appreciable pricing power' even as economic growth was increasing. Again, Greenspan cited the FOMC as continuing to see an unwelcome fall in inflation as a greater risk than a rise in inflation.

DEFLATION DISAPPEARS IN 2004

If the perception of the possibility of deflation in the modern U.S. economy was a remarkable macroeconomic development, its disappearance was equally curious. In a speech to the American Economic Association in early January 2004, Greenspan (2004a) reviewed monetary policy since he became Chairman of the Federal Reserve Board in 1987. He stressed the difficulty of forecasting macroeconomic activity based on traditional models and the challenge that the stock market bubble and its bursting had presented for monetary policymakers. The word 'deflate' was used in the context of a denial that monetary policy could have stopped the stock market bubble: 'our experiences over the past two decades suggests that a moderate monetary tightening that deflates stock prices without substantial effect on economic activity has often been associated with subsequent *increases* in the level of stock prices.' While Greenspan spoke of 'disinflation' in connection with the achievement of price stability, the only indication of a concern about deflation outside the stock market was that 'inflation risks had become two-sided for the first time in forty years' (ibid.). In his closing remarks, Greenspan stated that the most prominent issue for future monetary policymakers is 'the appropriate role of asset prices in policy,' an issue that will remain high on the research agenda of banks.

There were only limited comments about deflation outside the stock market in that speech. Greenspan opened the speech with praise for the monetarist policies of Volcker and the theoretical insights of Friedman and hailed the disinflation that had led to price stability. Global competition, government commitment to stable prices, and increases in productivity were also cited as factors. With respect to policies during 2002-2003, Greenspan appeared to play down the possibility that the economy was vulnerable to deflationary forces. The federal funds rate had been aggressively lowered because 'inflation risks had become two-sided for the first time in forty years' (2004a). Federal Reserve policymakers, operating under a 'risk-management paradigm . . . intended to provide insurance against especially adverse outcomes,' had adopted 'an easier stance of policy aimed at limiting the risk of deflation *even though baseline forecasts from most conventional models at that time did not project deflation*' (ibid., emphasis added). It was largely a matter that monetary policymakers had little confidence in 'the ability of models fit to the data of the moderate inflations of the postwar period to accurately predict what the behavior of the economy would be in an environment of aggregate price deflation' (ibid.).

In April 2004, Greenspan reported to the Senate Banking Committee that threats of deflation were no longer a monetary policy concern. Pre-tax profits of non-financial corporations had risen sharply due to increasing productivity and 'quite modest' increases in real wages. In fact, the ratio of employee compensation to gross non-financial corporate income had fallen 'to a very low level by the standards of the past three decades' (2004c). The economy had now reached a point at which 'the worrisome trend of disinflation presumably has come to an end' while the combination of productivity growth and 'a sizable margin of underutilized resources' was holding inflationary pressures in check (ibid.). While raising the federal funds rate was not needed at the moment, the Federal Reserve was ready to act to ensure the maintenance of price stability. In response to a question from one of the Senators, Greenspan stated that 'Threats of deflation, which were a significant concern last year, by all indications are no longer an issue before us,' and 'That clearly is a change that's occurred in the last number of weeks, and it's a change . . . that's been long overdue and is most welcome' (Gongloff 2004).

The statement released from the May 2004 meeting of the FOMC reported that the economy still needed an accommodative monetary policy, but 'the risks to the goal of price stability have moved into balance' (FOMC 2004) although the economy still needed an accommodative monetary policy. The cover of the June 19, 2004 issue of *The Economist* announced in its inimical eye-catching style that the type of inflation experienced in the 1970s might be returning on a worldwide basis.

SUMMARY OF DEFLATION CONCERNS

We will conclude this chapter with a summary of what was revealed in Greenspan's and Bernanke's statements about the Federal Reserve's concern about deflationary forces in 2002-2003. Because of the emphasis on debt and innovations in the deflation theories of Veblen, Fisher, Schumpeter, and Minsky, how and to what extent those two factors appeared in the commentaries on deflation merit particular attention.

What Was Seen as Constituting Deflation?

While Greenspan acknowledged that the term 'deflation' was used to describe several different sets of prices, he focused largely on falling stock prices with only limited attention to falling prices of newly produced goods and services. Bernanke was more conventional, defining deflation as a general decline in broad-based price indexes for goods and services, with much less attention given to stock prices. In shifting the concern to 'disinflation,' Bernanke acknowledged the difficulty of recognizing empirically when 'an unwelcome fall' in inflation becomes 'deflation.'

Why Was Deflation Being Discussed?

Obviously, deflation concerns for the U.S. economy stemmed, in part, from the experiences of Japan in the 1990s, the Asian financial crisis of 1997, and the Russian financial crisis (default on government debt and the stock market crash) in 1998. In particular, the Asian crisis showed that falling asset prices can feed back into the real economy. But the real concern was that the achievement of near-price stability was leaving the economy vulnerable to deflationary forces. While no significant risk of deflation was evident, low inflation could actually be deflation if conventional price indices tend to overstate the rate of inflation. Other than Greenspan's limited comments that most corporations lacked pricing power, there were no explicit explanations as to why prices in general would actually fall. Unemployment was attributed in large part to 'sticky' wages, but there was no comparable consideration of 'sticky' prices in oligopolistic product markets.

Why Worry About the Occurrence of Deflation?

The first reason for concern about deflation was that it has negative economic consequences. The zero-bound on nominal interest rates threatened ever-rising real rates if prices continued to fall. 'Manageable' nominal debt levels could be turned into corrosive rising levels of real debt and real debt service if prices continue to fall, raising the purchasing power of the dollar. Rising real interest rates hurt capital investment and rising real debt burdens threaten a fragile financial system. If nominal wages are 'sticky,' as Greenspan believed, the rise in real wages as prices fall will result in excessive unemployment. The second reason for concern involved monetary policy. This was addressed in the greatest amount of detail by both Greenspan and Bernanke. While they acknowledged that the zero bound on nominal overnight interest rates is a problem for monetary policymakers, both insisted that the Federal Reserve had other ways of stimulating aggregate demand and the general level of prices.

What Was the Cause of Deflation?

Both Greenspan and Bernanke dealt primarily with the consequences of deflation and with the policy actions the Federal Reserve could take should deflationary forces materialize. Their limited statements on the causes were curiously different. Greenspan asserted that Friedman was correct about deflation being a monetary phenomenon in the long run, but then explained the current situation with respect to the general level of prices as being created by aggregate supply growing faster than aggregate demand. His greatest fear seemed to be that falling stock prices could precipitate deflation through the reverse wealth effect on aggregate demand and the adverse impacts on financial balance sheets. In contrast, Bernanke explained deflation as due to the collapse of aggregate demand, which could be dealt with through expansionary monetary and fiscal policies.

Whose Theories of Inflation Were Cited?

Greenspan credited Friedman with being correct in stating that deflation is a monetary phenomenon in the long run, but admitted that did not apply in the medium term. No other theories were mentioned by Greenspan. Bernanke cited no theories of deflation but both he and Greenspan briefly mentioned Fisher's recognition that increases in real debt burdens during deflation have negative impacts on the level of economic activity and the functioning of the financial markets.

The Role of Innovations

In his rhetoric about the 'new economy,' Greenspan repeatedly asserted that both technological and financial innovations were giving rise to growth in productivity and efficiency that was allowing the economy to grow faster in the 1990s without generating inflationary pressures. With wage levels held in check, productivity increases allowed profit margins to remain relatively strong even as corporations lost pricing power. But cost-reducing productivity gains was one of the intermediate-term factors that Greenspan identified as contributing to the potential for deflation in the U.S. economy. However, the extent to which he explicitly related innovations to deflation was very slight. For the most part, his message was that innovations combined with the stock market had created a 'virtuous cycle' of rising aggregate demand, which further stimulates investment. Only in the general sense that productivity had contributed to world aggregate supply increasing more rapidly than aggregate demand during the early 2000s was deflationary forces related to innovations.

The Role of Debt

Neither Greenspan nor Bernanke considered household debt to be a causative factor of deflation. On the contrary, the record high debt of households in 2002-2003 was viewed as providing anti-deflationary support to aggregate demand and as evidence of the positive contributions of financial derivatives combined with an accommodative monetary policy. The negative aspects of debt were in the consequences of deflation on real debt burdens, turning 'otherwise *relatively manageable* level of nominal debt held by households and businesses into a corrosive rising level of real debt and real debt service costs' (Greenspan 2002f, emphasis added). But that was far from about to happen as the levels of household and business debt were 'not a significant cause for concern' (ibid.).

But debt was definitely involved, if only at the periphery. Greenspan's concern that deflation forces could be unleashed by a bursting bubble in asset prices raised the question of debt and stock prices. As we noted, Greenspan began speaking about deflation in 1998. In an August 1999 speech, he stated that the crisis in financial markets following the Russian default and Asian crises in 1997 illustrated that financial markets can experience 'discontinuous' adjustments *especially when positions are highly leveraged'* (Greenspan 1999, emphasis added). And in booming financial markets, there is a propensity to leverage both realized and unrealized capital gains. Yet, in his remarks about how monetary policy could respond to bubbles, Greenspan did not connect debt with speculative markets. He has repeatedly disagreed with critics who argued that the stock market bubble of the late 1990s could have been 'deflated' by raising the margin requirements. His defense was that the amount of margin debt was very small (less than 2 percent of the market value of stocks), and that some of the debt was used to finance short-sales and transactions in securities other than stocks. Since speculators could borrow from other sources, raising the margin requirement would not reduce the use of debt to purchase stocks. It would, however, force the 'small investors' out of the markets since they have limited access to other credit. The only causal effect would be that speculators would interpret the rise in margin requirements as a signal that the Fed was going to tighten monetary policy sufficiently to burst the bubble by depressing aggregate economic activity.

In a speech in November 2002, Greenspan dismissed the threat of debt, in part, by arguing that the risk of debt had been efficiently allocated by extensive use of new highly complex financial derivatives, including credit default swaps. But he acknowledged that the highly leveraged nature of financial derivatives is an 'Achilles' heel.' Historically, such high leverage induced speculative excesses that culminated in financial crises and human nature has not changed. In an admission of a 'too-big-too-fail' policy stance, Greenspan stated that central banks, as lenders of last resort, have come to accept some of the risk of derivatives, providing 'what essentially amounts to catastrophic financial insurance coverage' (2002e). He insisted that such public subsides, which create 'moral hazards,' are to be provided on only the 'rarest of occasions.'

Similarly, Bernanke (2003a) noted that while aggregate household debt and debt service burden had risen to fairly high levels in recent years, it had actually fallen somewhat in 2002 because real disposable income rose (in large part due to tax cuts) and interest rates fell. Personal bankruptcies rose to a new high in 2002 and continued to be elevated. But Bernanke argued that household debt was very manageable because of the increase in mortgage debt facilitated by 'subprime mortgage lending.' The tax reform act of 1986 had encouraged a substitution of mortgage debt for consumer credit and refinancing mortgages had allowed consumers to pay down non-mortgage debt with part of their equity. He denied that the restructuring of debt had 'come at the cost of a dangerous increase in leverage' (ibid.).

With respect to business debt, Bernanke noted an 'evident deterioration in aggregate credit quality' (ibid.) for the corporate sector. Many companies had their credit ratings reduced and corporate bond defaults in 2002 rose above the peak during the recession of 1991. But he noted that much of the weakness was concentrated in a few 'seriously distressed sectors' — telecommunications, airlines, and energy trading firms. Moreover, lower interest rates were allowing firms to restructure their debt through refinancing, significantly reducing their interest rate charges. Firms were also substituting long-term debt for short-term, reducing the ratio of current debt to assets.

Although Greenspan did not connect growing debt with the prospective deflation, other astute economic analysts did, particularly those associated with the Levy Institute. In November 2002, the Levy Institute's Macro Modeling Team raised the issue of whether personal debt in the U.S. economy was sustainable, and argued that it was not. Their report stated that 'The long economic expansion, dating from 1992 to 2000, was fueled by an unprecedented rise in private expenditure relative to income, financed by a growing flow of net credit to the private (household and business) sector' (Papadimitriou, et al., 2002). They noted that accompanying the boom that started in 1992 had been an unprecedented increase in the ratio of the private sector's debt to income. While there was at the same time a spectacular increase rise in the nominal values of the private sector's financial assets, it did not match the run-up in debt. But this was never a match between equals. There was a fundamental inequality between debt commitments that had to be met by actual flows of interest and repayments and the potential valuation compounded out of earnings and expectations that were highly illusory. While the huge drop in business investment resulted in no new acquisition of debt by the corporate sector, the household sector continued to borrow, although at a somewhat lower rate.

In a Levy Institute Public Policy Brief, Wray and Papadimitriou (2003) observed that most of the analyses of the possibility of a 'protracted period of price deflation' lacked 'a clear discussion of the causes of the deflationary pressures that seem to afflict economies today on a global scale'. That was certainly true for Greenspan and Bernanke. Wray and Papadimitriou provided a brief Fisher-Minsky perspective. Our purpose is to engage in a thorough examination not only of Fisher's and Minsky's theories of deflation, but also those presented by Veblen and Schumpeter. To set the stage, in the next chapter we briefly review the traditional monetary theories of the determinants of the general price level, and the so-called monetary theories of business cycles.

3. Monetary Theories of Deflation

The assertions by Federal Reserve officials and others that in the long run deflation is a monetary phenomenon bring into focus the traditional theory of the general level of prices — the quantity theory of money. That is especially true since both Greenspan and Bernanke cited Milton Friedman, who essentially resuscitated the quantity theory with his restatement in 1956. Greenspan opened his speech to the Economic Club of New York on December 19, 2002 with the statement: 'Although the gold standard could hardly be portrayed as having produced a period of price tranquility, it was the case that the price level in 1929 was not much different, on net, from what it had been in 1800' (2002f). The obvious incompatibility of prices between those two time periods aside, the gold standard and the quantity theory of money were often linked. That was implied by Greenspan in his assertion that 'a persistent overissuance of money' between 1933 (when the U.S. went off the domestic gold standard) and 1979 was responsible for a half-century of chronic inflation.

There is a substantial literature on the origin, development, and meaning of the quantity theory of money. For our limited purpose of distinguishing the deflation theories of Veblen, Fisher, Schumpeter, and Minsky from the traditional theory, it is briefly reviewed in the first part of this chapter. Because Fisher was so closely associated with what is regarded as the neo-classical version of the quantity theory, we focus on his reconstruction of the theory in *The Purchasing Power of Money*, first published in 1911.

The quantity theory was associated with both the classical and the neo-classical school and was directly or indirectly applied in the arguments between proponents of the banking school and proponents of the currency school. Our interest, however, is to the extent to which earlier economists associated with the classical school related credit/debt and deflation. Humphrey (2004) has explained why classical economists feared the effects on the real economy of deflation that was caused by monetary developments. Kindleberger (2000, p. 14) interpreted Minsky's model as being 'a lineal descendant of a model, set out with personal variations, by a host of classical economists including John Stuart Mill, Alfred Marshall, Knut Wicksell, and Irving Fisher'. In the second section of the chapter, we review Adam Smith's comments about credit and debt in *Wealth of*

Nations, and John Stuart Mill's theory of credit and financial crises, in which he cited the work of Thomas Tooke.

The assertions by Greenspan and others that deflation is a monetary phenomenon in the long run also bring monetary theories of business cycles into the picture. For the purpose of distinguishing the deflation theories of Veblen, Fisher, Schumpeter, and Minsky from the monetary theories of business cycles, the representative theories of Hawtrey and Hayek are briefly reviewed in the last section of the chapter.

THE QUANTITY THEORY OF MONEY

Friedman stated that 'The quantity theory of money is a term evocative of a general approach rather than a label for a well-defined theory' (1956, p. 3), and observed that 'Whatever its precise meaning, it is clear that the general approach fell into disrepute after the crash of 1929 and the subsequent Great Depression'. Similarly, Hegeland observed that 'Throughout its history, the quantity theory of money (which will always be referred to as the quantity theory) has been stated in so many different ways that there has been little agreement concerning it' (1969, p. 1). He identified three versions. The first was simply a statement that 'average prices are always in proportion to the quantity of money' (p. 1). The second stated that 'if other things remain the same, changes in the quantity of money *causes* proportionate price changes' (p. 2). The third version focused primarily on the effects of changes in the quantity of money upon the rate of circulation of money, with the effect of changes in the quantity of money on prices becoming a secondary question. Hegeland asserted that the second version was not a legitimate interpretation of the quantity theory and that the third, which is built on the first, was the most correct one.

Laidler noted that when the quantity theory reached the peak of its development in the period 1870-1914, it was 'conceived of as a theory of the general price level' (1991, p. 1). In *History of Economic Analysis*, Schumpeter argued that what has been received as the 'quantity theory' really should be termed the 'quantity theorem' because it was 'not a complete theory of money but merely a proposition about the exchange value of money' (1954, p. 312). He defined the quantity 'theory' as meaning four things. First, the quantity of money is an independent variable with respect to prices and volume of transactions. Second, velocity of circulation is independent of prices and volume of transactions, and remains constant or changes very slowly. Third, output or transactions is independent of the quantity of money. Fourth, changes in the quantity of money 'act mechanically on all prices, irrespective of how the money is used and in which sector of the economy' (ibid., p. 703).

Fisher's Interpretation of the Quantity Theory

Historically, the 'golden age' of the quantity theory coincided with the long period of deflation in the U.S. that ended in the mid-1890s and the formal adoption of the gold standard by the U.S. in 1900, but also with the 'golden era' of high agricultural prices for American farmers from 1897 to 1914 (Laidler 1991, p. 1). That 'golden age' corresponds to what Hegeland (1969) defined as the 'neo-classical' version of the quantity theory. Laidler (1991) noted that, as an explanation of general price levels, the quantity theory was formulated in terms of the stock supply and demand for money approach by Marshall and his followers in Britain and by Fisher's transactions approach in America. For our purposes, we will limit our review to Fisher's version.

In *The Purchasing Power of Money*, first published in 1911, Fisher (1963) lamented the loss of prestige of the quantity theory among economists. The theory had been incorrectly stated as prices vary proportionally with the quantity of money, which is true only if velocity and volume of trade or goods remain constant (ibid., p. 14). But the low state of the quantity theory at that time was also attributed to political attempts to use it as a basis for 'unsound currency schemes,' such as the free silver movement (ibid., p. 15). Fisher proposed to reconstruct the theory to demonstrate that it was a scientific principle that could be precisely formulated, and to develop the methodology for statistical and historical verification of that scientific principle (ibid., p. vii).

Fisher's theoretical construction utilized his equation of exchange. With M representing the average amount of money in circulation, the product 'MV' represented total expenditure, E, with V being E divided by M. With respect to the quantity theory itself, Fisher started with the equation $MV = \sum pQ$, where the p's represent the prices of the various individual goods and services and the Q's the total quantities of those goods and services purchased at those prices. With P becoming the weighted average of the p's and T as the sum of all the Q's, the equation can be rewritten as: $MV = PT$. Thus, P represents the level of prices and T represents the volume of trade (1963, pp. 24-27).

Fisher's three theorems were set forth as follows. First, if velocity and quantity of trade remain constant, the price level will vary proportionately with changes in the quantity of money. Second, if the money supply and the quantity of trade remain constant, the price level will vary proportionately with any changes in velocity of circulation. Third, if both the money supply and velocity remain constant, the price level will vary proportionately (but inversely) with changes in the volume of trade (ibid., pp. 26-27). For Fisher, the first of these 'theorems' constituted the true 'quantity theory of money' (p. 29).

To give the equation of exchange greater value as an analytical tool, Fisher brought 'credit' into the picture. 'Credit' referred to demand deposit balances, M', while V' represented the velocity of deposit money. The equation of exchange then becomes $MV + M'V' = PT$ (1963, p. 48). Because Fisher argued that M' *normally* varies directly with changes in the quantity of money, its inclusion magnifies the relationship between money and prices without distorting it (ibid., pp. 54-55). Nor does the introduction of M' alter the relationship between prices and changes in either velocity or volume of trade. But during what Fisher called 'periods of transition,' the ratio of M' to M is not constant. While several changes can constitute a transition, the most important is change in the quantity of money. If the money supply should be doubled, the price level would ultimately also be doubled. But there would be 'temporary effects' during the transition period in which a series of changes would be initiated by rising prices but involving changes in interest rates.

Fisher asserted that the 'peculiar' effects of both rising and falling prices on the rate of interest during periods of transition were 'largely responsible for the crises and depressions in which price movements end' (1963, p. 56). Because business people are accustomed to thinking of the monetary unit as being stable, the nominal interest rate is slow to adjust to changing purchasing power of the dollar. Consequently, the real interest rate falls below its normal level when prices are rising. Where debt costs are involved, business money profits will rise faster than prices. Business borrowing will increase to finance expansions and the short-term loans by banks increase M'. The resulting increase in money will increase prices, leading to further increases in profits ahead of prices and, hence, more borrowing. Lenders are encouraged by rising nominal interest rates to make even more loans, which are seemingly secured by rising prices inflating the collateral values pledged.

In the process, the ratio of M' to M increases above its normal level. There are also 'disturbances' in the form of 'unhealthy increases' in the volume of trade (T), which will be stimulated by 'easy terms for loans' and optimistic expectations of business operators. In contrast, workers find their incomes lagging behind rising prices (1963, pp. 61-62). Prices start rising with the increased spending of the new (or 'surplus') money, which is initially spent at nearly the original prices. But while there is some increase in volume of trade, an increase in money cannot alone increase trade substantially because such factors as population, invention, and productivity cannot be increased. The rise in prices will also increase V and V' because its value depreciates as prices rise (p. 63).

This comes to an end when the nominal interest rate finally catches up with the rise in prices, so that the real interest rate returns to its normal level. Banks have to raise rates because the abnormal increases in loans threaten their reserve positions, which are limited not only by law but also by the amount of money available for reserves. The rising interest rates curb the borrowing and lower the prices of securities that are collateral for loans. A financial crisis ends the prosperity. Firms begin to fail because they are unable to obtain new loans or have their existing loans called. That generates fears among the public that their bank deposits are not safe, leading to a desire to hold money instead, which reduces bank reserves. As the liquidity squeeze worsens, bankruptcies increase, as firms in desperate need for money are unable to obtain it. Fisher stressed that 'monetary causes of crises are the most important *when taken in connection with the maladjustments in the rate of interest*' (1963, p. 66). As loans and deposits contract, velocities decrease and prices fall somewhat below their peak levels as M' contracts. Business expectations become negative as firms with debts are hardest hit. Money may become so scarce (a 'money famine') as to lead to some resort to barter (p. 69). But, after some time, normal conditions begin to return. The nominal rate of interest falls to a level relative to the lower price level and the real interest rate is back to normal. The process then reverses. Prices begin to rise and there is a repetition of the upward movement (p. 70)

This 'pendulum' movement of prices up, down, and back up was the complete credit cycle which Fisher asserted takes about a decade to complete. These are 'abnormal oscillations' that are caused by 'some initial disturbance' (1963, p. 70), so that while the 'pendulum' is always seeking equilibrium, there are frequent disturbances that prevent such stability from being achieved. The most common of those disturbances, according to Fisher, are an increase in the money supply, a shock to business confidence, crop failures (in an age in which agriculture was still so important), and invention (ibid.).

Behind those direct influences on the price level are a number of indirect factors, including conditions that affect the volume of trade, conditions that affect the velocities of M and M', and conditions that affect the quantity of money. The latter included export/import of gold, melting and minting coins, and what Fisher termed 'monetary and banking systems' (1963, p. 90). Fisher then devoted a chapter to assessing the extent to which the five direct factors — M, M', V, V', and T are really '*causal*' factors (p. 151) affecting price, which is passive. But his conclusion was that 'we find nothing to interfere with the truth of the quantity theory that variations in money (M) produce normally proportional changes in prices' (p. 183).

Interestingly, Schumpeter (1954, p. 1102) argued that Fisher cannot be classed with the quantity theorists except in a special sense. First, Fisher stopped short of the theorem by admitting the influence of T on both V and M, which weakens the theorem considerably as a long-run proposition. Second, the theorem holds only for a state of equilibrium, and not for what

Fisher called 'transition periods,' during which he gave careful attention to interest rates adjusting in a lagged manner to rising or falling prices. Third, Fisher emphasized that M, V, and T were only 'proximate causes' of P, with almost a dozen indirect influences to be considered.

CREDIT, DEBT, AND CRISES: SMITH AND MILL

Humphrey (2004) has explained that while classical economists generally agreed that the quantity of money has a neutral effect on the real economy in the long run, they recognized that deflation caused by monetary changes had non-neutral effects in the short run. They were cognizant not only of the redistributive effects of rises in real debts and real burdens of taxes, but also that the lagging of wages and some prices behind the general trend in prices resulted in rising costs of production, which led to reduced output and employment. In addition, they recognized that aggregate demand would be negatively impacted by hoarding due to expectations of rising purchasing power of money. Our particular interest is in the extent to which classical economists considered the role of debt in the determination of the price level. For the most part, that must be seen as the other side of credit, which did receive some attention by Adam Smith, Thomas Tooke, and John Stuart Mill.

Adam Smith on Credit and Prices

In a footnote comment, Fisher (1963, p. 14) asserted that Adam Smith was one of a long line of political economists who accepted the 'often crudely formulated' quantity theory. Hegeland (1969, p. 47), however, noted the absence of an explicit statement by Smith to that effect. In *The Wealth of Nations*, Smith ([1776] 1976) distinguished between nominal prices and real prices, and between market prices and natural prices. Real prices were defined as the real cost of commodities in terms of labor commanded, while nominal prices were simply the monetary prices. As long-run equilibrium prices in perfectly competitive markets, the natural prices of commodities were equal to their exchange values, which, in turn, reflected the relative amounts of labor they could command in exchange. Market prices were short-run prices that could be higher or lower than the natural prices but would adjust to the natural prices in competitive markets.

In most of Smith's discussion of prices and value, the focus was on individual prices or relative prices. But there was at least a hint of a deflationary trend in Smith's labor theory of value and the general level of real prices. He stated that 'In that original state of things, which precedes both the appropriation of land and the accumulation of stock, the whole produce belongs to the labourer' ([1776] 1976, p. 82). If that 'state' had continued, the division of labor would have enhanced the productivity of labor to the extent that all commodities would have become cheaper because they could be produced with less labor.

That did not happen, of course, because capital ownership emerged and the natural profit (along with the natural rent) joined with the natural wage as components of the natural price. But there is a definite suggestion of a deflationary trend in Smith's theory of the effect of capital accumulation on profit. In the long run, as more capital is accumulated and employed by businessmen, more output is produced and the increased supply reduces the (apparently natural) prices. Smith stated that:

> In a country fully stocked in proportion to all the business it had to transact, as great a quantity of stock would be employed in every particular branch as the nature and extent of trade would admit. The competition, therefore, would everywhere be as great, and consequently the ordinary profit as low as possible. ([1776] 1976, p. 111)

If ordinary profit means the same as the natural profit, that clearly implies that natural price falls. Similarly, Smith argued that higher profit resulted in inflation. Prices will only rise in arithmetical proportion to a rise in wages, but in geometric proportion to a rise in profits. The effect of rising wages on prices was like the effect of ordinary interest on the accumulation debt, while the effect of a rise in profits on prices was like the effect of compound interest on debt ([1776] 1976, pp. 114-115).

With respect to money, Hegeland (1969, p. 49) argued that Smith did agree with the essence of the quantity theory — that the main function of money is circulation of goods. But the value of money was determined by applying the labor theory of value to the production of gold and silver. Smith argued that only a certain quantity of coins, constituting a given amount of labor commanded, could circulate a given quantity of goods. Any increase in coins will result in the excess coins being exported (Smith [1776] 1976, p. 294). The quantity of money in circulation is a passive factor that is determined by the demands of circulation and the costs of producing the gold or silver. If the production costs fall, more money will circulate the same goods. If the labor cost of producing a quantity of goods increases, more money will be required to circulate the same goods, but the rise in price is based on the greater amount of labor involved in production of the goods (ibid., pp. 49-51).

The importance of credit (and hence debt) was emphasized in Smith's statement that: 'A man must be perfectly crazy who, where there is tolerable security, does not employ all the stock which he commands, whether it be his own or *borrowed* of other people' ([1776] 1976, p. 285, emphasis added). But the relationship between credit/debt, and prices was most fully stated in Smith's discussion of paper bank notes as circulating money. The notes were promissory notes of banks that were issued in the extension of credit. Hence, the borrowers incurred debts, and received in exchange paper notes that represented debts of the issuing banks that were (nominally, at least) payable on demand in specie. A net expansion in the notes was an expansion in bank credit and debt, but what was the effect on the money supply?

Smith argued that as long as the notes were required by law to be redeemed upon demand in specie, the money supply could not be increased above the amount of gold and silver the notes replaced. Any bank issuing excessive notes would find those notes being immediately returned for redemption in specie. But there would be an expansionary effect in the real economy. The amount of circulating capital would be increased by the efficiency gains from replacing gold and silver with paper note and that increase would be employed to increase 'the quantity of the materials, tools, and maintenance' (Smith [1776] 1976, p. 296). This was analogous to a technological improvement allowing old machinery to be replaced with lower cost new machinery, with the cost-savings becoming a transfer from fixed to circulating capital (ibid.). In the case of paper bank notes, the freed-up specie would be used to purchase foreign materials and goods that would be used in manufacture at home (p. 295).

Smith disagreed with the argument that increasing the amount of paper money diminished the value of the 'whole currency' and thereby raised prices. Since the quantity of paper money just replaces gold and silver, the whole money supply was not increased (p. 324). As case examples of the positive effects of paper money, he noted the low prices of 'provisions' in Scotland when paper money was in great circulation, and that prices of corn were lower in England than in France even though there was more paper money in the former (pp. 324-325). But that was true only if bank notes were required by law to be redeemed upon demand in specie. If banks could delay redemption, the value of paper money would fall and prices in paper money would rise as banks increased credit (p. 325).

In Smith's day, bank notes were issued chiefly in the discounting of merchants' bills of exchange. But he praised the new practice of the Scottish banks of offering 'cash accounts.' Credit up to a specific amount (several thousand pounds) would be granted to individuals who could get two people with 'undoubted credit and good landed estate to become surety for him' ([1776] 1976, p. 299). The loans were repayable upon demand, but 'easy terms' were granted for repayment on a 'piece-meal' basis, essentially an installment loan. Merchants and manufacturers having 'cash accounts' themselves formed a large network in which they not only readily accepted bank notes when they needed money from the banks, but encouraged the circulation of the notes among their customers (ibid.).

Smith noted that the older Scottish banks were cautious in extending credit, requiring frequent and regular payments from all their customers and dealing with people who were not regular customers. Frequent and regular repayments allowed them to effectively monitor the creditworthiness of their customers and also 'secured themselves from the possibility of issuing more paper money than what the circulation of the country could easily absorb and employ' ([1776] 1976, p. 306). As a matter of economic principle, banks should only make short-term commercial loans and avoid lending the whole circulating capital needed by merchants, or even a very large portion of it, since the whole return is too distant. Long-term loans for fixed capital and property development should be provided by wealthy individuals in the form of mortgages and bonds, which would not involve issuing bank notes that circulate as money (p. 307).

Smith observed that bankers in Scotland were severely criticized by 'traders and undertakers' for being too restrictive in their lending and not expanding credits in proportion to increases in trade ([1776] 1976, p. 308). But the 'trade' that businessmen had in mind was extending their own projects beyond what their capital and private credit would allow. The folly of bankers attempting to oblige that 'trade' was illustrated by the failure of the Ayr Bank that was established to supply such demands for credit and failed after issuing large amount of notes for such loans. The impact of excessive note issues was largely in allowing the businesses to go much deeper into debt, resulting in greater losses for themselves and their creditors, thus doing the economy more harm than good (p. 314).

Smith also noted a practice that had come from England to Scotland called 'the practice of drawing and re-drawing' of bills of exchange, also called 'raising money by circulation' (ibid., p. 310). Essentially, this was a process in which someone in London kept extending a loan to a merchant, with interest owed and commission charged being compounded each time the loan is extended. Smith stated that while this practice was well known by businessmen, they did not necessarily understand the effects of it and the effects of it on banking were not well understood even by the businessmen. Accordingly, he explained it in some detail (pp. 308-312). The 'customs of merchants' included accepting at discount short-term bills of exchange because the person(s) presenting the bill by endorsement back to the drawer of the bill would be liable for payment. A merchant in Edinburgh might draw a bill on someone, B, in London, who agrees to accept the bill under the condition that he can draw a similar bill (with a commission and interest added) on the Scottish merchant before the first bill comes due. Before that second bill comes due, the Scottish merchant draws a second bill against B in London, which B accepts under the condition of drawing a similar bill (with commission and interest added) on the Scottish merchant. This might be repeated over several years, with the interest and commission owed by the Edinburgh merchant accumulating. Smith noted that expensive way of securing credit supported 'many vast and expensive projects' at a time when ordinary profits were in the 6-10 percent range, because the promoters 'had in their golden dreams the most distinct vision of this greater profit' but seldom found it (p. 310).

Banking came into the picture because the Scottish merchant discounted the bills drawn on the London agent and received Scottish bank notes, and the London agent discounted the bills drawn on the Scottish merchant and received Bank of England notes. The result was a creation of paper money in excess of the specie that would have circulated, and the notes would be returned for redemption in gold or silver. Bankers were unaware that they were advancing capital based on fictitious bills because the 'projectors' of the scheme might involve a circle. Even if a banker did realize that the discounted bill was fictitious, he might fear that refusing to discount any more would ruin not only the 'projectors' but him as well. Smith noted that the caution used by the Bank of England, other major London banks, and the older Scottish banks that restricted discounting bills enraged the 'projectors,' who clamored that their own distress was the nation's distress caused not by themselves but by 'the ignorance, pusillanimity, and bad conduct of banks' (Smith [1776] 1976, p. 312).

Smith denied that private debt could cause macroeconomic problems. He stated that

> Though some particular men may sometimes increase their expence very considerably although their revenue does not increase at all, we may be assured that no class or order of men ever does so; because, though the principles of common prudence do not always govern the conduct of every individual, they always influence that of the majority of every class or order. ([1776] 1976, p. 295)

Similarly, he declared that

> It can seldom happen, indeed, that the circumstances of a great nation can be much affected either by the prodigality or misconduct of individuals; the profusion or imprudence of some being always more than compensated by the frugality and good conduct of others. ([1776] 1976, p. 341)

One of the beneficial results of men's constant striving to better themselves is that there are more 'prudent and successful undertakings' than 'injudicious and unsuccessful ones' (ibid.). Only a small number of enterprises end in bankruptcy because 'the greater part of men . . . are sufficiently careful to avoid it'.

Where debt can cause problems is when it is acquired by government. Smith declared that 'Great nations are never impoverished by private, though they sometimes are by public prodigality and misconduct' ([1776] 1976, p. 342). In the last part of *The Wealth of Nations* on the subject of the public debt, Smith declared that 'enormous debts . . . at present oppress, and will in the long-run probably ruin, all the great nations of Europe' (p. 911). Yet, Smith had one positive observation about government debt. The progress in the public debts was essentially the progress made by merchants and manufacturers. For public debts to expand, merchants and other lenders had to have sufficient confidence in the ability and willingness of the government to enforce the law of contracts and property, enforcing payment of debts by all those who have the abilities to pay. In such a nation, the government does not need to accumulate 'treasure' to finance its extraordinary expenses. It can readily borrow from the merchants and manufacturers who have the funds to lend and are accustomed to lending in their economic activities. In Smith's words:

> The same confidence which disposes great merchants and manufacturers, upon ordinary occasions, to trust their property to the protection of a particular government; disposes them, upon extraordinary occasions, to trust that government with the use of their property. ([1776] 1976, p. 910)

He noted that there are definite advantages to businessmen who fund government debt. Lending to government serves to augment rather than to reduce their 'trading capital.' The government is willing to borrow on terms advantageous to the lender, and government securities are readily traded in the markets at prices that yield capital gains to the original purchasers. That was verified by the competition for participation in new government loans (ibid., pp. 910-911).

But Smith also argued that capital loaned to government is switched from paying productive laborers to paying unproductive laborers, and will 'be spent and wasted, generally in the course of the year, without even the hope of any future reproduction' (ibid., p. 924). While the marketability of government securities allowed businessmen to conduct their business by being able to borrow from others using the securities as collateral (or selling the securities), the 'new' capital acquired was simply transferred from some other 'productive' use (pp. 924-925).

The Tooke-Mill Credit Theory of Crises

In his *History of Monetary and Credit Theory*, first published in 1938, Rist gave high marks to Thomas Tooke, the leader of the British Banking School, for his theory of crises (which Rist claimed that historians had almost completely ignored (1966, p. 214).) Tooke rejected the arguments by members of the 'Currency Principle' that crises were caused by excessive issue of bank notes, and argued instead that 'a crisis is accompanied by an excess of credit in *all its forms*' (ibid.). The 'abuse of credit' was due to what he called the 'spirit of speculation' or 'overbanking,' which followed a speculative rise in prices.

In Tooke's theory, an increase in demand is spawned by a speculative development in markets for some commodities which results in rising prices. An increase in the money supply does not cause that development. But an expansion in money and credit occurs as speculators seek to take advantage of it by obtaining credit and their debt-financed spending drives up prices. Since the permanent incomes of consumers do not allow purchase of all the commodities at the higher prices, those prices will fall back to their 'general' levels. A crisis or 'collapse of credit' occurs when there is 'a cessation of the excess of confidence, terminating in distrust' (quoted in Rist 1966, p. 216).

After a chapter in *Principles of Political Economy* that dealt with 'Credit as a Substitute for Money,' Mill (1961) devoted a chapter to explaining the 'Influence of Credit on Prices,' in which he extensively cited and quoted Tooke. By 'credit' Mill meant all forms of that create 'a distinct purchasing power,' and not simply money loaned by one person to another. Essentially following Smith, Mill began with credit that enables capital that would otherwise remain idle to be put to productive use. But he subsequently observed that 'a more intricate portion of the theory of Credit is its influence on prices' because where commercial activity is extensively conducted on large amounts of credit 'general prices at any moment depend much more upon the state of credit than upon the quantity of money' (p. 514).

Turning to the influence of credit on prices of commodities, Mill remarked that the 'permanent value of money' (by which he meant the cost of producing gold and silver) and, hence, the 'natural and average prices of commodities' would not be affected by credit, but only the 'immediate and temporary' prices (1961, p. 523). An increase or decrease in the quantity of money in circulation would certainly raise or lower prices. But 'Credit' in any form would do the same. The demand for commodities that affects prices is the quantity of money offered for those commodities. While money that is being held out of circulation does not affect prices, Mill noted that 'the money offered is not the same thing with the money possessed' (p. 524). Credit affects prices by offering money that is not being possessed. Payment by checks, while not money in possession, is still money to which the buyer has a right. But transactions made in money that is only expected in the future, or is 'pretended' to be expected (p. 525), affect prices exactly as if they had been made in money.

Thus, the amount of purchasing power that a person can exercise consists of the money that he possesses or that is due to him, and all the credit that he can obtain. The whole of that purchasing power will be fully utilized only 'under peculiar circumstances,' but it is always there (1961, p. 525). An example of the 'peculiar circumstances' in which merchants are inclined to use all of their credit to increase their demand for commodities was when they expect rises in the prices of some commodities due to some 'accident' such as the opening of a new foreign market or indications that some commodities will be in short supply (ibid.), while the expectation of rising prices originally rests on 'some original grounds' that lead the merchants into spending all their money and using all their credit on the commodities in question. But prices rise by more than the 'original' reasons would explain. In response to the expectations of rising prices, speculation is unleashed in several 'departments,' and imitators are drawn in by the public perception that those holding the commodities are in a position to realize substantial gains. The speculative inflation, which spreads to totally unrelated markets, is facilitated by a great expansion in credit, which occurs not only because of the demand for loans by speculators but also because lenders more easily extend credit as the borrowers seem to be realizing unusual gains. As a 'generally reckless and adventurous feeling' comes to prevail, lenders become highly willing to lend to borrowers who 'are not entitled to it' (p. 527).

The speculative inflation based on credit used to drive up prices of commodities will end in a crisis. At some point, some holders of commodities will perceive that prices are irrationally high and will start selling. As prices fall, there will be a rush to sell, causing the prices to fall more than they rose so that the average level of prices during the 'commercial revulsion' falls below their original level. If the purchases had been made in money possessed, they would have drawn money from other transactions, creating a decrease in prices in other markets. Credit becomes overly tight and those with money want to hold onto it and those to whom it is owed want it returned. Panic conditions erupt as those in desperate need for money are forced to sell at any price in attempts to obtain it and will borrow it for short periods at extremely high interest rates (1961, pp. 526-527).

Not all credit contractions are preceded by speculative expansions in credit, as shown by the 1847 episode. Circumstances resulting in a withdrawal of a considerable portion of the capital usually going to the 'loan market' and, when that happens, firms needing credit are denied credit and are unable to pay their debts to other firms. A panic similar to the one described above (e.g., the 1825 panic) may result (1961, pp. 528-529). While all forms of credit will have the same general influence on prices, those that allow the greatest extension of credit will have the greatest influence, e.g., bank notes more than bills, bills more than book credits. But credit will not be used unless the 'circumstances of the markets, and the state of the mercantile mind, render many persons desirous of stretching their credit to an unusual extent' (p. 531).

MONETARY THEORIES OF BUSINESS CYCLES

R. G. Hawtrey has the reputation for being the 'best-known exponent of a monetary theory of the cycle' that was set forth in a number of books and articles (Estey 1956, p. 191). In Hawtrey's theory of business cycles, equilibrium exists when money outlays equal money income, with cash balances of consumers and traders holding constant and banks neither increasing nor decreasing bank credit. But this equilibrium is easily disturbed by changes in the cash balances. In most cases, that is caused by wholesalers or traders spending cash to increase their inventory stocks and an increased willingness of banks to make loans, thus increasing the cash. Households releasing cash balances by increasing their consumption spending is less likely to be a factor. Traders will release cash balances if their expectations for sales improve, while banks will increase their lending if they think reserves can be safely lowered. Because interest is a significant component of the cost of carrying inventories, the working capital of traders is highly sensitive to changes in interest rates. Thus, with banks lowering interest rates to encourage borrowing, traders borrow to add to their working capital.

As the releasing of cash balances by firms and banks leads to increases in consumers' income, consumption spending begins to rise. The increase in effective demand causes a reduction in traders' stocks which leads to further release of cash by traders, who borrow from banks when they have exhausted their idle balances. As money income and effective demand continue to increase, the general level of prices comes under increasing pressure as productive capacities are used up and labor shortages emerge. The price inflation adds to the expansion as lags in wage levels allow traders' revenues to rise faster than costs and, with interest rates also lagging, borrowing by traders continues to increase.

The expansion ends when banks are forced by their declining reserve positions to raise interest rates. Because banks are slow to do so, the expansion has gone to the point that a tightening by banks sets off a drastic and cumulative reverse reaction. Traders reduce orders for stock, which causes producers to reduce output and employment. While consumers may continue spending by pulling down idle balances, ultimately they have to reduce spending as their incomes falls. Traders see inventories rising, and reduce orders again and start paying off some of their debts, which reduces the total supply of money. All of these cause the price level and profits to fall. With deflation expectations building, cash balances are held and the velocity of money falls, which weakens prices even more.

The deflation eventually ends as a buildup of reserves in banks increases. As deflation and depression set in, the need for money is low and a return flow to the banks occurs while banks have reduced their lending. In industry, costs and inventories are lower and, as banks lower their rates of interest because of larger reserves, dealers become more willing to borrow and spend for inventories and the expansionary process begins again.

Business expansions and depressions may be caused by non-monetary factors but Hawtrey argued that those have no periodicity. The periodicity of business trade cycles is due to their monetary effects, with their actual behavior resulting from cumulative variations in bank credit (see Hawtrey 1927, p. 472). Individual banks wanting to maximize returns on their reserves will create new bank credit as long as their reserves permit. To protect their reserves during the contractions, they will reduce lending. The monetary cause of cycles could be eliminated by the central bank applying the appropriate monetary policies. Because bank reserves are too slow to indicate when there is a need for restraint of an expansion, policies should not be based on the state of bank reserves.

Schumpeter (1954, p. 1121) argued that Hayek's theory was not a pure monetary theory of business cycles. The commonality in Hayek's and Hawtrey's theories was that both start with banks offering easy conditions for loans. But, in Hawtrey's theory, investment spending by wholesalers is the link to booming conditions, while it is investment spending by producers of durable capital in Hayek's theory. A criticism of the pure monetary theory of cycles is that it fails to provide an explanation of why the production of capital goods fluctuates so much relative to the production of consumption goods. Because of the way in which that is explained in Hayek's theory, it has been described as a 'monetary overinvestment theory' (Estey 1956, p. 207).

Production occurs in both the capital goods industries and the consumption goods industries, but the allocation of resources across the various stages of production is determined by the spending-saving decisions. Saving means that society wants more capital goods produced while spending means that more consumption goods are wanted. With the money supply held constant, the equilibrium real interest rate equates saving by society with investment spending for capital goods. If the allocation of income changes, so that saving increases or decreases, the real interest rate falls or rises and investment by entrepreneurs increases or decreases.

Over-investment occurs when banks become eager to lend, reducing their lending rates below the equilibrium real rate level at which full employment existed. Entrepreneurs increase their borrowing and the new money created by banks in making new loans is spent for the purpose of increasing production capacities. As the increased demand for capital goods drives prices in industries producing those goods, resources are reallocated from the production of consumer goods to the production of capital goods. As the aggregate output of consumer goods falls, prices of those goods rise. Forced saving by households occurs as consumption is reduced because the entrepreneurs can bid the resources away. But money incomes rise as owners of producers' goods and inputs receive higher payments from the entrepreneurs' purchases of producers' goods. As soon as their money incomes permit, households increase their spending in an attempt to restore the old level of consumption. The result is more inflation in consumer goods, which encourages more production of consumer goods. With demand for producers' goods now declining, investments in producers' goods to fail to meet expected rates of return. For a while, the banking system continues to increase the volume of credits as the prices of consumer goods seem to offer the hope of extra profits for producers. But that only keeps the spiral of inflation going as, again, rising consumers' income increases their demand for consumption goods, which further drives up those prices.

At some point, banks will have to stop increasing bank credit and a reversal in the structure of production sets in, with many investment projects becoming abandoned. As production in capital goods industries decreases, prices of those goods fall and employment of labor is reduced. Temporarily, the demand for consumer goods continues to rise and mobile labor and capital is transferred to producing consumer goods. But the consumer goods industries cannot absorb all the labor that is freed from the capital goods industries and unemployment rises. A general deflation accompanies the shrinkage of activity as bank credit is reduced and the velocity of circulation falls as hoarding by businessmen and consumers occurs. Since prices of producers' goods fall more than prices of consumer goods, the producers' good industries become even more depressed.

Once the cycle has been initiated, there is no possible action that policymakers can take to ameliorate it. If credit is advanced to consumers, the depression will only be prolonged. While idle resources may be absorbed for a while, it is artificial stimulus that temporarily supports an artificial structure of production, setting up a new crisis when the credit ends. Additional credit to the producers could be justified because the deflation has made the structure of production shrink more than the voluntary distribution of saving and spending justifies. But that is not possible because policymakers lack knowledge as to how much stimulus is needed and precisely when to withdraw it to avoid starting another cycle. The cycle that ends in depression can be prevent only by taking away the ability of banks to increase the money supply.

Schumpeter wrote that Hayek's theory when presented to the 'Anglo-American community of economists, met with a sweeping success that has never been equaled by any strictly theoretical book that failed to make amends for its rigor by including plans and policy recommendations or to make contact in other ways with its readers' loves or hates' (1954, p. 1120).

The strong critical reaction that ensured underlined the success of the theory at first, but then the economics profession turned 'to other leaders and other interests.' (ibid.). It was apparent that the main 'other leader' to which Schumpeter referred was Keynes. In a footnote, he stated that other, more popularly received, theories did not have the 'spectacular quality' of Hayek's. In particular, Keynes' theory was not comparable because 'whatever its merit as a piece of analysis may be, there cannot be any doubt that it owed its victorious career primarily to the fact that its argument implemented some of the strongest political preferences of a large number of modern economists. . . . Politically, Hayek's swam against the stream' (pp. 1120-1121, fn.).

4. Debt, Innovations, and Deflation in Veblen's Theory

In *The Theory of Business Enterprise*, published in 1904, Veblen presented an analysis of developments in corporate finance, industrial technology, and business practices in light of the economic trends of the post-Civil War period, especially the last two decades of the 19th century. A key part of that analysis explained how a combination of institutional and technological factors made debt-deflation and chronic depression the normal course under the modern business enterprise system, with intermittent episodes of speculative inflation initiated by exogenous developments that end in financial crises. We begin this chapter with a review of the historical setting in which Veblen developed his theory of debt-deflation/chronic-depression. That is followed by an examination of how processes that are endogenous to modern business enterprise and industrial technologies tended to result in trends of deflation and chronic depression.

We close out the chapter with an examination of Veblen's revised theory in *Absentee Ownership*, published in 1923, that a 'new order' had emerged in the post-World War I era in which sustained credit-inflation had replaced the tendency toward deflation and chronic depression. Veblen's analysis of the 'new order' was based on observations of institutional developments that occurred between 1904 and the early 1920s. With the exception of the establishment of the Federal Reserve System in 1913, those developments were already well under way when Veblen was writing *The Theory of Business Enterprise*, and were simply accelerated by the economic effects of America's participation in World War I.

HISTORICAL SETTING OF VEBLEN'S DEBT-DEFLATION THEORY

During the last four decades of the 19th century, the U.S. economy experienced substantial economic growth and development in all dimensions but with great volatility. The growth was due to a combination of factors that included an increase in population; major technological advances and expansions in industry, transportation, communication, and energy that involved substantial investments in new capital equipment, and abundant natural resources. But business and financial conditions failed to allow full use of the increases in capacity and productivity as the economy experienced several cycles of prosperity and depression with a general long-run trend of price deflation.

This was a period in which the modern industrial system (broadly defined as including transportation, energy, mining, and communication as well as manufacturing) rapidly emerged on a large scale. That was attended by the growing importance of the engineers, technicians, and skilled workers who collectively created and operated the enormously complex industrial and transportation systems that increasingly required close coordination of all of the functioning elements.

On the business side, virtually every important sector of the industrial system was marked by the growth and consolidation of large operating corporations. New organizational forms emerged to increase the control of a few powerful businessmen over operating corporations. In the 1870s, the pools emerged in which producers in particular markets agreed on such items as prices, production, or market territories but those arrangements were not enforceable by law and the participants were not under effective control by the pool organizers. Collusive arrangements of a much more effective form began with the organization of the Standard Oil Trust organized in 1879 that allowed the Rockefeller interests to control nearly 90 percent of oil pipelines and refineries. A trust was formed by those holding the majority stock in competing corporations turned over their voting control to a group of trustees. By the end of the 1880s, trusts had been organized in most of the basic industries. When the courts ruled those arrangement were illegal, the holding company, as a legally charter corporation, quickly replaced the trusts and the era of big business became firmly entrenched.

The growth of large corporations and the consolidation of economic power were facilitated by important developments in corporate finance and banking. The huge investments in new plants and equipment had to be financed, as did also the numerous mergers and consolidations. Growth in the commercial banking sector facilitated the working capital needs of business, although the absence of a central bank left the American system of many independent state and national banks highly susceptible to crises. The most important new development in corporate finance was the emergence of the large investment bankers, as exemplified and personified by J. P. Morgan.

Financial control over operating companies was well underway by the time that Veblen published *The Theory of Business Enterprise* in 1904. But equally important were the heavy dependency on bank loans by businessmen and the pricing of corporate securities in the stock and bond markets. Along with efforts to engage in monopolistic practices in corporate production and pricing, the late 1800s and early 1900s was an era of virtually continuous financial manipulation of corporate securities that often had serious negative effects on the real economy. Veblen, who drew heavily upon the Industrial Commission's report to the House of Representatives in 1900, noted that it was chiefly in this manner that the 'great modern fortunes' had been realized (1904, p. 167).

Deflation and Depression

In the immediate post-Civil War period, the U.S. economy suffered a mild recession. But by 1869 a general prosperity had begun, which survived a short recession and panic that resulted from the unsuccessful attempt by Jay Gould and Jim Fisk to corner the gold market in 1869. But that prosperity ended with the Panic of 1873, which was followed by one of the longest periods of economic contraction in American history. In 1878, the economy began to revive and enjoyed a period of prosperity that ended in a recession in 1883, which turned into several years of depression. From 1886 to 1893, an inflow of foreign capital and trade surpluses contributed to generally favorable economic conditions. But a financial crisis in Europe was precipitated in 1890 by the failure of the British banking house, Baring Brothers. The U.S. economy experienced a short recession that was largely caused by a stock-market crisis. The situation became worse in 1893, when a financial panic led into several years of depression. Revival began in 1898 and, until the Panic of 1907, the economy enjoyed a prosperity that was interrupted by a mild recession 1903.

With the economic groups in the U.S. becoming more unequal in terms of wealth and power, the periods of depressions had different impacts on the economic positions of those groups. Farmers and some businessmen were negatively affected by low prices and most workers suffered unemployment. But depressed economic and financial conditions were very favorable for large bankers and industrialists, enabling them to establish and increase their dominance in particular markets by buying up competitors and other bankrupt businesses at reduced prices. John D. Rockefeller substantially increased his holdings in the oil business during the depression period of the 1870s.

The rapid growth in capital expenditures for new plant and equipment, much of which implemented technological innovations, resulted in a three-fold increase in labor productivity between 1869 and 1900. But while the real economy in terms of per capita production of goods increased substantially over this period, the price trends were generally deflationary. On an index with the period 1851-59 as the base, consumer prices rose nearly 80 percent during the Civil War and then went into a long decline that finally ended in 1898. Although there were occasional weak upturns, consumer prices were still lower in 1897 than in the 1850s. The wholesale price index with 1926 as the base, fell from 120 in 1865 to a low of 50 in 1897 before rising to around 70 in 1910 (Fite and Reese 1965, pp. 305, 481).

While workers as a group realized real gains in wage incomes, there were great variations with skilled workers gaining and unskilled workers doing less well. In sectors where wages rose, labor costs were held in check by increasing productivity. Wages in the manufacturing, mining, and construction sectors nearly kept up with increasing labor productivity (Fite and Reese 1965, p. 392). The downward trend in farm prices had particularly serious effects on the incomes of the large portion of the population that depended upon farming for a living. Whether prices of agricultural commodities fell more than or about the same as the prices of manufactured goods depends upon the indexes used. A Senate Finance Committee reported that the prices of non-farm commodities fell about 8 percent between 1860 and 1891, while the prices of non-farm commodities fell by only 3 percent over the same period. While prices of both wheat and cotton increased in some of the years during that long period, the general trend was downward, as shown by the decline in the average price of wheat from $1.52 in 1866 to $0.49 in 1894 (ibid., p. 436).

A Popular Version of the Quantity Theory of Money

A popular perception among farmers, small businessmen, and debtors, in general, was that the deflation was caused by an insufficient supply of money. Hence, the solution was for the government to increase the total amount of paper currency and coins in circulation. That popular version of the quantity theory of money gave rise to two political movements — the Greenback party and the free-silver movement.

The supply of paper currency at the end of the Civil War consisted of national bank notes and the 'greenbacks' that had been issued by the federal government. The total amount of national bank notes was limited by an act of Congress and, moreover, each national bank could only issue bank notes equal to 90 percent of its holdings of government bonds. An organized political movement emerged that sought to get the government to increase the number of 'greenbacks' in circulation. In the presidential election of 1868, the Democratic Party supported the 'Ohio Idea,' which called for inflating the currency by paying off the federal government's debt in 'greenbacks' rather than in gold. Paying in gold would provide an enormous profit for those who had bought the bonds with paper money during the war, when paper money was worth less than gold. With a Republican victory in the presidential election, the bonds were redeemed in gold. After the amount of 'greenbacks' had declined from $433 million in 1865 to $356 million in 1870, the government issued an additional $26 million in 1873. But in 1874 President Grant vetoed a bill passed by Congress that would have raised the amount to $400 million. In 1875 the Resumption Act required redemption of 'greenbacks' in gold, which involved gradually reducing the amount of greenbacks to $300 million.

Against that backdrop, the Greenback Party held its national convention in 1876, with a platform that called for repeal of the Resumption Act and increasing the issue of 'greenbacks.' The party received scant votes in the 1876 presidential election but did better in the mid-term elections of 1878 with a broader platform. Fifteen Congressmen were elected who endorsed Greenback principles. But, as farm prices began rising in 1880, farmers temporarily lost interest in the money issue and the Greenback Party's presidential candidate received less than 200,000 votes.

The rise in farm prices did not last and, by 1892, many farmers had come to consider inflation of the currency as the most important solution to their price problems. With the decline of the Greenback movement in the early 1880s, the 'inflationists' turned to free and unlimited coinage of silver as a practical means of expanding the money supply. After 1834 very little silver was being coined and, in 1853, Congress stopped coining silver except for the dollar. In 1873 coinage of silver dollars was also discontinued. Since the market value of the silver content of a dollar was greater than a dollar, the Coinage Act of 1873 drew little attention. But in the mid-1870s, the market price of silver began dropping because of an increase in the world's supply of silver. The newly unified Germany went on the gold standard and the German states sold their reserves of silver. At the same time, silver mines in the western U.S. began producing large amounts of silver.

Proponents of expanding the money supply with silver were successful in getting two acts passed by Congress and signed into law by the President. The Bland-Allison Act of 1878 authorized the Secretary of Treasury to purchase $2-$4 million worth of silver bullion per month and coin it into silver dollars. This amounted to a large subsidy for silver producers, since the market value of the silver content of the dollar coins was less than a dollar in gold. The second act, the Sherman Silver Purchase Act, was passed in 1890, after the general price level had continued to decline. The price of silver bullion also continued to fall, hitting $0.72 in gold in 1889. The act authorized the U.S. Treasury to purchase 4.5 million ounces of silver bullion per month, paying in treasury notes that were redeemable in either gold or silver although the Treasury, in practice, backed its notes in gold. As the price of bulk silver continued to fall, the ratio of the value of gold to the value of silver appreciated from 16-1 in 1873 to 22-1 in 1889. The deflation in prices of agricultural commodities continued to the extent that a $1,000 mortgage for a wheat farmer could have been paid off with a sale of 1,031 bushels of wheat in 1890 but would have required the sale of

1,775 bushels in 1894 (Fite and Reese 1965, p. 451). Farmers blamed the appreciating value of gold relative to silver for the deflation.

But the free silver movement spread beyond the rural economy. In 1892 the Populist Party campaigned for free silver and, in 1896, the Democratic Party backed free silver against the Republican's support of the gold standard. Republicans and pro-gold Democrats, such as President Cleveland, blamed the 1893 panic on the abasement of the money supply by the 1890 Sherman Silver Purchase Act. As European investors sold their American assets and took the dollars in gold, the Treasury's gold reserves fell below the level that was thought necessary to back the Treasury notes in circulation. Since silver could be sold at the Treasury for notes that could be redeemed in either gold or silver, and gold was more valuable than silver on the market, President Cleveland was persuaded that the drain on gold reserves was caused by the conversion of silver into notes that were then redeemed in gold. He succeeded in pressuring Congress to repeal the 1890 act.

The long period of deflationary trends and recurring recession came to an end in the late 1890s. Between 1897 and 1913 the farm sector experienced a rise in prices that has become known as the 'golden age' of American agriculture. While concern over the elasticity of paper currency for bank deposit withdrawals would be a factor leading to the establishment of the Federal Reserve System in 1913, concerns about the aggregate money supply dissipated for several reasons. The supply of gold was substantially increased by a combination of new mines and technological innovations that allowed more gold to be extracted from ores, which allowed the U.S. to formally adopt the gold standard under the Currency Act of 1900. More importantly, economists had begun to understand importance of deposit money created by banks.

THEORY OF DEBT, DEFLATION, AND CHRONIC DEPRESSION

In *The Theory of Business Enterprise*, Veblen interpreted the developments in the U.S. economy since the 1870s as creating a situation in which the 'ordinary course of affairs in business' was one of chronic depression that was intermittently disturbed by extraneous 'transient circumstances' (1904, p. 253). As the normal condition of modern American business enterprise, 'dull times' were in 'the course of nature' while the 'brisk times' were 'an exceptional invention by man or a rare bounty of Providence' (p. 184). To some extent, that was true also for England but less so for the continental European economies. Why chronic depression had become the ordinary course and what type of extraneous circumstances might be 'invented by man' or come as a 'rare Providential bounty' to irregularly disturb but not derail that course, Veblen explained in his analysis of the interplay between the business system (including the financial system) and the industrial system in the U.S. at the beginning of the 20th century.

Veblen's theory of business enterprise was an analysis of the behavior of businessmen and financiers in a modern industrial-financial economy within the broader context of a social environment that had been shaped historically by cultural values and institutional practices inherited from the 1700s and was continuously being conditioned to some degree by the impact of the demands of the modern industrial system and the mental influence of modern industrial technology. As a critical part of that analysis, Veblen substantially expanded and modernized the earlier economists' focus on the role of credit and debt in influencing the level of prices and the extent to which the productive capacity of the economy was utilized. That was accomplished within the framework of a sophisticated analysis of the role of credit and debt in the modern concept of business capital as a pecuniary valuation rather than as instruments of production or even the replacement cost of those instruments.

Why debt-deflation and chronic depression was the normal course of the modern business enterprise economy was one aspect of Veblen's famous dichotomy between production of vendible goods for business profits and production of serviceable goods for people. That has been described as 'making goods versus making money.' Technological forces determine the nature and mechanical functioning of the modern industrial system that is administered by the engineers and technicians. But the institutions, principles, and practices of modern business govern, determining how and to what extent the industrial capacity and available labor force will actually be employed. Because pecuniary values rule, financial institutions, instruments, and practices play particularly important roles. A key element in Veblen's explanation of debt-deflation and chronic depressions is that market prices of capital goods are highly influenced by financial markets and institutions and, in turn, market values of capital goods have a heavy influence on the financial aspects of the business enterprise system.

The economy's productive capacity is determined by modern machine technology that results in an industrial system that grows ever larger and more complex. The efficient functioning of that system requires a very fine balance of all of its components. Close attention to coordination is demanded, establishing the critical importance of technicians and engineers who have the specialized knowledge to understand the workings of the parts of the system. In contrast, the business enterprise system is one of many markets tied together by an ever-expanding set of financial contracts that are based on prices expressed in the standard monetary unit. Within this price system, disturbances in any one of the markets spread to other markets by destabilizing financial relations. Any financial disturbance will disturb the functioning of the industrial system that is under business control. Indeed, it is largely because of the highly interdependent functioning of the industrial system that a financial disturbance in one sector is quickly transmitted throughout the economic system as a whole, creating unemployment and decreased material welfare due to reduced outputs of goods.

But the industrial system is not a static system. On the contrary, it is subject to dynamic evolutionary change as continuous advances in technology are implemented in the industrial system. Here again, the dichotomy of administration is present. Improvements in industrial technologies are the work of the engineers, technicians, and skilled workers. The influence of the mechanical cause-and-effect relationships on their mentality leads to a habitual interest in production efficiency and ways to maintain and improve that efficiency. But the pecuniary institutions of the modern business enterprise system determine not only how and to what extent the industrial capacity will be used but also the rate and timing at which new technologies will be introduced through business investment. Here, the financial sector plays an important role in determining the rate of new investment and the business consequences of old investments through the valuation of the capital of business enterprises and the relationship of debt to capital.

Capital and Debt

A major contribution by Veblen was to modernize the concept of capital in the business enterprise system as it developed during the second half of the 19th century. From its beginning in the 1700s, the driving force of business enterprise has been the profit motive. In determining how the productive industrial capacity would be used, the only consideration was to market prices and costs in the quest for profitable returns. But, in the earlier periods, the profitable interests of those who owned and operated the productive units generally coincided with the interests of the consumers of the products. That changed in the 19th century, especially during the second half. A key development was the emergence of corporate finance to link banking and the securities markets to the management of large corporate enterprises and, thus, to the real economy. Here, evolving concepts of capital and investment added a new dimension to the pursuit of pecuniary profit.

As the modern technological system developed in the industrial sector on a large-scale operational basis, large corporations under the direction of businessmen emerged to control how and to what extent the industrial processes is used. Businessmen became increasingly removed from the actual production processes to focus almost exclusively on the financial operations of large firms. That was especially the case for large firms organized as corporations with limited liability provided for the absentee owners of the corporate stocks. In the modern era, businessmen systematically invest in the mechanical processes of industry for pecuniary profits and the industrial plants and processes are capitalized on basis of their profit-yielding capacity (1904, p. 85). In contrast to earlier periods, when gains on investments were regarded as 'fortuitous' events, modern businessmen expect a 'normal' rate of return on investments (pp. 86-89). Veblen's debt-deflation theory of chronic depression emerges from the combination of an institutional expectation that business investments must pay 'normal' returns, business capital being enhanced by debt, continuous technological improvements that lower the costs of industrial equipment and, hence, the costs of goods produced by that equipment, and competitive markets that force prices ultimately to fall in line with production costs.

Veblen emphasized that extensive use of credit is an essential feature of the modern business management of the industrial system. Business credit takes a number of forms, ranging from contracts of purchase and sale on credit to loans by commercial banks and the issuance of securities by corporations. But the real focal point in Veblen's analysis was the relationship between credit/debt, stock prices, and capital during periods of prosperity, crisis, and depression.

Capital as a modern business concept is the capitalized value of expected future corporate earnings. The values of corporations' capital assets are set by the prices of their stock as currently quoted on the stock market. In emphasizing that the managers of modern corporations use debt to maximize capital, Veblen essentially gave new meaning to Adam Smith's statement that: 'A man must be perfectly crazy who, where there is tolerable security, does not employ all the stock which he commands, whether it be his own or borrowed of other people' (Smith [1776] 1976, p. 285). But whereas Smith was thinking of 'stock' in terms of either commodities to be used in production or as 'circulating capital' used to pay the wages of workers employed in production and had a very dim view of joint-stock companies and their financing, Veblen recognized that, in modern corporate finance, debt had a different purpose and effect. A business firm that operates with debt would gain a competitive advantage in terms of the rate of return on equity investment, provided that other firms did not follow suit. But the competitive nature of business enterprise leads every firm to seek the same advantage, so that all are forced to incur debt up to the limit set by the collateral value of the firm's capital. A key point in Veblen's theory was that the distinction between capital and debt is very blurred. In the emergence of a period of speculative prosperity, capital becomes enhanced by debt and the increase in capital facilitates further increases in debt.

Speculative Prosperity and the Accumulation of Debt

Price inflation and deflation occur with business cycles that follow the pattern of 'prosperity' or 'exaltation,' 'crisis,' and 'depression.' Veblen defined 'prosperity' and 'depression' in terms of business values — market prices, valuation of capital, and rates of return on investment, which come in the regular course of business (1904, p. 183). Although depression and prosperity are bound together in some measure, a depression may occur without a preceding period of prosperity (ibid.). Veblen criticized the conventional economic theory of crises and depressions for focusing on the industrial side rather than the business side. A 'tenable theory' must recognize the role of prices, earnings (both expected and actual), and capitalization of both tangible and intangible business assets (p. 185). Such a theory must also deal with the fact that prosperity and depression are 'at least in their first incidence, of the nature of psychological fact, just as price movements are a psychological phenomenon' (p. 186).

Prosperity occurs when prices are rising (1904, p. 198), but the general form is a 'speculative prosperity' that involves a 'speculative inflation in industrial investments' (p. 247). An 'inflation in capitalization' (pp. 243-244) is initiated by 'some favorable disturbance of the course of business' (p. 194), typically in the form of an increase in demand in some industry or sector of the economy. That Veblen recognized the possibility of a monetary-induced inflation but was dealing with a different set of factors is indicated in his comment that the

> . . .usual and more effectual impetus to an era of prosperity, *when it is not an inflation of the currency*, is some form of wasteful expenditure, as, e.g., a sustained war demand or the demand due to the increase of armaments, naval and military, or again, such as an interference with the course of business as is wrought by a differentially protective tariff. (1904, pp. 210-211; emphasis added)

Presumably an expansion in the money supply from new discoveries of gold would be a case of prosperity wrought by the 'providence of nature.' But the other factors cited in that statement explain what Veblen meant that 'brisk times' being 'an exceptional invention by man' (1904, p. 184). In a footnote, he attributed the prosperity of 1897-1902 to the 'demand for supplies caused by the Spanish-American War, though other favorable circumstances acted to give it volume' (p. 194, fn).

In that same footnote, Veblen cited with evident agreement an article in which the author (identified as 'Mr. Carver') argued that the price increases are necessarily in the 'producers goods' sector because those prices are more sensitive to changes in profits whereas consumer goods prices are more sensitive to 'entire demand' (1904, pp. 194-195). Thus, the main focus of Veblen's analysis was on the prices of capital goods, which relate closely to the capital of business enterprises and the use of the capitalized values of businesses as going concerns as collateral for new debt. Firms in the industries or sectors experiencing increasing demand respond to the rising prices for their outputs by attempting to increase supply to meet the increase in demand. In addition to extending the operations of existing plants, they make new investments, thus increasing demand for producers' goods and capital goods, which raises prices in supplying industries or sectors. Although consumer goods prices rise, the most volatile fluctuations occur in the prices of producers goods (p. 194) and, because capital is most 'vendible' in those sectors, that is where the price rises start in prosperity, and also where they break at the crisis (p. 181).

With labor costs lagging, the rising prices increase the profits of firms in the sectors experiencing the actual or anticipated increases in demand. As soon as prices and profits begin rising, an expansion in credit (and debt) becomes a major factor. The increased use of credit may be either a cause or an effect of the acceleration in business activity, but Veblen declared that in most cases it was both (1904, p. 190). As the stock market capitalizes the higher profits in higher stock prices, corporate management immediately issues bonds or borrows from banks, using the higher capitalization as collateral. Credit is extended under 'somewhat easy scrutiny of the property values' that serves as collateral for the loans (p. 198). Veblen essentially describes an endogenous process by which the money supply is effectively increased as he recognized that the new loans expand the aggregate spending power, which further increases demand and, thus, inflation of prices, leading to expectations of yet higher profits, which are again collateral for more new loans.

In a very substantial way, prosperity quickly becomes a 'psychological phenomenon' (1904, p. 195) as purely speculative expectations of increases in profits permeate through the economy, which are capitalized through rising stock prices. Business debt increases as corporate managements quickly issue more bonds and all businesses take out more loans based on the increased capitalization of their corporate assets. Thus, Veblen described this as both a 'speculative inflation' and a 'credit inflation' (pp. 99-100).

There may be a modest gain in the 'aggregate material welfare' during a period of prosperity. At times, Veblen seems to treat the total output of new capital goods as relatively constant so that the increased demand for capital goods results in the primary inflation. But, at other times, he indicated that there may be some increase in the stock of industrial equipment (1904, p. 210). Although nominal wages lag behind prices, there is some increase in the general level of real labor income due to greater opportunity for employment in 'brisk times.' But that gain is largely offset by the increased cost of living as prices rise, suggesting that any increase in the output of consumer goods tends to be quite limited.

The inflationary increase in prices, however, is partially countered by the effects of business investments in cost-reducing industrial technologies. Veblen noted that during a prosperity there is to 'an uncertain but commonly appreciable extent . . . a progressive cheapening of the processes of production' which helps to maintain the profit margin even when labor costs begin increasing (1904, p. 200). But the efficiency gains from new industrial technologies will play a more important role as a major cause of deflation and chronic depression that in curbing the price rises during a period of speculative prosperity.

Crisis and Liquidation: The Initial Deflation

The initial deflation comes as the immediate aftermath of the ending of a speculative prosperity, which often involves a financial crisis. In a general sense, prices of outputs are mainly a function of consumption demand and, for the value of output in demand terms to rise as fast as business capitalization rises, the nominal incomes of consumers would have to increase at the same rate as inflation (1904, p. 109). As nominal wages lag behind prices until near the end of the prosperity, aggregate consumer demand lags behind inflation. But nominal wages do eventually begin to rise, which reduces the profit margin on which prosperity rested (pp. 211-212). At some point, the original increase in demand that started prices rising in the first sector dissipates and, in the late stages of prosperity, nominal wages begin to rise. The combination of rising labor costs and weakening demand for output eliminates opportunities for higher corporate earnings. The false prosperity may continue for a time for two reasons. First, there are numerous contracts that must be filled, which supports demand for outputs in those industries. Second, the psychological effects of prosperity produce a 'habit of buoyancy, or speculative recklessness, which grows up in any business community under such circumstances' (p. 196).

With actual earnings capacities now falling below the previously expected earnings capacities, the capitalized valuations of business assets pledged as collateral for loans begin to fall. As Raines and Leathers (2000, pp. 74-75) have noted, there is the suggestion of the efficient markets hypothesis in Veblen's explanation of what happens. When the stock market perceives the discrepancy between actual and previously expected corporate earnings, stock prices begin to fall, which lowers the capitalized values of business assets. That alerts banks and other creditors to the deficiency in collateral and they begin to call loans or demand that additional collateral be posted. A crisis looms as the liabilities of firms have become 'in some degree, bad debts' (Veblen 1904, p. 202). The initial deflation is caused by distress selling of goods and business assets by firms needing liquidity. As Veblen observed, the liquidation by one firm 'involves cutting under the ruling prices of products, which lessens the profits for competing firms and throws them into the class of insolvents, and so extends the readjustment of capitalization' (p. 205).

Chronic Depression: Deflationary Trends

Like prosperity, depression is a business phenomenon involving prices and profits. It affects businessmen by reducing their profits to losses and turns debts into liquidation of assets and outputs and, ultimately, bankruptcies. Depression comes 'in the regular course of business,' and while it follows every period of prosperity, a preceding prosperity is not required (Veblen 1904, p. 183). During the last decades of the 19th century, the periods of prosperity became less frequent and were weaker while depressions became more frequent and severe. While a 'mild but chronic state of depression' had become the normal condition of industrial business, 'brisk times' were either 'an exceptional invention of man or a rare bounty of Providence' (p. 184).

Veblen observed that while crises had received much attention from economic historians, economic theory had not addressed sufficiently the relatively newer and more obscure phenomenon of 'protracted depression' that arises from the nature of modern business enterprise (1904, p. 212). In his theory, the two main causes of chronic depression are business debt (together with an interest rate) and new investments that implement new and improved industrial technologies. But before discussing those, attention needs to be given to the underlying psychological factor.

Veblen noted that, like prosperity, depression is, at least in the first instance, in the nature of a psychological phenomenon but there are two differences between depression and prosperity. First, the features of depression are less pronounced and, hence, have not attracted the attention of economists in the same way as crises. Second, the limits to the run of a depression are less definite than for a prosperity (1904, p. 212). Chronic or protracted depression is possible for reasons that will be explained shortly, but prosperity (whether it ends in crisis or not) is unsustainable as was explained above.

The psychological factor behind depression is that businessmen and lending institutions conventionally suffer from the illusion that the monetary unit has 'invariable value' (1904, p. 105). Investments are expected to realize the same rate of return, which means paying back the same number of nominal dollars, when deflation is raising the purchasing power of those dollars. Those holding corporate bonds and contracted debt of businesses expect to receive the same rate of interest (the same amount of interest in nominal dollars) on those debts and to receive the same number of nominal dollars loaned when the debt is paid off. Thus, the indebted businesses are required by law to pay that same rate of interest on debts incurred at an earlier time, when the purchasing power of the monetary unit was less, and to pay back the same number of nominal dollars as was borrowed. The real hardships that depression brings to the general population is unemployment and reduced production of consumption goods because businessmen see no advantage in producing if prices are not expected to assure 'ordinary' profits.

Debt, Interest Rates, and Competitive Markets

The first factor responsible for the indefinite limits to deflation and depression stems from the financial aspects of business enterprise — debt, interest rates, and profits, and from the determination of prices in competitive markets. When deflation occurs, the fixed costs of interest charges on firms' debts reduce the margin of profit and make it difficult to shut-down as long as outputs can be sold at prices that cover variable costs (in Veblen's words, the fixed interest costs 'preclude shutting down, except at a sure and considerable loss' (1904, pp. 217-218)). But the chronic depression and deflationary trend stems from the consequences of lower interest rates and the emergence of new firms in markets that are still highly competitive, such that prices are set by the firms with the lowest costs of production and operation.

Although Veblen included 'perturbations of the rate of interest' among the substantial and far-reaching 'secondary effects' of the liquidations that are forced by financial crises (1904, pp. 111-112), he emphasized that the *level* of interest rates does not cause depressions. In addition to affecting the capitalized valuation of business assets and securities that pay fixed amounts of interest (bonds), interest rates are important because the rate of expected earnings must exceed the rate of interest to make debt worthwhile. While interest rates set a limit on the advantage of using loan credit, that limit is 'somewhat elastic.' What businessmen regard as fair prices and reasonable profits necessarily use current interest rates as a sort of zero line below which profits should not fall. In times of 'ordinary prosperity,' the rate of earnings exceeds the interest rate by an appreciable amount and even more so during 'brisk times' (p. 96).

While the use of credit tends to be somewhat restricted during depression, it is not due to an absence of credit. On the contrary, credit is readily available on good security. But low or declining interest rates do depress the business situation because of the entry of newly organized firms (or reorganized firms coming out of bankruptcy) with credit obtained at the lower interest rates. With lower interest costs, the new firms are able to realize a reasonable profit while selling output at the lower prices. In markets that are still highly competitive, prices are set the lowest cost producers. The older firms carrying the higher interest costs are forced to sell at those lower prices, suffering losses which leads to more distressed selling and bankruptcy (1904, pp. 220-224).

Technological Innovations, Investment, and Competitive Markets

An important feature of Veblen's analysis is his explanation of how a period of stable prices and interest rates turns into a period of deflation and depression. Low interest rates could explain chronic depression only if they progressively fall, which they never do (1904, pp. 224-225). Even if interest rates and prices have been stable, deflation and chronic depression will still occur because of the competitive pressure on prices arising from new investments in cost-reducing industrial technologies.

Veblen's theory of business investment spending was clearly stated: 'New investments are made on the basis of current rates of interest and with a view of securing the differential gain promised by the excess of prospective profits over interest rates' (1904, p. 218). Businessmen have a motive to innovate because the adoption of more efficient, time-saving industrial processes increase profits (p. 94). On the technology side, innovations in the industrial equipment are constantly occurring as 'Machine processes, ever increasing in efficiency, turn out the mechanical appliances and materials with which the processes are carried on, at an ever decreasing cost; so that at each successive step the result is a process having a higher efficiency at a lower cost' (p. 229).

Here now is an explanation of why the limits to depression and deflation are indefinite. Veblen's analysis heavily emphasized the effects of technological improvements in the production of capital goods. In competitive markets, the prices of capital goods trend downward as the production costs of industrial equipment progressively falls. That cost reduction is passed on in the form of lower prices of outputs produced by the new equipment. Moreover, the new capital goods have higher efficiency in use so that the cost of producing the final output prices fall yet again (1904, p. 229). Veblen described an 'acceleration' effect of increasing efficiency of machine technology that arises 'out of a persistent divergence between the past cost of a like or equivalent equipment at any subsequent date, — supposing that there had been no inflation of prices and no extraneous cause making for a speculative advance' (pp. 226-227). In a competitive market for capital goods, the prices of those goods fall with cost to all buyers. But those buyers are chiefly the new investors who start new ventures or extensions of existing industrial establishments. The newcomers will under-price their competitors, causing the profit margins for the older firms to decrease as they are forced to sell at lower prices (p. 230).

The effect of cost-reducing innovations in industrial technologies being progressively implemented by business investment was so important that it provided a 'simple' explanation of why 'the ordinary course of affairs in business, when undisturbed by transient circumstances extraneous to the industrial system proper, has been chronic depression' (1904, p. 253). As a result of the rate of reduction in the cost of producing capital goods and with competitive prices falling, a persistent decline in profits had not permitted a consistent speculative expansion to get under way. When a speculative movement had been initiated by extraneous factor, the persistent and relatively rapid decline of earning-capacity of older investments brought the speculative inflation to book before it became strong enough to bring on a violent crisis (p. 255).

REMEDIES FOR CHRONIC DEPRESSION

Veblen identified four possible remedies for deflation/chronic depression, none of which were judged to have much prospect of being effective as things stood at the beginning of the 20th century. Several of the remedies involved stimulation of aggregate demand or demand in some sectors that subsequently spreads to the broader economy. Others involved retardation of aggregate supply.

Monetary Remedies

Stimulation of aggregate demand could come from an increase in the money supply. Veblen gave the most explicit attention to the effects of an increased supply of gold such as occurred in the 1890s, when gold was discovered in Alaska, Colorado, Australia, and South Africa and new technologies allowed more gold to be extracted from low grade ores. In that discussion, Veblen appeared to generally accept the quantity theory but added three insights of his own.

First, an increase in gold occurs only under very exceptional circumstances (Veblen 1904, p. 237). Second, technological advances have different effects on business when they occur in mining of gold than when they occur in other industries. While the latter contribute to chronic depression by lowering the prices of the goods produced, the increased supply of gold 'is the most fortunate material circumstance for the business interests that industrial activity can bring, because it puts off depression by keeping up price' (pp. 235-236, fn). But since gold has primarily a monetary use and is not consumed, any additional gold produced constitutes a small fractional increase in the total money supply (p. 236) and, thus, normally will have only minimal countering effects against depression (p. 237).

Third, the most important effect of an increase in gold is psychological, the excitement that it gives to 'speculative inflation' (1904, p. 237). But that tends to be only a short-lived phenomenon. Thus, even though the level of prices rose by 32 percent from 1897 to 1902 after the discovery of gold in Alaska, Australia, and South Africa and the improved technology in producing gold from low-grade ores (Williams 1994, p. 11), Veblen believed there was little potential for increases in specie to prevent the protracted depression arising from the combination of funded debt and cost-reducing industrial technologies in competitive markets.

Veblen also recognized that the money supply could be increased through inflation of the currency and by the 'more facile use of credit instruments as a subsidiary currency' (1904, p. 235). With the exception of a brief footnote observation that only a fractional reserve of gold backed the notes of national banks (p. 101), Veblen did not discuss an expansion of the currency. But he repeatedly acknowledged that credit extended by banks under fractional reserve banking (ibid.) created purchasing power, which allowed property in use to be 'coined into means of payment' (p. 103). That gives rise to inflation as the business borrowers spending the newly created purchasing power bid up the prices of capital goods. The reverse holds during depression, although the depression conditions may be somewhat thwarted or at least delayed by leniency on part of creditors. Banks and other large lenders may be hesitant to foreclose due to 'short-sightedness and lack of insight beyond the conventional routine,' fearing that forced liquidation of their debtors would depress the money value of the property involved (p. 207). But such leniency would be inconsequential when over-capitalization of borrowers was large and widely prevalent (p. 206).

There is the hint of a government-provided monetary policy in Veblen's statement that 'a well-advised and discreetly weighted extension of credit by the government to certain sections of the business community' had helped to avert a recent crisis (1904, p. 205). Veblen did not expand upon that statement but it would seem to pertain to actions by the Secretary of Treasury in the fall of 1902. Taus (1943, p. 97) noted that, between 1896 and 1912, the Secretaries of Treasury in the U.S. assumed extraordinary central banking powers. When the cash reserves of the New York banks fell below 25 percent in the fall of 1902, Secretary Shaw took what was considered to be 'drastic steps' to strengthen bank reserves. His actions included prepaying the interest and principal on government bonds, which provided banks with funds they did not have to pay out until the interest and principal payments were actually due, purchasing bonds at extremely high premiums, and telling banks they did not need to keep cash reserves against holdings of federal government funds (p. 104). But clearly Veblen dismissed any possibility of a monetary remedy as having anything more than a mild episodic braking of protracted depression.

Government Expenditures

Of the other three remedies that Veblen identified, two involved government policies. The most effective remedy was some form of 'wasteful' or 'extra-industrial' spending (1904, pp. 210-211, 252). In a footnote, Veblen explained that while these expenditures were wasteful in terms of using the industrial processes to produce outputs that resulted in 'unproductive' consumption, by generating prosperity they may have an indirect effect of inducing fuller use of the industrial capacity so that there may be some net increase in 'serviceable' outputs (p. 252, fn).

There was little hope that a sufficient level of wasteful spending could come from the private sector. While wasteful consumption spending is substantial during prosperity (1904, p. 210), it would be inadequate to offset the increased productivity of new industrial technologies (p. 255). Business principles leading to saving and investment are too ingrained in the mental habits of modern man to admit an effective reduction in the rate of saving (p. 256). Thus, 'wasteful' government expenditures in the form of 'a sustained war demand or the demand due to the increase of armaments, naval and military' (p. 211), 'public edifices, courtly and diplomatic establishments' (p. 256), or 'colonization, provincial investment' is required. The most recent speculative inflation had been generated by the Spanish-American War.

Government expenditures financed by borrowing results in securities being exchanged for private saving, giving the illusion that private saving has not been reduced while at the same time reducing the real saving rate (1904, p. 252). Expenditures financed by taxes would be less expedient in that respect. But indirect taxes, i.e., excises, 'have the peculiar advantage of keeping up the prices of the goods on which they are imposed, and thereby act directly toward the desired end' (p. 256).

Veblen noted that if the level of wasteful government spending should slacken, a depression would ensue and, if such spending was abruptly ended, there would be 'a crisis of some severity' (1904, p. 252). But problems emerge even if the level of public expenditure stays constant. There is an early anticipation of the Harrod-Domar growth model in Veblen's observation that a progressive increase in government expenditures would be required to 'offset the surplus productivity of modern industry' (ibid.). Veblen also noted that time spent in military reduces the purchasing power of those who serve.

Restricting Aggregate Supply: Protective Tariffs

While monetary expansion and 'wasteful' expenditure raise prices by stimulating aggregate demand, the other two remedies to protracted depression raise prices by reducing aggregate supply by reducing competition. One of those involved government policies. The U.S. and Germany in the late 19th century provided case studies of the prosperity-inducing effects of both 'wasteful' government expenditures for military purposes and reducing foreign competition by protective tariffs. While Veblen did not mention it, the increase in import duties imposed by the Dingley Tariff of 1897 was followed by gold inflows for the U.S. (Williams 1994, pp. 13-14). In both countries, the 'primary incidence' of the tariffs was 'a waste of industrial output or energy,' but the prosperity achieved must be recognized as a beneficial outcome in the form of heightened industrial activity and increased comfort for the industrial classes (Veblen 1904, p. 211).

Restricting Aggregate Supply: Collusion

The other approach to reducing aggregate supply was collusive efforts by businessmen to 'curtail and regulate' production levels (Veblen 1904, p. 258). Veblen remarked that 'Barring providential intervention . . . the only refuge from chronic depression . . . is thoroughgoing coalition in those lines of business in which coalition is practicable' (p. 263). The pools and trusts in the late 1800s were organized in efforts to replace prices established under free competition with 'collective selling' at prices based on 'what the traffic will bear,' which meant prices that will maximize the aggregate net earnings of the businessmen involved (p. 258). Prices might be lowered to stimulate larger sales and lower costs by exploiting economies of scale with increased production. But Veblen noted that monopoly pricing virtually always results in less output and higher prices (pp. 258-259). The modern machine process by being incompatible with competitive selling and simultaneously making it practicable to form such coalitions in virtually all industries, makes such a remedy appear both 'efficacious' and 'reasonable' from the perspective of businessmen (ibid.). But unless the whole industrial system is under the control of one monopoly, which had not been accomplished in 1904, the coalitions actually increase competition that depresses prices. Because of the concentration of income in the hands of a few businessmen with large saving rates, there is an acceleration of the increase in investments that creates downward pressure on price by potentially increasing supply and lowering production costs (p. 264).

HISTORICAL SETTING OF VEBLEN'S CREDIT-INFLATION THEORY

Veblen did not discuss collusive control over credit by large bankers in *The Theory of Business Enterprise*. But nineteen years later, in *Absentee Ownership*, he argued that such control in the hands of investment bankers had changed the tendency toward debt-deflation and chronic depression to well-entrenched chronic 'credit-inflation.' To a very large extent, the 'New Order of Business' that Veblen described in *Absentee Ownership* (1923, p. 205) was the most recent form of the institutional system that had been evolving for decades through cumulative changes. The one new institutional development that loomed large in the background was the establishment of the Federal Reserve System. Both the inflationary effects of government financial policies during World War I and the psychological effects of appeals to nationalism and patriotism had accelerated and heavily influenced the path and pattern of evolutionary development (1923, pp. 3, 218, fn). Veblen repeatedly made reference to such things as the 'crisis of unexampled privation, such as these years since the War' (p. 217) and 'the state of things brought on by the War and perpetuated by the businesslike Peace which has followed' (p. 218).

The most important way in which the war had shaped this 'New Order' was related to the emergence of credit-inflation rather than deflation and chronic depression as the 'normal' condition of the modern business enterprise system. Not surprisingly, Veblen seemed out-of-step with other observers of price trends in both *The Theory of Business Enterprise* and *Absentee Ownership*. According to Fisher (1925), the economy experienced a long period of inflation that started in 1896 and culminated in 1920. But, in 1904, Veblen was focusing on debt-deflation and chronic depression, not inflation. Similarly, while Fisher stated that the period of inflation ended in 1920, and was followed by 'drastic deflation' in 1920-1922 (1925, p. 180), Veblen identified inflation as being a chronic condition in 1923.

Veblen asserted that the inflation was induced by the war, which provided a launching pad for persistent credit-inflation as a normal phenomenon of the 'New Order.' The U.S. economy began experiencing war-induced inflation prior to the U.S. entering the war in 1917. Demands by the allies for American goods and the large inflows of gold resulted in wholesale prices rising by 43 percent by the time that the U.S. declared war on Germany. Farm prices also rose but by less than the increase in the prices that farmers paid, so the parity ratio fell from 100 in 1913 to 94 in 1916 (Fite and Reese 1965, p. 511).

Initially, the expansion in debt that helped to fuel the inflation came largely from the borrowing by the Allies. The Morgan banking firm handled the financial affairs of the allies, which involved contracting for $3 billion of U.S. war supplies and floating the English and French loans to pay for those supplies (Fite and Reese 1965, p. 512). When the U.S. entered the war in 1917, the nature and role of debt became greatly increased as two-thirds of the cost was financed by government borrowing. The inflation that ensued was due to the increase in government spending combined with a transfer of economic resources and manpower from production of private civilian goods to military use. While official statistics showed that prices in 1923 were 60-70 percent above their 1914 level, Veblen asserted that the 'effectual inflation' was 'appreciably' higher (1923, p. 219) as the inflation in credit, including loan credits and 'fiduciary currency,' was 'rated at something like 100 per cent., (sic) rather over than under' (p. 218).

When the U.S. entered the war in 1917, the government imposed a comprehensive set of economic regulations that included price controls over certain commodities. But neither the fiscal policies nor the price regulations effectively contained inflationary pressures and the Federal Reserve's monetary policy was subordinated to the Treasury's need to fund much of the war expenditures by public debt. The federal government used the constitutional authority to tax incomes granted under the 16th amendment but the contractionary effects on disposable incomes were more than offset by the inflationary effects of government borrowing. While the purchase of bonds by individuals reduced disposable income spent for consumption, the practice of allowing bonds to be purchased with funds borrowed from banks had just the opposite effect. Two other factors contributed further to inflationary credit conditions. Individuals were allowed to use government bonds as collateral for private loans and the Treasury anticipated bond receipts by selling certificates to banks. The Federal Reserve's policies were subordinated to the credit demands of both government and business. Member banks were not required to keep a reserve against federal deposits and they were allowed to increase their reserves by borrowing from the Federal Reserve Banks at low interest rates. In addition, the general reserve requirements were lowered by Congress (Degen 1987, pp. 32-36).

The price regulations imposed by the War Industries Board were based on negotiated agreements on maximum prices with the producers of certain basic commodities. The agreements were only for three months and were subject to renewal or revision at their expiration. Most of the revisions were upward and the regulated prices continued to rise throughout the war. The War Industries Board's primary concern was with prices of basic commodities. Little attention was paid to consumer prices. With food supplies critically short in Britain and France, a food control program was imposed in the U.S. which limited the amounts of certain foods that could be purchased. That was accompanied by posted warnings that anyone attempting to buy more would result in serious trouble for both the consumer and the grocer involved (Fite and Reese 1965, pp. 516-519).

As orders for war materials slowed in the fall of 1918, prices and economic activity began a gradual decline that lasted until the spring 1919. Prices then began rising in response to a booming market for exports financed by government loans to wartime allies and a strong surge of domestic demand for civilian goods as both business and labor incomes rose. With prices of farm commodities rising and easy mortgage money available from country banks, prices of farmland surged. A surge in consumption spending was further fueled by sales of Liberty bonds that households had purchased during the war. Between March 1919 and January 1920, the economy experienced an inflationary boom driven by speculation in commodities, inventory accumulation, and spending on luxuries. Wholesale prices rose by 21 percent from May 1919 to May 1920 (Williams 1994, p. 64). Although the money supply grew by 15 percent, a major factor was speculative inventory accumulations that reduced supplies. At the same time, unemployment and labor discontent over low wages and rising profits during a period of price inflation resulted in numerous labor strikes during 1919.

By the summer of 1920, the economy was moving into a deep but short depression that hit bottom in the third quarter of 1920 (Williams 1994, pp. 64, 74-75). When Veblen published *Absentee Ownership* in 1923, the inflation had largely subsided in nominal prices and the economy had recovered from the depression (with the exception of agriculture). But inflation in Veblen's analysis was a broader and deeper concept. In some instances, the term was used in the conventional way, referring to the current level of prices in comparison to an earlier period. But more fundamentally, it was a matter of even stable prices being high in relation to the unit costs based on the productive capacity of industrial system. Essentially, the inflation that Veblen perceived was a case of monopolistic prices relative to what prices would have been in competitive markets.

The Federal Reserve

When Veblen wrote *The Theory of Business Enterprise*, there was no central bank in the U.S. and efforts by the U.S. Secretary of Treasury to use government deposits to help banks had minimal effects. But the Panic of 1907 impelled political action that resulted in the establishment of the Federal Reserve System, which became operational in 1914. The ability to play a role in supporting the nation's private credit and banking system, however, was delayed until after the federal government's war finance activities ended. The subordination of the Federal Reserve to the U.S. Treasury's need to borrow was enhanced by the Secretary of Treasury serving the *ex officio* chairman of the Federal Reserve Board and a wartime law that gave the President the executive authority to transfer Federal Reserve powers to the Treasury if the need arose. At the same time, the prestige of the Federal Reserve was enhanced in the financial community by successfully assisting the Treasury in marketing and managing the government debt and by becoming the depository for the federal government funds.

In 1919, the Federal Reserve had to support the Treasury's last big issue (the Victory loan), which made it unable to raise the discount rate to counter the credit expansion that financed much of the speculation in commodities. In January 1920, just as the economy was weakening, the Federal Reserve banks increased the discount rate, raised it again in June 1920, and waited until May 1921 to begin lowering the rate. Consequently, the Federal Reserve received much blame for the depression of 1920-1921. Veblen, however, saw the Federal Reserve as a contributor to chronic inflation, as we will note shortly.

Two important post-war developments escaped Veblen's explicit attention but were entirely consistent with his views concerning the role of the Federal Reserve in *Absentee Ownership*. First, the Federal Reserve's ability to affect the credit-creating abilities of commercial banks was increased with the discovery of open market operations in 1922. Second, in 1923 the 10th annual report of the Federal Reserve Board defined the Fed's role as an independent central bank. For the purpose of maintaining aggregate economic activity at a satisfactory level and to avoid inflation and recession, credit should be restricted to productive uses. In proposing to deny credit for speculative purposes, the Federal Reserve Board was reacting to the inflation in commodity prices in 1919-1920 that was caused by speculators accumulating excessive stocks of commodities with borrowed funds (Degen 1987, pp. 43-44).

CREDIT-INFLATION AND FINANCIAL STABILITY IN THE 'NEW ORDER'

In Veblen's 1923 analysis, the three factors that determined the price level were the rate of employment of the existing productivity capacity (the level of aggregate output), the creation and stability of credit/debt, and improvements in industrial technologies that continuously reduced the costs of producing industrial capital goods. In contrast to the situation described in *The Theory of Business Enterprise*, the first two factors were now being effectively managed by the 'One Big Union of Interests.' The effective elimination of competition had largely nullified the price-depressing effects of the third factor.

The institutional form of business enterprise that had recently evolved as the 'New Order of Business' (1923, p. 205) derived its 'newness' from two intertwined distinct characteristics. The first was an effective collusive control of the majority of corporations in the 'key industries' so that 'a reasonably concerted check on production in these key industries is a manageable undertaking' (p. 213). Veblen asserted that even during the 'crisis of unexampled privation' in the post-war years, the interests that now controlled production maintained a retardation of output (p. 217). Since the Armistice in 1918, business firms had continuously been seeking additional funds, but not by increasing production. On the contrary, they had been operating at half-capacity, believing that increased production would result in 'a calamitous liquidation, in which a greatly inflated credit situation would collapse, and would involve a cancellation of, perhaps, one-half of the money-values now carried on the books of the business community' (p. 95). To create demand for their products at the higher prices, businesses engaged in extensive and intensive efforts of salesmanship to create consumer demand for their outputs at the higher prices.

Business retardation of production and heavy reliance on salesmanship were integral to Veblen's theory of business enterprise. The current situation was truly a 'New Order' because of the second distinctive characteristic, which made credit-inflation a persistent condition. The large investment banks and their affiliated groups had gained effectual control over banks and other financial institutions as well as control over the corporations in the 'key industries' through use of the holding company, interlocking directorates, and the marketing of credit instruments. With the backing of the Federal Reserve, the large investment banks were using their collusive control over the financial system in a way that had largely nullified the debt-deflation syndrome. They were not only preventing financial crises due to over-indebtedness. By continuously increasing the amount of credit and debt such that debt-funded expenditures would continuously rise, they were assuring steady and stable increases in price levels and, thus, steady and stable increases in business profits, prices of securities, and hence, capitalized value of the corporations they controlled. This management of credit-creation was so well established that 'there should no longer be any serious apprehension that the credit system may break down at an opportune moment or that the price-level will suffer any material decline' (1923, p. 328). With aggregate production effectively restrained, the price level 'rises and continues to rise to meet the rising volume of purchasing-power that is thrown loose on the market at large by the current ubiquitous recourse to credit' (p. 359).

There is a subtle but important difference in the financial aspects in the new system from that which Veblen had described in *The Theory of Business Enterprise*. In the 1904 book, the creation of credit came largely as businessmen sought additional loans whenever the capitalized values of their businesses increased. But in the new system things are reversed. In a seemingly endless process, the investment banks market new securities that create the increase in aggregate purchasing power that raises prices, which increases the profits of the related corporations and, thus, their capitalized values (1923, pp. 390). It was unlikely that a financial crisis would disrupt that 'self-propagating' expansion of credit, purchasing power, prices, profits, capitalization of assets because 'the Federal Reserve and One Big Union of Interests' had sufficient control over credit to expand its growth on a 'reasoned plan' while keeping the growth of output sufficiently checked (pp. 290, 340).

In contrast to the undisciplined prosperities of the 19th century that ended in headlong liquidation, panic, crisis, and depression, Veblen described the inflation of capital and prices in the New Order as 'an orderly advance under the conservative surveillance of the Federal Reserve and One Big Union of Interests' (1923, p. 391, fn). While the dominant investment banks can effectively punish any financial institution that lends at such a high rate as to threaten the orderly increase in credit (and hence values of securities), the Federal Reserve might take some offsetting action to curb price rises should they become threatening to the orderly advance of inflation (p. 179). So the expectation was that the price level would continue to rise progressively, with the economy producing at below capacity levels and workers suffering unemployment and falling real wages (p. 403).

The Nature of Inflation and Vestiges of Deflation

The new arrangement was not fully developed, and there were still vestiges of deflation in the form of 'partial deflation' that may periodically interrupt 'habitual credit-inflation' (Veblen 1923, p. 327). But credit inflation would not only regain ground lost to deflation but would ordinarily run at a higher level than before. In modern terms, the 'credit-inflation' phenomena that Veblen described suggested a form of 'stagflation' due to a combination of supply-side reduction in output and a controlled increase in aggregate demand by credit-creation to support the higher supply prices. In *The Theory of Business Enterprise*, a speculative prosperity ended when nominal wages rose to eliminate the margin of profit that supported the increase in credit, setting the stage for financial crisis, deflation, and depression. But in the 'New Order,' not only were workers suffering from unemployment, but wages were remaining constant or declining as the cost of living rose.

The nature of inflation in Veblen's analysis sometimes seemed to suggest some version of the quantity theory of money as the total volume of credit-instruments — banknote currency and 'deposit currency' — was a multiple of specie reserves (e.g., 1923, p. 327). That was reflected in Veblen's statement that the price level was 500 to 1,000 percent higher than it would have been in the absence of bank credit. As long as Veblen was citing statistics showing that prices were 60-70 percent higher over their 1914 level (1923, pp. 218-219), there was no question that inflation had occurred. But how could there be a continuing inflationary situation when the conventional indicators showed the economy was experiencing price stability in 1923? The answer is found in the effects of 'irrepressible new technological advances' that were 'forever running out new ramifications of industry' (p. 232). Veblen explained that the continuing reductions in cost of production from the advancements in industrial technologies were offsetting or minimizing the increase in prices from the inflation of credit, so that 'any statistical presentation of the actual course of prices during the period will not show in any adequate fashion how greatly the inflation of credit has acted to inflate prices' (pp. 90-91; see also p. 349).

In a footnote in *Absentee Ownership*, Veblen sounded surprisingly like a conventional neo-classical economist praising the efficiency and tendency toward full-employment of a competitive market system which, in *The Theory of Business Enterprise*, had a tendency toward deflation and depression. In that footnote, he asserted that if competitive market conditions had been imposed in both financial and product markets:

> a drastic liquidation of the country's business affairs would doubtless have gone into effect in due course and brought on an effectual retrenchment in capitalization and prices; whereupon the country's industries would have shortly got under way and would speedily have made good the wastes of the War and supplied all ordinary goods. Indeed, there is no reason to doubt that the resulting industrial production, if it had been allowed to run free, would by this time (1923) have added as much to the tangible wealth of the country as would equal the book-values of those inflated assets which their financial guardians have been safeguarding with unemployment and commercial paper through these years of privatation and unrest. (1923, p. 329, fn)

The Political Context of Credit-Inflation

An important cultural factor in Veblen's analysis of the credit-inflation was government support of the ability of the coalition of financial interests to retard production to keep prices high while continuously increasing credit in the financial arena to generate the aggregate demand needed to support those prices. How was that possible in a democratic order when the economic welfare of the 'underlying population' was negatively impacted by policies and practices that served the pecuniary interests of the large business and financial interests? Why did the 'common man,' who collectively possessed the political power to change government and policies, not exercise that power to serve his own interests? In his earlier works, Veblen had analyzed the nature of modern constitutional government as based on institutions of economic liberty, natural law, and rights of property that developed in and were compatible with economic conditions of the 18th century, i.e., before the modern industrial system and modern business system developed. But his analysis of government policies under democracy serving the interests of large businessmen was further developed in conjunction with the entry of the U.S. into WWI and its aftermath in *The Vested Interests and the Common Man*, and other writings, culminating in *Absentee Ownership*.

Veblen viewed the common man's acceptance of a government that supported the vested interests in the post-war environment as simply a continuation of behavioral tendencies under the influence of archaic cultural institutions that were of a barbarian nature. In particular, the influence of business principles in conjunction with religion and patriotism or nationalism deludes the common man, resulting in his electing and supporting governments that function in the interest of the large businessmen and 'absentee owners' at his expense. People had 'been schooled in the practice of salesmanship until they believe that wealth is to be created by sharp practice, and that the perfect work of productive enterprise and initiative consists in "cornering the market" and "sitting tight,"' (1923, p. 34). The common man 'whose sense of the realities is palsied with this manner of hip-shotten logic is also fit to believe that "the foreigner pays the tax" imposed by a protective tariff or that a ship subsidy is of some benefit to someone else than the absentee owners of the ships.' (ibid.).

Citing Lincoln's comment that all the people could not be fooled all the time, Veblen noted 'in the case where the people in question are sedulously fooling themselves all the time the politicians can come near achieving that ideal result' (1923, p. 34). In reference the Republican administration that advertised itself as a 'business administration,' Veblen stated that the

> constituted authorities of this democratic commonwealth come, in effect, to constitute a Soviet of Business Men's Delegates, whose dutiful privilege it is to safeguard and enlarge the special advantages of the country's absentee owners. And all the while the gains of the absentee owners are got at the cost of the underlying population. (1923, p. 37)

Under the illusions of nationalism, ordinary people believed that the common good was served by the gains of the large businessmen that it had 'become an axiomatic rule that all the powers of government and diplomacy must work together for the benefit of the business interests of the larger sort' (1923, p. 114). In democratic America, governing authorities constitute a Business Administration to enforce the provision of the U. S. Constitution that provides that the property of citizens, interpreted as the large business interests, must be protected and advanced at any cost to the taxpayers (pp. 296-297).

In *The Vested Interests and the Common Man* (1919), Veblen explained that the common man supports international policies that are beneficial only to the large business interests under the irrational belief that he receives a 'ratable share' of the 'imponderable,' i.e., the illusion of intangible property in the form of national prestige and honor. The government procures and safeguards foreign investments and concessions for businessmen and the common man willingly accepts the burden of the costs. Subsidies and credits are provided to those businessmen who profit from shipping and the cost is willingly borne by the common man (1919, pp. 136-137). The only difference between the dynastic state and the democratic commonwealth is that in the latter 'the common man has to be managed rather that driven — except for minor groups of common men who live on the lower-common level, and except for recurrent periods of legislative hysteria and judiciary blind-staggers' (p. 127). Such management of the common man by governmental representatives of the businessmen is not difficult to achieve as 'he is helpless within the rule of game as it is played in the 20th century under the enlightened principles of the 18th century' (p. 163).

The retardation of production by the large businessmen for their own pecuniary gains is supported by the government because in a 'civilized nation,' the national government has the general care of the nation's business interests in its charge and is in a position to 'penalize excessive or unwholesome traffic.' Indeed, through regulations and excise taxes, Congress and the Administration 'will have some share in administering that necessary modicum of sabotage' needed to assure maximum pecuniary gains for the large business interests (Veblen 1921, pp. 19-21).

5. Fisher's Debt-Deflation Theory of Great Depressions

In a curious way, the stock market crash of 1929 and the Great Depression of the 1930s invalidated both Veblen's and Irving Fisher's interpretations of economic and financial developments in the 1920s. Until the latter part of the decade of the 1920s, Veblen's credit-inflation theory in *Absentee Ownership* seemed to be at least partially credible. Although there was little explicit inflation in prices of goods and services, price stability with productivity gains from technological improvements corresponded to at least one of Veblen's concepts of inflation — prices not falling as costs of production fall. But there was great price inflation in the stock market, which as Galbraith (1988) emphasized in his classic *The Great Crash 1929*, rested on a pyramid of debt. While it might be argued that the Federal Reserve was able to prevent the speculative Florida land market bubble fiasco in 1926 from spreading to the financial system proper, it did not prevent the speculative bubble in stocks from developing in 1928-1929, the 1929 stock market crash, the bank failures, nor the depression itself. Ironically, the stock market crash and the depression appeared to emphatically revalidate Veblen's 1904 debt-deflation thesis.

Fisher viewed developments in the 1920s with confidence and enthusiastic approval, famously assuring the public that stocks had reached a new permanent high plateau in 1929. He lost his own fortune and much of his reputation as prices of stocks fell from 1930 to the summer of 1932 and the economy sank deeper into depression. Beginning with his immediate efforts to explain the stock market crash in *The Stock Market Crash — And After*, which was finished in December 1929, Fisher spent several years developing what he would call his 'debt-deflation' theory of great depressions. While the purpose of this chapter is to examine Fisher's theory, our review of the historical setting allows us to also reflect on why Veblen's 1923 interpretation of financial stability failed to be validated and what the developments meant for his earlier debt-deflation/chronic-depression theory.

HISTORICAL SETTING: FROM PROSPERITY TO CRISIS AND DEPRESSION

When Veblen published *Absentee Ownership* in 1923, both the inflation of the war years and the post-war inflation caused by speculation in commodities, which resulted in losses of real income for workers and shortages of commodities, were well into the past. For the rest of the decade of the 1920s, consumer and wholesale prices were relatively stable and the economy experienced a vigorous expansion. Prices were lower in 1929 than in 1919-1920 but most of the decline had occurred by 1922. Real gross domestic product rose by more than 8 percent in 1925 and by another 5.5 percent in 1926. Between 1922 and 1929, national income rose about 23 percent and the annual per capita income in 1926 prices rose from $563 to $625. The index of manufacturing production rose by almost 50 percent and there was a 17 percent increase in employment (Fite and Reese 1965, pp. 529-530).

At least through 1927, business investment spending was strong, with gross capital formation averaging around $17 billion annually. Labor productivity in manufacturing rose 3.8 percent annually, and many new products and improved versions of existing products were brought into common use. The boom was fueled to a large extent by the production and sales of automobiles but other industries were expanding and investments that implemented new technological product and process innovations were strong. Wages of labor, however, showed little gain, with the increase in hourly wage rates averaging less than 1 cent per year. The agricultural sector, which had enjoyed boom times during the war, was particularly troubled throughout the 1920s by high costs and low prices. Even with substantial reductions in tax rates, the federal budget was kept in surplus under the Republican administrations of Harding and Coolidge by reducing government expenditures to minimal levels. While government debt decreased by 25 percent, household debt took on greater importance in the later 1920s. In addition to mortgage debt rising, consumer demand for automobiles and other durable goods was stimulated by installment payment plans (Fite and Reese 1965, pp. 530-531).

While prices of producer and consumer goods and of commodities remained stable, there was substantial inflation in stock prices in the second half of the decade. Demand for stocks was encouraged by lower taxes on higher incomes, high corporate profits (and expectations of even higher future profits), and relatively easy money encouraged demand for stocks. A speculative frenzy in Florida land collapsed in 1926 but the stock market provided fertile ground for a speculative mania in stocks to develop that Galbraith chronicled in *The Great Crash 1929*. While credit-inflation in the sense of rising prices (as opposed to stable prices with decreasing costs) was absent from product markets, it became virulent in financial markets. Brokerage firms borrowed heavily in the call market, using the funds to both acquire blocks of stocks and bonds they intended to sell to clients at profits and make margin loans to their customers. In 1928-1929, speculators were able to purchase stocks with loans from their brokers on a 10 percent margin.

In October 1929, the stock market crashed. Over a two-day period, the Dow-Jones Industrial Average lost 30 percent of its value. But the worst was still to come. After a brief period in which stability seemed to be possible, the stock prices began a downward slide in a long bear market. At the low point in the summer of 1932, the market values of stocks in general were only 14-16 percent of their pre-crash highs in 1929. During that time, the economy sank deeper and deeper into depression and there were three waves of banks failures between 1930 and 1933. The economic statistics paint a very dismal picture. Gross domestic product fell by 28 percent between 1929 and 1932; per capita disposable income by 24 percent; the index of manufacturing production by 48 percent; the level of employment by nearly 19 percent; the index of wholesale prices by 32 percent; the average hourly earnings in manufacturing by 21 percent; and bank deposits by 22 percent. Corporate profits fell from about $10 billion in 1929 to losses of $3 billion in 1932. At the same time, the federal debt rose from $17 billion in 1929 to nearly $20 billion in 1932. The rate of unemployment, by conservative estimates, was 25 percent in 1932, with many of those who remained employed working less than a full week (Fite and Reese 1965, pp. 579-584).

VEBLEN: INVALIDATED AND RE-VALIDATED

What did the developments after 1923 suggest about Veblen's credit-inflation analysis? Dirlam (1958) challenged the 'factual validity' of Veblen's assertion that corporate expansion and increased capitalization was funded by debt, noting that internal financing provided the source of funding (pp. 212-214). But, as Galbraith noted, debt was definitely a major factor behind the rising stock prices which were the basis for the capitalization of public corporations. In his analysis of corporate finance in *The Theory of Business Enterprise*, Veblen argued that corporate stocks were essentially another form of debt contracts. From that perspective, the substitution of stocks at rising prices for corporate debt in the 1920s would be viewed as merely changing the form of debt. In addition, while Veblen wrote *Absentee Ownership* before the popularity of consumer installment debt, that type of debt became important in temporarily sustaining aggregate demand in 1928-1929 in the face of level wage incomes and increased capacity to produce.

Veblen stated in *Absentee Ownership* that serious financial crises and depressions could still occur only if the 'One Big Union of Interests' decided to take deliberate action to make it happen (1923, pp. 328-329). But that was hardly to be contemplated. Seeming to confirm Veblen's perception that the Federal Reserve was assisting the 'one big union of financial interests' in stabilizing the financial system while expanding debt, the Federal Reserve Board's 1923 annual report defined the Federal Reserve's role as that of an independent central bank that would pursue economic activity at a high and stable level, permitting credit to be extended to support productive investment, production, and consumption, but not to speculative accumulations of stocks of commodities. By restricting credit to productive uses, excessive credit creation would be avoided and, by preventing credit to finance speculative accumulations of commodities, recession could be avoided (Degen 1987, pp. 43-44).

For a while at least, the Federal Reserve seemed to be able to use its monetary control powers to stabilize the economy, applying the brakes when the expansion became too vigorous and stepping on the accelerator when the economy weakened. When the 1921-1923 expansion appeared to become too rapid, the Federal Reserve raised the discount rate and used its newly discovered tool of open market operations, selling securities to reduce bank reserves. The economy entered a mild recession but recovered when the Federal Reserve then lowered the discount rate and purchased securities. When the economy gained steam in 1925 and there was a real estate boom (with speculative buying of Florida land), the Federal Reserve seemed to bring things under control by tightening the monetary brakes. Subsequently, the mild recession of 1926-1927 was met by an expansionary policy and the prosperity continued.

But the Federal Reserve would ultimately fail to control the stock market speculation and the financial instability associated with it. Critics maintained that lowering the discount rate in 1927 to assist the Bank of England in its efforts to stem the outflow of gold from London encouraged the speculation in U.S. stock markets. There were also important changes in the American banking sector in the 1920s, with the composition of bank loans shifting away from commercial loans to security and real estate loans. Consumer debt became increasingly important as installment credit for purchasing automobiles and consumer durables was provided by finance companies which, in turn, borrowed from banks. Banks also increased their investments relative to loans, purchasing bonds not only of federal, state, and local governments, but also of domestic corporations and foreign debtors. Large city banks also had investment bank affiliates that underwrote new issues and speculated in securities as dealers. In that atmosphere, regulation of bank activities was relaxed in various ways.

By 1928, stock market speculation became the Federal Reserve's biggest concern but there was an internal dispute over what actions should be taken. After lowering the discount rate in 1927, the Federal Reserve became increasingly concerned about the accelerating rise in stock prices. Critics charged that the easy money policy was funding speculation in stocks, pointing to loans to stockbrokers by New York City banks as an indicator of speculative finance. Other sectors of the economy complained that bank credit in general was being denied to them, going instead to high-rate call loans to brokers. In the spring of 1928, the New York City Federal Reserve Bank was allowed to raise its discount rate and the Federal Open Market Investment Committee sold government securities, draining reserves and forcing banks to the discount window. Those actions stemmed the growth in the money supply and raised the interest rates on call loans, but that had no effect on the stock market boom. On the contrary, stock prices accelerated in the second half of 1928, taking the Dow Industrial Average to nearly a 50 percent gain for the year.

In 1929, the Federal Reserve Board and the Federal Reserve Bank officials became increasingly split over the appropriate policy to curb stock market speculation. The New York Federal Reserve Bank wanted an increase in the discount rate, while the Federal Reserve Board preferred to punish commercial banks making loans to stock market speculators by denying them access to the discount windows of Federal Reserve Banks. In August 1929, the Federal Reserve Board finally allowed the New York Federal Reserve Bank to raise its discount rate but in early September the stock market was already up nearly 27 percent for the year, even as the economy had entered into a recession. The speculative bubble began to break, faltering in early October, then rallying before the Great Crash of 1929 occurred, with October 24 becoming known as 'Black Thursday,' and October 29 as 'Black Tuesday' because of the volume of selling on those days. Over the two-day period, October 28-29, stock prices fell by 30 percent.

Institutional Developments

Veblen's debt-deflation and credit-inflation theses were both very much in keeping with his general theory of evolutionary change within the institutional genre of the modern business enterprise system. The protective tariff rates that were established by the Fordney-McCumber Act of 1922 were consistent with the counter-deflationary measures that Veblen had mentioned in *The Theory of Business Enterprise*. That was followed in 1930 with the infamous Hawley-Smoot Tariff Act. But just as institutional developments had created the conditions that favored the credit-inflation thesis in the early 1920s, continuing institutional and technological developments subsequently undermined the collusive control of financial institutions and the stability of the credit-expansion. That allowed a vigorous resurgence of conditions for debt-deflation.

One of those institutional developments was increased competition from new investment banks. Investment banking in the U.S. evolved through three stages which Edwards described as pre-Morgan, Morgan, and post-Morgan eras (1938, pp. 227-228). The first stage was associated with the rise and decline of Jay Cooke and the 'speculative capitalists,' which ended with the Panic of 1873. In the second stage, Morgan and his group gained dominance over the system of security capitalism in the latter decades of the 1800s, and held that position until the 1920s. The preeminence of the Morgan house was largely due to influence over the supply of capital through its relations with commercial banks and life insurance companies. The firm followed a policy of distributing securities to wholesale dealers or a small group of institutional buyers or large individual buyers.

The post-Morgan stage began in the 1920s as the power and influence of the Morgan-type groups over financial markets was weakened by several developments. Direct investment in stocks and bonds by individuals increased, resulting in a diffusion of security ownership and making it more difficult for one firm and its group to influence investment of funds. A complete transformation in the organization of investment banking occurred in the 1920s, as not only the number of investment banks increased but they were spread geographically across the entire country. The increase in investment banks resulted in what Edwards called 'overcompetition' as two essential operations of investment banking underwent change (1938, p. 229).

First, the close relationship that existed between investment banks and the corporations whose securities they underwrote in the Morgan era gave way to open competition to underwrite new issues, with investment banks offering inducements to corporations to gain their business. Whereas investment banks during the Morgan era would not underwrite speculative capitalists, in the new highly aggressive competition, investment banks rushed to provide financial resources where credit positions did not warrant.

The second change was in the sense of responsibility on the part of the investment banks for the issues they had financed. During the Morgan era, the investment banks generally assumed a continuing obligation to do whatever was possible see that the corporation was managed in a manner that would support the securities they had placed. In the 1920s, the new investment bankers not only failed to exercise any control over the financial policies of the corporations they financed, but often did not even keep any current information on file about the performances of those firms. Combined with that were unsound selling practices, e.g., the formation of syndicates to place large issues that 'pegged' the after-market at artificially high levels for a time after the placement, which gave the illusion of a sound stable market. The result was a decline in the quality of bonds placed and an over-issue of new securities. Highly aggressive marketing of brokerage services aimed at selling out an issue on the day of its flotation, which often involved hard selling of 'difficult' issues (Edwards 1938, pp. 227-235).

Another institutional factor was financial innovations that encouraged debt-funded speculative excesses. The holding company that Veblen observed was used by Morgan and other investment bankers to gain control over the operating companies in key industries became an instrument that in the 1920s was used most extensively in public utility finance. Edwards noted that the benefits of 'well-managed holding companies, were only too often offset by the unsound financial and technical policies of unscrupulous holding companies' (1938, p. 247). What transpired was very Veblenian in character and form. Holding companies competed with each other to acquire operating companies, paying prices far above the values based on earning power. The acquired properties were then capitalized on the basis of the high purchase prices and used as the basis for issuing the securities of the holding companies. In many cases holding companies were dominated by super-holding companies, so that small blocks of closely held voting stock at that level frequently controlled an entire system with capitalization of hundreds of millions. As an example, one dollar of stock of Middle West Utilities Corporation ultimately controlled $1,750 of the assets of Georgia Power. In order for the stock of the Insull Company to earn a 6 percent return on its market value, the net income would have to be 44 percent of its actual invested assets (Edwards 1938, p. 248).

Similarly the investment trusts, which were supposed to provide investors with diversification and management expertise, were often used as a convenient dumping ground by investment banks for stocks that they could not sell to their clients (Edwards 1938, p. 249). More importantly, the investment trusts were devices for super leverage (see Galbraith 1988, pp. 46-51), adding to the instability of the financial system that increasingly became beyond the control of the 'One Big Union of Interests.'

But perhaps the most important institutional development in the 1920s confirmed Veblen's 1904 observation that large and increasing government expenditures would be required to offset the tendency toward chronic depression. In the 1920s, the fiscal policies of the Republican administrations did just the opposite. Reducing government spending and running budget surpluses contributed to the deficiency of aggregate demand, while reducing tax rates on higher incomes contributed to speculative excesses in the stock market. The 1920s also validated Veblen's recognition that wage incomes would not rise sufficiently for consumption spending to increase in proportion to the capacity to produce.

Technological Innovations

Developments in the 1920s draw particular attention to a puzzling oversight in both Veblen's 1904 and 1923 analyses. While the prosperity of the 1920s did become highly speculative and rested on mounting debt, it was initiated by investment spending to implement innovations in the form of new products and industrial technologies that ultimately increased capacity well beyond what aggregate demand under the existing distribution of income could absorb. While Veblen recognized the key role of technological improvements, reducing the cost and increasing the efficiency of industrial machines, in his 1904 debt-deflation/chronic-depression analysis, he never seemed to recognize (or at least to acknowledge) that prosperity could be initiated by waves of investment spending on product and process innovations. The consequence was that in both *The Theory of Business Enterprise* and *Absentee Ownership*, Veblen appears to have ignored the impact of technological innovations as initiators. He could not, of course, have foreseen the big wave of technological innovations that was implemented by a heavy wave of investment spending between 1924 and 1927 (see Brockie 1958, p. 127). But as a long passage in *Absentee Ownership* reveals, continuous technological innovations were a particularly powerful force in the 'New Order.'

> New processes, new materials from near and far, are continually being turned to account, and new methods of turning old materials to account and of coordinating known processes for the more efficient use of old resources, as well as for incorporating new resources into the routine of the day's work, — these improvements and accelerations in the industrial arts continue to insinuate themselves into the fabric of the industrial system, in spite of the uniformly conservative management on part of the business community as touches all new projects and project-makers in the industrial field. (1923, pp. 419-420)

FISHER ON DEBT AND STOCK PRICES IN THE 1920S

In his *History of Economic Analysis*, Schumpeter traced the roots of Fisher's debt-deflation theory to his monetary theory. He described Fisher as the 'most eminent sponsor' of the theory that an expansion in bank reserves makes banks more willing to lend, and the result is credit inflation owing to low money rates of interest until those rates catch up with prices, and reverses the process (1954, p. 1122). After first stating that theory in an 'unsophisticated manner' in 1911 in *Purchasing Power of Money*, Fisher continued to emphasize the monetary phenomenon until he had broadened the basis of his analysis to end up with the Debt-Deflation Theory (ibid.). In a footnote, Schumpeter identified the following as the 'main stepping stones' to Fisher's Debt-Deflation Theory: Fisher's 1922 article 'The Business Cycle Largely a "Dance of the Dollar",' his 1925 article 'Our Unstable Dollar and the So-Called Business Cycle,' the book *Booms and Depressions*, and the summary version that Fisher presented in the 1933 *Econometrica* article 'The Debt-Deflation Theory of Great Depressions' (ibid.).

But missing from Schumpeter's 'stepping stones' was Fisher's book *The Stock Market Crash – And After*, which was published in 1930 but had been written by mid-December 1929. Fisher's interest in explaining the stock market crash was as both a professional economist, whose public reputation had been challenged by his pronouncements on the stock market, and a personal investor who, at the time of writing that book, had no idea how much he would ultimately lose as stock prices continued to fall in 1930-1931. *The Stock Market Crash – And After* should be considered one of the 'main stepping stones' to the debt-deflation theory because of the role of debt in the inflation and deflation in stock prices.

In his biographical study, Allen noted that while Fisher campaigned to promote his ideas on money illusion and the scheme for a sound dollar, his attitude toward developments in the 1920s and his own behavior in the stock market suggested otherwise. Over the second half of the decade, Fisher went from being 'a university professor to a business publicist and financial tycoon, from small businessman to a board member of important corporations, and stock-market prophet' (Allen 1993, p. 179) whose paper wealth grew as stock prices surged upward. Fisher was both a speculator in the stock market, exercising stock options and buying Remington Rand and other stock on the margin, and a public advocate for speculation and rising stock prices.

With the booming stock market making him a millionaire in terms of paper wealth, Fisher viewed the future with unlimited optimism, praising investments in common stock as being safe and sound, profitable to the individual and good for the country. His writings during this time largely dealt with 'money, making money, and financial markets' (Allen 1993, p. 179). Allen asserted that Fisher actually believed the popular myth of the day that purchases of common stock on the stock market provided businesses with funds to be used for expansions, and had also come to believe that the bull market would continue on a sound basis (p. 207). There was an ironic echo of Veblen's 1923 analysis, albeit with very different normative implications, in Fisher's belief that the Federal Reserve could keep a stable prosperity going by modestly increasing the money supply through use of open-market operations. Price stability would be achieved, which would encourage stocks to keep rising. It is worth noting that

Greenspan came to express a similar view with respect to the rising stock prices and the 'new economy' of the late 1990s, leaving expressions of concern about 'irrational exuberance' somewhat in the background.

On October 17, 1929, Fisher was reported in the newspapers as telling members of the Purchasing Agents Association that stock prices appeared to have reached a permanent high plateau and would probably go even higher over the next few months. On the eve of the October 24th stock market panic, he was quoted in the newspapers as expecting a recovery in stock prices. In 1930 Fisher published *The Stock Market Crash – And After*, which he indicated in the *Preface* was actually written in early December 1929. Fisher acknowledged that he had been mistaken in asserting that while stock prices had reached their peak, there would not be a crash. But he insisted that developments in the market in the weeks following the crash had proven that his earlier assurance that 'the new plateau would survive any recession' had been true (1930, p. vii). Thus, his main purpose was to explain the crash, presenting both his own interpretation and a host of other explanations that had been presented at that time.

A similarity exists between Fisher's optimism in the closing month of 1929 and Greenspan's optimistic expectations in 2001 that corporate earnings would continue to rise due to continuing opportunities for increasing productivity. Fisher argued that expectations of rising stock prices in the 1920s were justified based on a realistic expectation of rising corporate profits from an increasing application of science and invention in industry. An inventor of some success himself, Fisher asserted that 'Inventing is now a profession. Invention is today recognized as having a high cash value and is eagerly sought after by progressive corporations' (1930, p. 119). That trend began during World War I, when science professors had been induced by the inflation to leave universities and go to industry. Industrial corporations were ready to make use of their research talents, in part, because of a growing recognition of how Germany had made use of technical science and invention (p. 124). To make the workers worth the higher wages, employers sought labor-saving inventions. With large corporations establishing 'gigantic research labs,' the higher profits expected from research and development (R&D) and use of new technologies justified the higher price-earnings ratios of stocks (pp. 140-141). Closely affiliated with scientific research and invention was the spread of 'management engineering' in industry (p. 142). The speedy implementation of scientific method or management engineering and more efficient flows of processes and information, which allowed closer coordination of sales and financing with production, resulted in increased production and cost efficiency and also stability (p. 156).

It should also be noted that Greenspan's optimistic (and somewhat self-congratulatory) statements about monetary policymakers' achieving price stability in the late 1990s seemed to be an echo of Fisher's optimistic statements about the seven years of a 'stable dollar' as commodity prices remained relatively stable after 1922 (1930, p. 182). By providing more safety in businessmen's expectations, price stability had resulted in prosperity with 'bigger earnings, better prospects, and a higher level of securities' (ibid.). Like Greenspan, Fisher credited the Federal Reserve with playing a contributory role to that stability in the 1920s through the newly discovered open market operations (pp. 188-189). Expectations of growing future gains led to a willingness to invest at lower immediate dividends, hence higher stock prices.

There seemed to be little of the debt-deflation theory at work in Fisher's enthusiastic account of the 'flight from bonds to stocks' with corporations converting funded debt into shares with ease (1930, p. 211). Again, there is a parallel between Fisher's analysis of the 1920s and views of a 'new economy' in the 1990s. As the bull market of the 1990s gained steam, a popular theme was that investors had recognized that stocks were less risky because of greater information, increased market efficiency, and greater sophistication on part of the investors. Fisher's version of that theme was that stock investors in the 1920s had come to recognize that bonds were more risky because of the unstable dollar while stocks were less risky for several reasons. He was especially enthused about the reduction in risks due to the rise of investment counsel and investment trusts (p. 197), which explained why stocks would be preferable to bonds whose values are subject to inflation risk. Fisher claimed that while neither stocks nor bonds are free of risks, there is less risk in investment trusts which 'with the aid of expert counsel' invest in 'well-selected diversified stocks and preferred securities' (p. 204).

Fisher repeatedly insisted there had been a solid economic reason for stock prices to remain high. His defense of the 1920s and also of his optimism even after the crash is illustrated in the following passage.

Thus, the change in the caution factor, reducing it to a much narrower margin from the true mathematical value of common stocks as the element of risk have been absorbed by intelligent diversification, has helped put the stock market on its higher plateau. It constitutes a permanent reason why this plateau will not sink again to the level of former years except for extraordinary causes. (Fisher 1930, p. 207)

An optimistic view was also expressed in Fisher's statement that 'the high plateau on which the stock market now moves — and still far above previous plateaus, despite the panic of 1929 — is, therefore, a result of improved order and efficiency in the investment market as well as in American business' (1930, p. 209).

So why did the stock market crash? Curiously, in identifying debt as the prime factor, Fisher offered two views that related to debt. One of those supported his optimism about the 1929 crash as being merely an adjustment downward of stock prices to the new high plateau. In citing data showing that the number of people holding shares had actually increased when the crash occurred, Fisher stated that many investors started buying with cash rather than margin loans after the crash because stock prices had become so attractive. They 'held back their purchasing power until they saw their favorite issues available, in many instances at the lowest level in two years or more' (1930, p. 210).

But Fisher's primary argument was that 'overspeculation' and debt had created the conditions that resulted in the crash. There was a limit to which the lower risk of stocks should lead to rising stock prices. Fisher recalled that in 1928 he had warned that 'cooperative buying of diversified stock securities should be done with full knowledge that it may be affected by *overspeculation*' (1930, p. 214, emphasis added). When deflation in commodity prices occur, as was the case after 1925, investors should hold bonds and preferred stock (ibid.). Fisher also distinguished between investment trusts proper as being very sound in their investments and investment companies that were called investment trusts and pools, which were highly speculative in their operations (ibid., pp. 214-216). But in contrast to what Galbraith would later reveal in *The Great Crash 1929*, Fisher claimed that debt was a minor factor for investment trusts (p. 217), and declared that 'in spite of the tremendous harm that has been done to common stocks during the panic of 1929, investment trusts have made it safer to invest in common stocks than ever before' (p. 268).

Fisher stated that while the contagion of the long bull market had encouraged 'unwise speculation,' the main trouble was it was being financed with so much borrowed money (1930, p. 218). Distinguishing between 'wise and beneficial speculation' and 'unwise and injurious speculation' (p. 219), Fisher declared that speculation 'would have been entirely proper had the speculators used their own money in following a generally sound judgement to profit by reasonably expected gain in the future' (p. 221). Speculation by 'unprofessional speculators' based on 'tips' is little more (but worse than) gambling (p. 220) but the 'prime fault lay in the credit structure' (p. 257). The real opportunities to invest were so 'golden' that people became over-eager to exploit them by using borrowed money.

The 'overextension of credits' in the form of brokers' loans was due, in part, to the failure of the Federal Reserve Board to raise discount rates in the fall of 1928 or spring of 1929, as proposed by the New York Federal Reserve Bank (1930, pp. 234-235). Fisher claimed that between two-thirds and three-fourths of the rise in stocks was justified. The other one-fourth or one-third of the rise was due to an abnormal increase in brokers' loans resulting in an enormous top-heavy credit structure, which Fisher described as a house of cards that was built on top of a solid mountain (pp. 259-260). With too many speculating with margin accounts, the market was rendered vulnerable to bear raiders, whose waves of selling caused thousands of small holders of stock to sell at lower prices (pp. 257-258). The end result was a 'panic shrinkage of brokers' loans' in October 1929. Fisher declared that if the margin accounts had not been so large, there would have been no panic (p. 263).

To prevent 'overextension' of stock market credits, Fisher endorsed the suggestion that Federal Reserve Banks be allowed to rediscount brokers' loans made by member banks. His rationale was that bankers would become less evasive about the nature of their loans and more subject to the advice, influence, and even discipline of the Federal Reserve (1930, pp. 250-251). But suggestive of Greenspan's continuous opposition to increased regulation of financial derivatives, Fisher suggested that a more comprehensive solution would be greater use of options as substitutes for brokers' loans (pp. 252-253). He also called for policies of higher interest rates when 'inventions' are offering increased future profits, arguing that higher rates would have curbed the 'overspeculation' facilitated by margin loans.

In mid-December 1929, Fisher was still very optimistic about the future of stocks and the economy, and concluded *The Stock Market Crash – And After* with the statement that 'For the immediate future, at least, the future is bright' (1930, p. 269). Stock prices at their post-crash levels had created 'one of the most wonderful bargain-counters ever known to investors' (p. 258). But he cautioned that the possibility of deflation was the one 'fly in the ointment' (p. 269). At that time, Fisher did not connect deflation with debt. Rather, still working with the quantity theory of money, he worried that there was the danger in a few years of gold shortage and long gradual deflation like the deflations after the Civil War and after the Napoleonic Wars. The world-wide growth of business combined with the slowing of the production of gold had reduced the surplus of gold which had enabled the Federal Reserve to stabilize money for seven years. Fisher cited concerns of many economists and businessmen, who saw declining commodity prices as the beginning of a long secular deflation similar to the post-Civil War experience (p. 192). But Fisher asserted there was still time at the end of 1929 to avert deflation by adopting wise banking policies and gold control (p. 269).

FISHER'S DEBT-DEFLATION THEORY OF DEPRESSIONS

Dimand (1994) noted that as the economy sank into depression in 1930-1932, Fisher began to focus on a gap in his analysis of business cycles in the 1920s, namely that his 'dance of the dollar' thesis needed to explain how such a deep and lasting depression could occur after some deflations but not after others. That resulted in the book *Booms and Depressions*, and the subsequent *Econometrica* article 'The Debt-Deflation Theory of Great Depressions.' Although the book was published in 1933, the date of the *Preface* was July 1932, which meant that it was written before Roosevelt became President. The article was published in October 1933 so it is possible that Fisher may have observed at least the early policies of the new administration.

Fisher reported that the interaction between waves of liquidation by debt-burdened businesses and deflation had first occurred to him in 1931 and he had developed his debt-deflation theory in lectures at Yale, presenting it publicly for the first time in January 1932 at a meeting of the American Association for the Advancement of Science. The book *Booms and Depressions* was then an elaboration of that address. In the *Preface*, Fisher stated that he had done little work in the 'vast field of "business cycles"' and was concentrating on nine factors that had 'the outstanding influence' on most major depressions and certainly on the current one (1933a, p. vii). That explained the subtitle 'Some First Principles.' The 1933 *Econometrica* article provided a more concise statement of those 'principles' in terms of the nine factors.

In the opening paragraph of the article, Fisher stated that since the debt-deflation theory had been presented in *Booms and Depressions*,

> its special conclusions have been widely accepted and, so far as I know, no one has yet found them anticipated by previous writers, though several, including myself, have zealously sought to find such anticipations. Two of the best-read authorities in the field assure me that those conclusions are, in the words of one of them, 'both new and important'. (1933b, p. 337)

Fisher did not identify those 'authorities,' but Wesley Clair Mitchell and Schumpeter would seem to be the most likely candidates. Fisher's claim to an original discovery is quite curious, not only because Schumpeter observed that it was Fisher's habit not to claim originality to his theories (1948, p. 228), but also because he only acknowledged Veblen's earlier work in a footnote comment that Mitchell had told him that Veblen had come nearest to a debt-deflation theory (1933b, p. 350). Schumpeter also observed in a footnote comment that it was a 'curious slip when Fisher wrote in 1932 (*Booms and Depressions*) that the field of business cycles was "one which I had scarcely ever entered before." His name would stand in the history of this field even if he had ceased to write in 1925' (1948a, p. 230, fn).

It seems doubtful that Fisher needed to be told about Veblen's debt-deflation theory in view of his 1909 published response to Veblen's critical reviews of Fisher's *The Nature of Capital and Income* and *The Rate of Interest.* Fisher (1909) attacked both Veblen's approach to economics and his criticism of the work of others, but said nothing about Veblen's theory of business enterprise. That omission is especially noteworthy because in his review of *The Nature of Capital and Income*, Veblen (1908) drew attention to the inflation of business capital through debt and the consequences in the following statement: 'The failure of classical theory to give an intelligent account of credit and crises is in great part due to the habitual refusal of economists to recognize intangible assets, and Mr. Fisher's argument is, in effect, an accentuation of this ancient infirmity of the classical theory' (1908, pp. 3-4). Seemingly, that would have drawn Fisher's critical attention to Veblen's own theory of capital, debt, deflation, and chronic depression, so that it would not have been necessary for him to learn about that theory from Mitchell.

Like Veblen, Fisher defined a depression as a business situation involving prices and profits, both actual and expected, a 'condition in which business becomes unprofitable' (1933a, p. 3). As 'Private Profits disease,' depression has widespread effects on employment, wealthy individuals, and 'some of the mightiest and best managed enterprises' (ibid.). Characteristically, Fisher framed his analysis in terms of the lack of a stable monetary unit. Profits are measured in money, and will be affected if money (a 'distributive mechanism') becomes 'deranged' (p. 7). The 'mystery of depressions' is that the dollar's purchasing power may (and sometimes does) increase faster due to deflation than the reduction in debts that are being paid off (p. 26). Because people are subject to 'money illusion,' they fail to realize that real debts change as do real wages when the price level changes (pp. 17-21).

Fisher rejected explanations of 'the so-called business cycles' as caused by such factors as 'over-production, under-consumption, over-capacity, maladjustment between agricultural prices, over-confidence, over-investment, over-saving, over-spending, and the discrepancy between saving and investment' (1933b, p. 340). Instead, he identified the two dominant factors in booms and depressions as being 'over-indebtedness' (the 'debt-disease') and 'price-level disturbances' (the 'dollar disease') (p. 341), While the other factors or conditions may be conspicuous, they are only the effects of the two dominant factors.

The 'Debt Cycle'

For a great depression to occur, 'over-indebtedness' and deflation must occur in combination because they react to each other, creating a 'debt cycle' in which nine tendencies are involved in the downswing to depression. Those are the debt factor ('over-indebtedness'), the currency-volume factor, the price-level factor, the net-worth factor, the production factor, the psychological factor, the currency-turnover factor, and the rates of interest. At some point, the depression ends and the cycle reverses itself through the nine factors.

The 'debt factor' or 'over-indebtedness' (the 'debt disease') is the beginning of the cycle. Fisher defined 'over-indebtedness' for an individual or business firm as 'whatever degree of indebtedness multiplies *unduly* the chances of becoming insolvent' (1933a, p. 9). But in the aggregate 'over-indebtedness' means that debts have become excessive in relation to 'other economic factors' such as assets, income, gold, and the liquidities of assets and liabilities (pp. 10-11). 'Over-indebtedness' is responsible for making 'over-investment' and 'over-speculation' important by being conducted on borrowed money; 'over-confidence' is likely to do harm only when it leads people to go into debt (p. 341).

At some point, over-indebtedness leads to distress selling, either by the creditors selling some of the debtors' assets or the selling by insolvent debtors in efforts to pay down debts (1933a, p. 13). In ordinary events, distress-selling is not responsible for lowering the price level since buyers gain the spending power that the sellers lose. But when a '*stampede liquidation*' (p. 14; Fisher's italics) occurs, the volume of deposit money decreases as debts owed to banks are reduced faster than new credits are created by bank loans (pp. 14-15). The 'currency-volume factor' results in a radical decrease in prices. The 'price-level factor' then changes the level of 'real debts' as money owed has greater purchasing power when prices fall. Fisher stressed that in the aggregate real debts are increased even as efforts are made to pay off the monetary debts. '*Money illusion*' is symmetrical as both debtors and creditors are unaware of the changes in purchasing power (p. 18; Fisher's italics).

A vicious spiral downward ensues. As deflation weakens the financial position of strong debtors (the 'net worth factor'), they liquidate to pay off their debts, which intensifies the deflationary process, thus weakening the financial positions of even stronger debtors, who are then forced to liquidate (1933a, p. 25). Banks join in by calling loans (p. 26). The fall in businesses' net worth results in more bankruptcies and a fall in profits (the 'profit factor') leads to business losses, which lead to a reduction in output (the 'production factor'), volume of trade, and employment. That causes pessimism and loss of confidence (the 'psychological factor'), which leads to hoarding (the 'currency-turnover factor'), which is particularly bad when banks begin doing it, and further decrease the velocity of money. Finally, all of these together cause 'complicated disturbances in the rates of interest' (1933b, p. 342). A cyclical tendency in indebtedness involves a cyclical tendency in interest rates such that money or nominal interest rates decrease as debts are paid off but real interest rates increase as deflation occurs (1933a, pp. 38-39). Fisher declared that deflation is 'the root of all the evils' (p. 39).

Fisher acknowledged that, in the real world, the nine factors do not follow in that pedagogical order. A table in Appendix 1 of *Booms and Depression*, which was included in the *Econometrica* article, provided some detail to chronological order of developments (see 1933a, pp. 161-162; 1933b, p. 343). Of particular note, the psychological effects of pessimism come in earlier, with 'mild gloom and shock' leading to a loss of 'confidence.' That leads to a slight decrease in the velocity of money and to the beginning of debt liquidation. The next development is that interest rates on unsafe loans rise while those on safe loans fall. Then come progressive increases in distress selling, with prices of both securities and commodities falling, and 'gloom' becoming progressively more intense. That is followed by rising real interest rates and real debts and further reductions in the velocity of money, with the money supply contracting as balances in deposit accounts shrink. Business losses and reductions in net worth lead to more liquidation and to a reduction in the volume of trades on stock exchanges. With construction activities, output, and trade decreasing, unemployment rises. Pessimism about economic conditions increases with each step and hoarding of money leads to runs on banks. Banks curtail loans for self-protection, sell investments, and bank failures occur.

Fisher stressed that, except for debt and interest rates, all of the fluctuations occur through deflation of prices of assets and commodities (1933b, p. 344). For a great depression to occur, both over-indebtedness and deflation must occur in combination as they react to each other. When over-indebtedness occurs without precipitating deflation, i.e., when inflationary forces are accidentally or intentionally present, the debt cycle does not occur (ibid.). And if deflation occurs for some reason other than debt, the consequences are very mild.

There was an element of the quantity theory of money involved. In the *Econometrica* article, Fisher stated that in the book *Booms and Depressions* he had perhaps understated the importance of the direct effect of the decrease in money and deposits and the velocity of money on the level of output (trade) and employment. As empirical verification, he noted that where emergency money had appeared locally, trade had revived (1933b, p. 342). The 'debt disease' precipitates the 'dollar disease,' making real debts greater as the purchasing power of the dollar rises with the fall in prices. Attempts to pay down debts may be more than offset by decreases in prices caused by the liquidation, with the end result being less money debts but greater real debts. Fisher declared that 'Then we have the great paradox which . . . is the chief secret of most, if not all, great depressions: *The more the debtors pay, the more they owe*' (p. 344). The timing of maturities is, of course, critical, as call loans and brokers loans being the most prone to 'debt embarrassment' (p. 345). In his concluding paragraph of the *Econometrica* article, Fisher indicated that feature of his debt-deflation theory that he thought was the newest and sought to stress the most was 'that when over-indebtedness is so great as to depress prices faster than liquidation, the mass effort to get us out of debt sinks us more deeply into debt' (p. 350). In that aspect, there does appear to be at least a superficial difference between his theory and Veblen's theory.

How 'Over-Indebtedness' Emerges

Since the emergence of 'over-indebtedness' is the initial factor, why does it occur? Fisher placed debt in two categories or classes. 'Unproductive debt' is that which has occurred because some 'misfortune' has 'cut a hole in the borrower's income-stream' and a debt is incurred to temporarily and partially cover that hole (1933a, p. 44). The examples that Fisher gave was an ill worker borrowing because of a loss of income and a nation borrowing to pay for war. 'Productive debts' are those that are deliberately incurred to take advantage of some perceived opportunity for economic gain. There is a difference in the psychology involved in the two cases. 'Unproductive debt' arises from the psychology of fear, gloom, and caution because of distressed circumstances. But such debts occur sporadically and are usually limited by security available. Except during war, 'unproductive debts' are not likely to be 'greatly overdone.' In contrast, 'productive debt' arises from the psychology of great optimism and enthusiasm and, usually, the opportunity to invest is the result of new inventions, discoveries, or business methods. 'Productive debts' are much more important in explaining economic crises and depressions, which is enhanced by a 'shady side' of investing giving way to speculation and fraud (pp. 44-45).

Fisher identified the 'debt starters' as many. The most common appeared to be '*new opportunities to invest at a big prospective profits*, as compared with ordinary profits and interest, such as through new inventions, new industries, development of new resources, opening of new lands or new markets' (1933b, p. 348; Fisher's italics). But Fisher declared that 'Easy money is the great cause of over-borrowing' (ibid.). He described the 'public psychology of going into debt for gain' as passing through several distinct phases, starting with the expectations of large dividends or gains in income in the remote future, which gives rise to growing public expectations of being able to realize substantial capital gains in the immediate future. That, in turn, gives rise to reckless promotions, which culminate increasingly in downright fraud that takes advantage of 'a public which had grown credulous and gullible' (p. 349).

Recovery

At some point, the liquidations finally reduce the size of real debt to the point that a situation of under-indebtedness develops (1933a, p. 41). Recovery begins as people who have the ability start buying assets and commodities at bargain prices. The nine factors are then reversed and recovery begins. The release of hoarded currency and new borrowing results in 'reflation.' For a time, nominal interest rates and nominal debts rise but real rates remain low so that real debts are diminishing. The increase in profits and net worth as prices rise encourages an expansion in output and employment. As the intensity of the recovery increases, a boom occurs which may turn into a vicious spiral upward, taking the economy above equilibrium with over-indebtedness again occurring (p. 43).

THE DEBT-DEFLATION THEORY APPLIED: THE GREAT DEPRESSION

In applying his theory to explain the current economic situation, Fisher argued that the unusual severity of the debt-deflation depression of 1929-1932 was due to the levels of nominal and real debts reaching historical highs in 1929 (1933b, p. 346), followed by a 40 percent increase in the real debt burden by 1932 due to deflation. The empirical grounds for that assessment was that while total nominal debts had been reduced by 20 percent through liquidation, the purchasing power of the dollar had increased by 75 percent (ibid.).

In addition to Fisher's textual discussion of the debts that led to the Great Depression in *Booms and Depressions*, he presented statistical data on various types of debts in Appendix III (1933a, pp. 168-185). The over-indebtedness that Fisher held responsible for the Great Depression began with the huge borrowing to finance World War I and the reconstruction that followed, which involved both private and government debts. A psychological factor was the sense of optimism and high expectations resulting from ending the war. In particular, the 'spirit of invention' was given new impulse and a 'New Era' of technological advancement was being talked about. While corporations turned to equity financing as stock prices rose, the burden of debt was shifted to individuals who bought stock with borrowed funds, largely those of the most dangerous type — margin loans subject to call. That debt became greater and less stable, and the situation was intensified by the investment trusts that pyramided debt.

Among the 'miscellaneous influences' were the high-pressure techniques of investment bankers, with a mixture of fraudulent enterprise, an inexperienced investing public that had become conditioned to securities investment by holding government bonds, and the capital gains tax which caused people to hold on to their stocks while borrowing to buy more (pp. 71-74).

While Fisher concentrated on borrowing by individuals to speculate in stocks, he also argued that the combination of technological improvements and growth in 'trade' allowed 'commodity' prices to remain 'steady,' so that profits of corporations to soared, which caused stock prices to rise. In such a period, commodities markets and stock markets tend to experience different movements. Prices in commodity markets tend to fall because of lower costs while stock prices tend to rise because of increased profits (1933a, p. 75).

Fisher also cited the increased debt to finance public facilities in Europe and gave special note of Germany's dependence on borrowing from the U.S., which included a quote from the head of Germany's central bank that distinguished between the merits of borrowing to purchase productive equipment and borrowing to spend for luxury consumption (1933a, p. 76). Farm debt and consumer installment debt were only briefly mentioned (p. 77), as were public debts (pp. 79-80). Fisher also argued that the expansion of credit based on the inflow of gold rested on a myth because the gold was subject to return to Europe. Here he mentioned the adoption of a policy by the Federal Reserve that would help return gold to Britain by lowering of interest rates in the U.S. through the period 1925-1928 (pp. 82-84).

But in keeping with the earlier book, *The Stock Market Crash – And After*, it was the borrowing for stock market purposes that Fisher emphasized. In *Booms and Depressions*, he stated that no single factor unites a decrease in the money supply and a slowing of the velocity of money as effectively as the type of stock market crash that occurred in October 1929. A large amount of deposit money becomes wiped out and the desire for liquidity greatly increases, reducing the velocity. The contribution to deflation is almost exactly the same as 'a bonfire of a large part of the nation's cash' (1933a, p. 35). Stock market crashes have a double impact as falling stock prices induce falling commodity prices. Although commodity prices at first fall more slowly than stock prices, the effects are more injurious to 'the foundations of the economic structure,' and panic selling may ensue (ibid.).

REMEDIES

Fisher distinguished between the leading 'substantive cures,' which he viewed as mere palliatives, and the real cure — currency reforms — that goes to the root of the disease. The role of money is indicated by his comments that end the chapter of *Booms and Depressions* entitled 'The Over-Indebtedness That Led To the World Depression.'

> In a word, we dismissed some of our gold foundation and at the same time built a debt structure over the place where the gold had been. Billions of debt and a gold base that was slippery — these two conditions had now set the stage for the collapse of 1929. (1933a, p. 84)

Among the 'palliatives' which will have only secondary effects (1933a, p. 114), Fisher strongly disapproved of government jobs programs, but approved of some form of unemployment insurance, reducing costs to increase profit margins by relaxing the anti-trust laws to permit mergers, cutting 'wasteful armaments' so as to reduce the tax burden, eliminating the capital gains tax as a means of 'retarding the debt disease,' reducing tariffs, making the accounts of investment bank affiliates of commercial banks more open to the public, banks becoming stricter in their lending standards, replacing 'flexible bonds' by options for refunding after five years, and debt 'scaling' of both private and governmental debts (but not debt 'regulation') (pp.115-120).

The real remedies were in credit control, even though the need for a reliable criterion for determining 'how much debt is too much debt' was still to be met 'in due time' (p. 120). Fisher began by illustrating fluctuating price levels or, conversely, what would be needed to stabilize the price level, with his quantity theory of money (pp. 122-123). But he stated that the same could have been shown without any recourse to the quantity theory of money. All that was needed was to 'assume that the quantity of the circulating medium has *some* tendency to raise the price level, and vice-versa' (p. 124). He denied that control of the quantity of money would be futile because factors other than money and credit are influential. Debt-deflation can be stopped or prevented by monetary policies based on price indexes that first 'reflate' the price level, up to the average level existing at the time when the outstanding debts were contracted by existing debtors and assumed by existing creditors, and then maintain that level. But when inflation is not being registered by price indices, as was the case with commodity prices in the 1920s, Fisher argued that stock prices will serve as an indicator (p. 121). That corresponds to the nature of inflation that Veblen perceived in 1923, where price levels failed to respond to falling production costs.

Fisher wrote *Booms and Depressions* in 1932, and therefore his monetary policy remedies preceded the United States going off the domestic gold standard, the creation of the Federal Deposit Insurance Corporation, the Securities Act that gave the Federal Reserve the power to set the margin requirement on stocks, and the re-organization of the Federal Reserve in 1935 that gave the Board the authority to change reserve requirements and created the FOMC. But Fisher's recommendations anticipated some of those reforms. On the monetary policy side, he called for regulating the volume of deposit money by changes in the discount rate, open market operations, and changes in the reserve requirement (1933a, pp. 126-131). The banking system needed to be strengthened through some form of deposit insurance, allowing branch banking, and the creating a 'unified banking system' by bringing state banks under the Federal Reserve System. In addition, Fisher suggested that the Federal Reserve control both the level of commodity prices and the level of stock prices, and should have the power to 'put special obstacles' to block the lending to brokers when such loans are judged to have become excessive (p. 133). There was also a suggestion that the U.S. Treasury carry out activities 'analogous to the "open market policy" of the Federal Reserve Banks' (p. 135).

On a broader basis, Fisher called for leadership that would restore the public's confidence in banks so they would stop hoarding cash and the velocity of money could be increased (1933a, pp. 140-142) and urged the adoption of the 'compensated dollar plan' on an international basis. Fisher noted that a form of a stamp tax on hoarding had not come to his attention before the book was written, but endorsed it as offering 'the most efficient method of controlling hoarding and probably the speediest way out of a depression' (p. 142).

When Fisher wrote the *Econometrica* article, he had had the opportunity to see at least the initial policies implemented by the Roosevelt administration. As evidence that it was possible to 'reflate,' Fisher cited the policies implemented by Sweden and Roosevelt's policies. He asserted that it would have been easier to do so if the 'reflating' policies had been implemented earlier, such as the Federal Reserve's policies that revived prices and businesses from May to September in 1932 before being changed. It would have been still easier to prevent the depression by attacking the 'debt-disease' before it can lead to the 'dollar disease.' He declared that if the Federal Reserve had followed Benjamin Strong's policies consistently, there would have been the 'debt disease' (the stock market crash) but not the deflation. The economy would have experienced 'the bad cold but not the pneumonia' (1933b, p. 347).

THE DEBT-DEFLATION THEORY AND FISHER'S EARLIER WRITINGS

How does Fisher's debt-deflation theory differ from his earlier writings on business cycles? In *The Purchasing Power of Money* ([1911] 1963), the pendulum swings to prosperity, then to depression, and eventually back to equilibrium occur because increases in the money supply result in temporary lowering of the interest rates below normal levels. Debt enters the picture in response to the lower interest rates as banks are eager to lend and businesses are eager to borrow, given the combination of rising expected profits due to inflation and lower than normal interest rates. At some point, banks raise interest rates and some of the outstanding loans become questionable. Credit conditions tighten, money and velocity decrease, and panic may result in runs on banks. In the 1923 article 'The Business Cycle Largely a "Dance of the Dollar",' and the 1925 article 'Our Unstable Dollar and the So-Called Business Cycle,' Fisher asserted that his seemingly novel idea was that alternate booms and depressions are due to alternate inflation and deflation and, more particularly, on the rate of change in the price level (1925, pp. 180-181). This was largely a statistical demonstration to serve as an 'inductive verification' that rising prices temporarily stimulate trade and falling prices temporarily depress trade. Since the price level explains so much, the business cycle is essential a myth (pp. 191-192). The price level is influenced by extraneous forces such as government inflation policies, banking policies, legislation, foreign trade, gold mining, and many other factors that have no regular pattern of occurrence (p. 194).

How does Fisher's debt-deflation theory differ from Veblen's 1904 theory of debt, capital, deflation, and chronic depression? Unlike Veblen, Fisher did not recognize the role of debt in close relationship to capital as systemic feature of modern business investment and operations. While Veblen recognized the changes in real debt burdens when deflation occurs, there was not Fisher's emphasis on the force of real debt increasing even as nominal dollar debt was being reduced. For Veblen, the importance of debt was its effect on the businessmen's required rate of profits and investors' required rate of return on investment. Perhaps the more important difference was that Veblen stressed the cost-reducing effects from investment in new capital goods purchased at lower prices, which enable the new firms to realize the required rate of profit even while selling at lower prices. In addition, new firms and those emerging from bankruptcy would have lower fixed costs associated with paying interest on the larger debts of the older firms. Fisher apparently had no concept of deflationary trends due to lowered costs of production from technological progress implemented by business investment.

RECENT INTERPRETATIONS AND MODIFICATIONS OF FISHER'S THEORY

Several interpretations and modifications of Fisher's debt-deflation theory have recently appeared that merit attention. One by Wolfson (1996) was in a Minskian context, therefore it will be reviewed in Chapter 7. Dimand (1994) noted that the importance of Fisher's theory that the 'sensitivity of real expenditure to deflation depended on the extent of nominal indebtedness' can be clearly seen in Tobin's three-equation 'Walras-Keynes-Phillips' model. In that model, the desired real aggregate expenditure is a function of the price level, expected inflation, and real income, with the money supply given. The output gap is related to the gap between actual and expected inflation, with expected inflation adjusting adaptively. Dimand observed that was reminiscent of Fisher's explanation of money interest rates as being related to distributed lags of past price changes. Since neither Keynes nor Walras used adaptive expectations, Tobin's model actually takes on a Fisherian character.

Dimand (1994) argued that Fisher's debt-deflation theory has implications for Tobin's stability condition. If inside debt denominated in money becomes sufficiently large, the 'Fisher effect' on inside debt (real debt increasing) could dominate the stock Pigou effect on outside money (lower prices increases the real money supply), so that a lower price level could reduce real expenditure. The model becomes necessarily unstable, with both real income and the price level moving further away from their equilibrium levels after an initial shock. The size of the derivative of desired expenditure with respect to expected inflation could also be expected, from Fisher's analysis, to depend upon the amount of nominal indebtedness. The larger that relative amount of that indebtedness, the less likely the model will be stable. That supports Fisher's explanation of why the U.S. economy returned to potential output quickly after the 1921 deflation but failed to do so after the 1929-1930 deflation due to 'overindebtedness.'

In another article, Dimand (1998) has offered an interesting comparison of the two paths for economics that had been laid out by Veblen and Fisher in 1909, focusing on their disagreement on neoclassical capital theory to illuminate the differences. It was not obvious in either 1909 or in the early 1930s that economics would follow Fisher's path rather than Veblen's (Dimand 1998, p. 462). Yet Dimand noted that Fisher's work as a macroeconomist had little direct influence on macroeconomics after the 1920s (p. 463). In both Veblen's and Fisher's cases, their debt-deflation theories remained outside mainstream economics but were resuscitated by Minsky.

6. Innovations, Debt, and Deflation in Schumpeter's Theory

In historical context, Schumpeter overlapped with Veblen and Fisher from the early 1900s to the 1930s. But he continued his critical analyses of institutional changes in the capitalistic system through World War II and the post-war years until January 1950. In his early classic *The Theory of Economic Development*, published in German in either 1911 or 1912 and published in English in 1934, Schumpeter presented a purely theoretical explanation of business cycles as a process of structural transformation resulting from the successful implementation of technological and organizational innovations by special individuals with unique vision — the entrepreneurs. In that theory, entrepreneurial ventures are financed by credit money (capital) created by banks, and both inflation and deflation occur as normal phenomena in the several phases of business cycles. Schumpeter stated in the *Preface* to the English Edition (1934) that all of the ideas that he presented in that book were developed by 1909, some as early as 1907. Thus, for all practical purposes *The Theory of Economic Development* was a historical contemporary of Veblen's *The Theory of Business Enterprise*, which was published in 1904.

But there is no indication in *The Theory of Economic Development* that either the period of deflation from 1867 to the mid-1890s in America or the emergence of large corporations and modern corporate finance had made the type of impression on Schumpeter that it had on Veblen. While both *The Theory of Business Enterprise* and *The Theory of Economic Development* presented socio-economic theories of evolutionary changes in the capitalist system that placed great emphasis on technological innovations, Veblen's theory was much more institutionally specific to the U.S. economy. He had drawn heavily on the reports of the U.S. Industrial Commission and focused his analyses on the development of large corporations and corporate finance in J. P. Morgan's America. In contrast, Schumpeter applied the abstractness of pure theory (albeit of a non-technical nature) with very little attention to real world developments of either a historical or current nature. Only in the last chapter on 'The Business Cycle' did Schumpeter mention, albeit very briefly and rather abstractly, 'the progressive trustification of economic life' and the 'great combines' (1934, p. 244). Some limited commentary, largely in footnotes, were added by Schumpeter in preparing the later English translation, e.g., the reference to the post-WWI depression as being 'not normal' (p. 246, fn).

That approach changed, however, in the two volumes of *Business Cycles*, published in 1939. In addition to expanding the theoretical framework from a single cycle to three cycles, Schumpeter also presented historical analyses of the long cycles that included detailed comments on economic and financial developments in the 1920s and 1930s. The great depression of the 1930s was explained as a coincidental converging of the downturns in all three cycles but, within that discussion, Schumpeter offered qualified approval of Fisher's description of debt-deflation phenomena while mildly criticizing Fisher for not presenting a true theory of the causes of depressions.

Overview

In the first part of this chapter, we review the roles of innovations, debt, and deflation in Schumpeter's business cycle theory and in his historical analyses of the periods of the long Kondratieff cycles. In the second part, we reflect on similarities and differences in Schumpeter's and Veblen's analyses, and in the third section, we review Schumpeter's critical comments about Fisher's debt-deflation theory of great depressions. In the fourth section, Schumpeter's analyses of debt in the 1920s and depression in the 1930s are reviewed. That is followed in the fifth section by an examination of Schumpeter's views on the prevention of and remedies for deflation and depression. In the last section, we note that, like Veblen, Schumpeter focused on sustained inflation in his later works and that, like Veblen, he associated the inflation with government policies under American democracy. But Schumpeter's views of the nature and causes of inflation in the 1940s were almost diametrically opposite to Veblen's views on the nature and causes of inflation in 1923.

DEBT, INNOVATIONS, AND DEFLATION IN SCHUMPETER'S BUSINESS CYCLES

Credit and debt play major roles in affecting prices in Schumpeterian business cycles, but those roles are quite different in the 'primary' wave (or 'pure model') and the 'secondary' waves of the cycles. In Schumpeter's pure model, the economy is assumed to be initially in equilibrium in a Walrasian circular flow model with labor and other factors of production fully employed. A 'primary' wave of prosperity is initiated by the launching of a cluster of successful technological or organizational innovations by entrepreneurs. The entrepreneurs need capital (i.e., money) to finance their ventures, and seek loans from banks. Bankers, as the capitalists, have the special talent and experience to recognize which innovations merit funding by virtue of having high potential for success and which do not.

In making loans to entrepreneurs, the banks create credit money, thus increasing the money supply. Because labor and other inputs are currently employed, the spending of the new money by the entrepreneurs for material inputs and labor generates temporary increases in the prices of outputs (and profits) of the supplying firms and in wages of those supplying labor. Thus, the inflation and prosperity may appear to simply be the result of an increase in the money supply. But the real source is the entrepreneurial visions of innovative products and processes which are endorsed by the bankers. The increase in the money supply is only the facilitating instrument that is necessary in a market economy.

The 'Secondary Wave' of Speculative Prosperity

A 'secondary' wave of speculative prosperity that becomes superimposed on the 'primary' wave will typically have much larger and more visible dimensions. Under the presumption that demand for their outputs will continue to increase, firms that are supplying materials and capital goods to the entrepreneurs increase their investment spending to expand capacity. Consumption spending rises as the households that are supplying labor to the entrepreneurs presume that their wage incomes will continue to increase. There will also be 'induced' investment spending by firms that adapt to the new technologies and products of the entrepreneurs. Much of this increased spending is financed by bank credit and serves to further accelerate the inflation that was created by the spending of the new money by the entrepreneurs.

The 'secondary wave' of general prosperity quickly becomes highly speculative in nature. A major factor is a change in the behavior of bankers who supply the new credit money. In Schumpeter's pure model, only bona fide entrepreneurs borrow and only banks create money (capital) to finance their ventures. The creation of that money is 'the monetary complement of innovations' (Schumpeter 1939, p. 111). As capitalists who bear all the risks, bankers must be independent agents, with no proprietary involvement in the ventures being financed, and must have the special ability to judge which innovations will be successful, denying credit to those that will not. But such ability is rare in the real world and, in the secondary wave, speculative business ventures are launched based on unrealistic expectations of rising prices and profits.

'Reckless finance' and 'easy money' facilitates speculative spending of all types, including pure financial speculation (Schumpeter 1939, p. 147). Bankers cease to be the responsible 'aphors' of the system who dispense credit only to the entrepreneurs with meritorious innovations to implement. Instead, credit creation spreads throughout the system to finance any kind of expansion. Credit/debt loses its relationship with innovation and becomes an instrument for financing business in general (Schumpeter 1939, p. 159). Schumpeter observed that 'Many things float on this "secondary wave," without any new or direct impulse from the real driving force, and speculative anticipation in the end acquires a causal significance' (1951, p. 226). In addition to low bank lending standards, many speculative new business ventures are funded through floating stocks on a rising stock market. As speculation drives stock prices higher, more speculation is encouraged.

In addition to extending loans for highly speculative business ventures that would be denied funding under responsible banking, consumer borrowing (which Schumpeter defined as both public and private, and which was left out of the pure model) attains great importance in the cyclical process. Based on developments in the 1920s, Schumpeter stated that 'consumers' borrowing is one of the most conspicuous danger points in the secondary wave of prosperity, and consumers' debt are among the most conspicuous weak spots in recession and depression' (1939, p. 110).

Deflation and Recession

The prosperity and the attendant inflation come to an end, beginning with the innovative ventures of the new ventures becoming operational. As entrepreneurs' demand for labor and material inputs to construct their plants subsides, wages and prices in the supplying markets begin to fall, which affects consumer demand and prices of consumer goods and services. Successful entrepreneurs use part of their monopolistic profits to pay off their debts, which reduces the money supply. Schumpeter labeled this shrinkage in the money supply as 'credit deflation' or 'autodeflation' (1939, p. 136), or 'the incipient self-deflation of business' (1939, p. 636).

But the key factor in changing inflation to deflation is the increased supply of new products and existing products that are being produced with new techniques. In *The Theory of Economic Development*, Schumpeter stated that even if the money supply did not shrink, 'this appearance of new products causes the fall in prices, which on its part terminates the boom, *may* lead to a crisis, *must* lead to a depression, and starts all the rest' (1934, p. 233; Schumpeter's italics). (In that early work, he was detailing a two-phase cycle, so 'depression' was the same as 'recession' in the four-phase cycle in *Business Cycles*.) Downward pressure on prices in general emerges as the supply of new products by the entrepreneurs and supplies of imitators catches up with demand. Since some of the innovations will be in the nature of cost-efficient ways to produce existing goods, that too will put pressure on prices as typically more must be produced to exploit the economies of scale that are involved. Prices will not only be below the levels reached during the boom but also below their levels before the boom (Schumpeter 1934, p. 234).

Schumpeter asserted that the history of prices verifies that the 'secular' price trend must fall (1934, pp. 234-235). The deflation process may be gradual as newly created purchasing power only partially disappears and borrowing by non-entrepreneurs, especially by states and municipalities, may step in. Entrepreneurs may pay off debts in gradual steps. But the deflationary tendency is operative and liquidation of debts by successful entrepreneurs takes place — so that deflation, even though in mild form, must always appear automatically when the boom has gone far enough. In *Business Cycles*, Schumpeter explained great depressions and long periods of deflation as the coincidental downturns in three cycles, which has significance for capitalism. Because prices fall more in the 'downgrades' of those cycles than they rise in their 'upgrades,' 'capitalist evolution produces a long-run (or "secular") tendency for prices to fall' (1939, p. 465). Indeed, Schumpeter declared that historical experience tends to show 'that neither capitalism itself nor the social institutions associated with it, democracy among them, can work efficiently and with comparative smoothness except on a falling trend of prices' (pp. 465-466).

The deflation quickly spreads through the economy. Wage incomes cease to rise and may fall, leading to less consumption spending. Many existing firms will be forced to lower their prices in efforts (often in vain) to stay in the market. The psychology of rising prices quickly changes to the psychology of falling prices. Individually, bankers will adopt defensive strategies, limiting credit and calling in loans. This is the normal adaptation of the economy to a new and higher equilibrium in terms of economic development. But at the new equilibrium, the level of prices is lower (1939, p. 137; see also 1951, p. 41).

Schumpeter scolded economists for putting too much emphasis on the price level, stating that: 'Businessmen, politicians, and many economists unite in drawing a picture which grossly exaggerates the role of price movements in the cyclical process' (1939, p. 449). While, for obvious reasons, there is some excuse for this in the case of businessmen and politicians, Schumpeter declared that only faulty analysis could account for it in the case of economists. The very definition of a crisis as 'a break in prices,' and propositions such as 'the collapse of the price system is the real cause of a depression,' are based on failures to understand that the business cycle is a process in which 'all elements of the economic system interact in certain characteristic ways and that no one element can be singled out for the role of prime mover' (ibid.). Schumpeter noted that falling prices do not necessarily increase debt load in the sense of creating economic problems.

Prosperity can start from a falling price level because innovations allow the entrepreneurial firms to realize profits at existing price levels (pp. 349-350).

Debt, Abnormal Deflation, and Depression

The 'reckless' financing of speculative ventures and financial speculation in the secondary wave of prosperity is responsible for the non-normal phases of 'depression' and 'recovery' in Schumpeter's four-stage business cycles in *Business Cycles*. Schumpeter distinguished repeatedly between his innovation-driven cycles and the monetary theories of cycles. 'Easy money' and 'reckless finance' are not the cause of the prosperity, but the availability of credit amplifies the expansion of the prosperity stage and intensifies the 'normal' recession stage, turning it into depression. 'Abnormal' deflation occurs in a depression. It is the result of the great build-up of debt allowed under 'reckless finance' and 'easy money' in the secondary wave and over-reactions by the banking community when the 'auto-deflation' begins in the recession stage. There is much more to liquidate than would be the case if tight lending standards had been maintained by bankers. Financial speculation may result in a financial crisis that leads to much excessive liquidation, eliminating firms that are fundamentally sound and deserving of credit. When a recession is under way or is expected by the banking world, banks endeavor on their own initiative to restrict credits. This factor is important and frequently starts a real crisis but it is an accessory and not inherent in the process (1939, p. 234).

SCHUMPETER'S AND VEBLEN'S THEORIES

It is curious that neither Veblen nor Schumpeter ever acknowledged the other's work on modern capitalism. However, similarities exist between their analyses of economic society as an evolutionary process; a focus on the dynamics of capitalism; and a profound concern about the origins and impacts of technology. Cramer and Leathers (1977) noted that in their views on the 'new imperialism' of the late 19th and early 20th centuries, both analyzed the nature of political and economic power in the social relationships of capitalist economies. Certainly, their normative perspectives on modern capitalism were at the opposite ends of the ideological spectrum. Schumpeter was a great admirer of 'unfettered' capitalism in a social-political environment in which aristocratic elements provided supporting leadership. Veblen was a caustic critic of the pecuniary value system of the corporate business enterprise system and its leisure class culture that retained strong psychological and sociological elements of the barbarian institutions of feudalism.

But Veblen and Schumpeter were exceptionally well-informed scholars who critiqued the writings of economists with whom they disagreed on a professional basis. With his great facility for languages, Veblen read books and articles written in German, French, and Scandinavian languages. The citations and footnote comments in *The Theory of Business Enterprise* indicate that he was very familiar with the business cycle theories of European economists. Veblen was surely familiar with Schumpeter's theory of economic development and business cycles, since Schumpeter was a visiting professor at Columbia in 1913-1914 and lectured at several American universities. Thus, it is curious that Veblen ignored Schumpeter's work when he was wrote *Absentee Ownership*. Similarly, Schumpeter was famous for having an encyclopedic knowledge of famous and less famous economists and he was certainly familiar with Veblen's work. In *History of Economic Analysis*, Schumpeter stated that *The Theory of the Leisure Class* was of 'considerable importance' in economic sociology, but an 'appraisal or even characterization' was 'impossible in the space of our command' (1954, p. 795). What is perhaps most important about that comment was that Schumpeter did identify Veblen as an 'economist' although he classified the subject of the book as 'sociology.' In other brief comments, Schumpeter stated that Veblen was particularly 'candid' in voicing hostility to the capitalist order (p. 802), came close to a 'depredation theory of entrepreneurial gain' or at least could be regarded as the scientific ancestor of the theory of unproductive entrepreneurs who 'prey upon the productive activity of others' (pp. 895-896), was one of the 'history-minded' or 'sociology-minded' critics of the economic theories based on marginal utility (p. 911). Thus, it is curious that Schumpeter failed to give critical attention to Veblen's analyses of the modern business enterprise system since he habitually acknowledged the works of numerous others with whom he disagreed.

One distinct difference in their analyses of cycles and trends was that Veblen attributed the beginning of prosperity to an increase in demand in some sector or industry. Such an increase would usually be due to government outlays for war although, over a longer period, expansions in the population and exploiting natural resources provided stimulus. As we noted in Chapter 5, Veblen failed to recognize that such an increase in demand could result from technological innovations, even though he recognized that new investment to implement new developments in technology routinely occurred even during periods of depression.

Schumpeter failed to acknowledge that his account of the 'secondary wave' of prosperity and the inevitable aftermath was very similar to Veblen's analysis of speculative prosperities and the deflation that follows.

There was, however, a major difference in their views on the individual reward system that is involved. Veblen contended that the bulk of personal fortunes acquired in the late 19th and early 20th centuries came from stock price manipulation by those business interest controlling the large corporate enterprises (1904, p. 167). In contrast, Schumpeter stated that 'the bulk of private fortunes is, in a capitalist society, directly or indirectly the result of the process of which innovation is the "prime mover." Speculative maneuvers which are responsible for some, are evidently incidents to the process of economic evolution' (1939, p. 106).

While Schumpeter did not mention how closely his 'secondary wave' resembled Veblen's analysis of speculative prosperities, a footnote summary statement of what happens in his secondary wave of speculative prosperity would also effectively summarize Veblen's theory.

This may be expressed by saying that in prosperity present earnings which are ephemeral and future earnings which are imaginary are capitalized. Excessive borrowing is facilitated thereby. A subsequent fall in prices then impairs these values and may enforce liquidation even before, and independently of, any default in interest payments. (Schumpeter, 1939, p. 147, fn)

There is certainly a close similarity in their views that technological innovations tend to be cost-reducing, and that competitive pricing based on unit costs of production means deflation as a secular tendency. But there is a very distinct difference between the recession phase of a Schumpeterian cycle and Veblen's chronic depression. While there will be structural changes that include rendering obsolete some industries, firms, and labor skills (the famous 'creative destruction'), Schumpeter's recession does not mean the usual unemployment and lower standard of living. On the contrary, the economy is moving to new but higher equilibrium. Unlike Veblen's chronic depression, real incomes will have risen (1939, p. 137). Yet, there is similarity to Veblen's observation that investment that implements new industrial technologies continues even during depression in Schumpeter's statement that recession is a period in which:

The new methods are being copied and improved; adaptation to them or to the impact of new commodities consists in part in 'induced inventions'; some industries expand into new investment opportunities created by the achievement of entrepreneurs; others respond by rationalization of their technological and commercial process under pressure; much dead wood disappears. Thus, there is a good deal of truth in the popular saying that 'there is more brain in business' at large during recession than there is during prosperity. (1939, p. 143)

SCHUMPETER ON FISHER'S DEBT-DEFLATION THEORY

In *Business Cycles*, Schumpeter discussed the phenomena of the 'secondary wave' in terms of 'Professor Irving Fisher's Debt-Deflation Theory not of cycles — the existence of which he denies — but of Great Depressions' (1939, p. 146). Schumpeter stated that he agreed 'entirely with *some* of the "49 articles" by which . . . Professor Fisher formulates his "creed"' (ibid., fn) but criticized Fisher for failing to understand the role of innovations as the basis for a theory of cycles and waves of 'creative destruction,' the nature and role of debt, and the remedies to depression.

Fisher's Rejection of Business Cycles

In a footnote in *Business Cycles*, Schumpeter cited Fisher's claim that the notion of the business cycle as a single self-generating cycle was a myth. In the sense that a business cycle does not consist of a single wavelike movement and is not 'simple,' Schumpeter agreed with that statement (1939, p. 35, fn). But he dismissed Fisher's claim that business cycles do not exist because the plus and minus deviations in Fisher's times series showed no conformity to 'certain arbitrary standards of regularity.' Schumpeter argued that such arbitrary standards were not appropriate tests of the existence of cycles and noted that 'In every other sense "deviations" do occur and indeed characterize phases. The writer here entirely agrees with Professor Mitchell, who unhesitatingly recognizes "recurrence" without "strict periodicity"' (pp. 143-144, fn).

In discussing the phenomena of the 'secondary wave,' Schumpeter drew attention to Fisher's use of italics in listing new opportunities to invest at a big prospective profit as the common 'starter' of a period of prosperity (1939, p. 146). Fisher was stressing historical facts (e.g., the Erie Canal and railroads) that came within Schumpeter's concept of innovations (p. 146, fn). Schumpeter could have also noted that in *The Stock Market Crash — And After*, Fisher gave substantial credit to inventions and scientific research and to increased efficiency in information use for the prosperity of the 1920s. Moreover, Schumpeter himself, in 1925, was quite sure future depressions would become milder because better statistical knowledge and theoretical understanding of the economy would allow businesspeople to make better decisions and because large corporations could afford to make investment decisions on basis of longer-term considerations (Stolper 1994, p. 335). By not recognizing that innovations are the starters of business cycles, Fisher failed to recognize that debt-deflation was part of the business cycle phenomena, and could not be the *basis* for a theory of booms and depressions. Schumpeter reported that, in their discussions of that subject, he had told Fisher: 'If a man dies of consumption, I say he dies of consumption and not of the fever which is one of the concomitants of the process' (1939, p. 146, fn).

In his 1948 article on Fisher's econometrics, Schumpeter stated that although Fisher's tendency to be a monetary reformer had impaired the scientific and the practical value of his contribution to business-cycle research, those contributions were more important than the economics profession had realized. In particular, the more important 'starters' in Fisher's debt-deflation theory only need the 'modus operandi' to be worked out to yield a satisfactory 'explanatory schema' of cycles (1948a, p. 230). That could be done by placing the 'starters' before 'overindebtedness' and the process of inflation. In Fisher's theory, the expansion and contraction of debt in association with rising and falling price levels 'land us again in monetary reform, the subject Fisher was really interested in' (1939, p. 230). In a footnote, Schumpeter added that debt-deflation, in itself, was just a piece of mechanism, part of the familiar spiral that is well understood but added that Fisher's 1933 *Econometrica* article was important because his theory of 'starters' and its implications stand out much better in the article than in the book *Booms and Depressions* (1948a, p. 231).

That combination of criticism and acclamation of Fisher's debt-deflation theory was repeated in *History of Economic Analysis*. Schumpeter stated that Fisher's debt-deflation theory was a continuation of his emphasis on the monetary phenomena but what he described applied to all recorded business cycles and, in essence, was not monetary at all. Fisher laid the burden on the fact that debts are accumulated during prosperity and the inevitable liquidations that occur when prices break constitutes the core of depression. While he did not fail to see the really operative factors that were behind this 'surface mechanism' — new technologies and their commercial possibilities — he assigned them to the secondary position of 'debt starters' (1954, p. 1122).

Productive and Unproductive Debt

While Schumpeter rejected the claim that debt-deflation could be a *basis* for a theory of booms and depressions, he credited Fisher with being right in emphasizing that '*over*indebtedness' was primarily induced by easy money. But Fisher did not adequately define '*over*indebtedness,' which to some extent defies definition (1939, p. 147; Schumpeter's italics). Curiously, Schumpeter did not mention Fisher's definitions of 'productive' and 'unproductive' debt, which we noted in the previous chapter, but his own interpretation of 'overindebtedness' was in terms of productive versus unproductive use of debt.

Schumpeter argued that debt incurred by entrepreneurs to implement innovations and by firms that are adapting to move into the 'New Economic

Space' created by the innovations is 'productive' because it results in increases in productivity and lower costs of production. Those types of debt cannot result in 'overindebtedness.' But debt that finances expansions in existing capacities under false expectations of continuing or increasing demand, consumption spending, and speculation do not increase productivity. The fall in prices that results from productive debt, the 'autodeflation' that is a normal part of the business cycle initiated by innovations, must be distinguished from the deflation that results from the build-up of such 'unproductive' debt (1939, p. 147).

In the previous chapter, we noted that Fisher's observance that the opportunity to invest, often the result of new inventions, discoveries or business methods, has a 'shady side' as investing gives way to speculation and fraud (1933a, pp. 47-48). That corresponds to some extent to the unproductive borrowing that occurs in Schumpeter's secondary wave of prosperity. It should be also noted that, for Veblen, business debt would be 'productive' in the Schumpeterian sense if the 'loan credit' served 'to transfer the management of industrial materials from the owner to a more competent user' (1904, pp. 104, 112). But such use of 'loan credit' was virtually insignificant, since Veblen assumed that the productive goods were already in the hands of the most competent users. Instead, business debt was both unproductive from a social welfare perspective by virtue of not leading to a higher level of production and unproductive in the Schumpeterian sense because it only resulted in inflated prices of both industrial and consumer goods in a speculative spiral.

Schumpeter's view of Fisher as an inveterate 'monetary planner' led to a warning that Fisher's theory could lead to a jump to misleading conclusions about the role of money. 'Easy money' and 'reckless finance' amplifies the increase in debt during prosperity, which intensifies the downturn when it comes, but is not the cause of prosperity. Fisher's recommendations for ending deflation by monetary policies aimed at 'reflation' were based on his failure to understand the true nature of what drives the prosperity (1939, pp. 147-148).

SCHUMPETER'S ANALYSES OF DEBT AND DEPRESSION

Schumpeter explained the depression of 1930-1932 in terms of a convergence of the Kitchens '40-month cycle,' the nine to ten year Jugular cycle, and the long-term Kondratieff cycle (see 1939, pp. 169-171). When all three cycles are in their recession stages simultaneously, the 'vicious spiral' that turns the 'normal liquidation' during recession into the 'abnormal liquidation' of depression is particularly severe and the phenomena that Fisher described in his debt-deflation theory become part of the cyclical mechanism (p. 925). The accumulation of business and household debt in the 1920s, which was facilitated by an easy money policy, played an important role in creating a situation that made the depression much more severe (p. 936).

There is a notable difference between Schumpeter's analysis of business debt in the 1920s and the type of business debt involved in speculative prosperities in Veblen's theory. In the latter case, the debt of corporate businesses increases as rising stock market valuations of business assets provide increasing collateral for loans. In contrast, Schumpeter noted that in the 1920s large-scale businesses substituted new stock issues in a rising market for long-term debt and used the 'monetary ease' to gain independence from banks (1951, p. 211). Schumpeter remarked that the 'plethora of money made it easy and profitable to embark upon a course which in itself appeals to executives who are always jealous of anything that involves a certain amount of supervision and who for this reason never love their banking connections' (1939, p. 860). As stock prices rose, money flowed easily toward corporate industry at below bank rates and large concerns took advantage of the situation by becoming creditors rather than debtors, eventually entering the depression with 'a financial outfit that was nothing short of luxurious' (ibid.), that enabled some corporations to finance investments in 1935-1936 with funds raised during the boom period of the 1920s (pp. 860-861).

In one area of business, however, Schumpeter saw 'over-indebtedness' as clearly becoming a problem of a Veblenian nature. That was in 'power finance,' where efforts to gain control of gas companies made use of 'the financial instrument of the holding company' to 'unprecedented dimensions' (1939, p. 770). The competitive bidding for strategic positions resulted in a huge structure of debt that was far out of proportion to any real gains that were achievable through rationalization of the industry's structure. In addition to providing 'food for purely financial maneuvers and speculative excesses,' the banking system was jeopardized because power securities constituted a large part of the collateral behind loans to the holding companies and the some large banks had become closely tied to the power industry (p. 771).

Schumpeter stated that although consumer installment debt increased in the 1920s, it 'behaved remarkably well' (1939, p. 938). But mortgage debt was a very different matter. The easy money policy of the 1920s that made it easy for everyone to go into debt for the purpose of building a home resulted in a debt structure that stood ready to collapse if rosy expectations about things in general failed to materialize. It was easy to understand

> why the load of debt that thus lightheartedly incurred by people who foresaw nothing but booms should become a serious matter whenever incomes fell, and

that construction would then contribute, directly and the effects on the credit structure of impair values of real estate, as much to a depression as it had contributed to the preceding booms. (1939, pp. 748-749)

Schumpeter declared that when prosperity ends, nothing is so likely to produce cumulative depressive processes as a vast number of households with such high mortgage debts financed by commercial banks (1939, p. 749).

Schumpeter offered a somewhat different perspective than Fisher on the role of brokers' loans and the stock market bubble of the 1920s. While those loans contributed to the irrationally high stock prices, the processes were related to the easy creation of funds outside the control of commercial banks' credit-creating activities proper. By 1929, banks had largely stopped contributing to the increase in brokers' loans and the boom in stock prices was entirely due to funds flowing to the brokers in the form of loans made through banks by non-banking businesses (1939, p. 874). Schumpeter saw that change as a symptom of the general over-abundance of money and the institutional changes that allowed the creation of funds to get out of control. With existing funds far exceeding the amounts needed by businesses, the excess funds flowed to the stock market (pp. 902-903).

Schumpeter argued that new stock issues were the most important link between stock exchange booms and easy money. He explained that brokers' loans increased when customers withdrew from their margin accounts the gains in market value of stocks being held as collateral and 'converted' the balances into bank deposit money. In that way, brokers' loans provided a way to inject the speculative paper gains on stocks being held into the stream of consumer and producer expenditures by 'coining' those gains into money without selling the stocks (1939, p. 873). But Schumpeter denied that the stock market boom was initiated by the abundance of funds available. Rather, the initiating force was industrial success but an abundance of money was a condition for speculators being able to easily convert capital gains into bank balances and for corporations to be able to sell such large quantities of new securities at high prices. Brokers' loans were further increased in 1928-1929 as part of the proceeds of those sales was re-loaned to brokers. It was a situation in which an 'abundance of "funds" created additional abundance' that for a time paralyzed the brakes that the credit system would normally have applied (p. 874).

American Banks and American Character

Schumpeter's repeated references to 'easy money' conditions of the 1920s bring the role of banks squarely into the picture. Although large-scale businesses reduced their dependence on bank loans in the 1920s, commercial banks were ultimately responsible for much of the increase in mortgage debt. Households borrowed heavily from banks and indirectly from banks through financing agencies that discounted with banks and the creation of installment paper (1939, p. 860). Although banks did not provide the bulk of brokers' loans in 1929, they still created money through loans to buyers of stocks and bonds, which swelled loans on securities. Schumpeter commented that 'In the midst of rioting stock markets creation (of money) went on at a pace very different from that which would have been set in bankers' conference rooms. The steering and balancing parts of the capitalist machine were seriously and perhaps permanently impaired' (p. 861).

Schumpeter attributed the bank failures of 1930-1932 largely to the weaknesses of the American system of large numbers of small and inefficient banks and 'the absence of the English tradition' (1939, p. 909). The failure of the banking system to evolve into a 'small number of giant banks' with extensive branches that would be 'impregnable to the impact of depression' was explained by the 'irrational attitude of the public mind' in America (1951, p. 214). Schumpeter declared that:

> The American debt situation and the American bank epidemics . . . are in a class by themselves. Given the way in which both firms and households had run into debt during the twenties, it is clear that the accumulated load — in many cases, though not in all, very sensitive to a fall in price level — was instrumental in precipitating depression. In particular, it set into motion a vicious spiral within which everybody's efforts to reduce that load for a time only availed to increase it. There is thus no objection to the debt deflation theory of the American crisis, provided it does not mean more than this. (1939, p. 909)

In a footnote, Schumpeter stated that while Fisher's claim that a fall in prices *always* impairs debtors' ability to pay was not correct, over-indebtedness and deflation are strong and indeed dominating factors in any serious depression. But the rate of increase in total debt in the U.S. during the 1920s was not a normal element of the downturn of Kondratieff cycles, nor was it even an 'understandable' incident like speculative excesses and the debts they induce. Instead, the huge accumulation of debt in the U.S. 'must be attributed to the humor of the times, to cheap money policies, and to practices of concerns eager to push their sales; and it enters the class of understandable incidents only if we include specifically American conditions among our data' (1939, p. 909). Schumpeter also declared that 'the ominous increase in the flotation of securities of investment trusts and financial and trading companies since 1926 . . . teaches much about the specifically American characteristic of the great crisis' (p. 877).

Under the sub-heading of 'Incidents, Accidents, and Policy in the United States,' Schumpeter described the situation in 1931 as due, in part, to the psychological effects of the abnormal burden of mortgage debt. The problem was not so much actual losses by banks and other creditors on bad debts, but rather the phenomena of Fisher's debt-deflation at work. The strain and drain of repayments of debts, together with the general awareness of that the value of collateral was impaired and the net worth of many people had become negative, had the effects of depressing prices, business output in general, and the level of employment (1939, p. 938).

PREVENTION AND REMEDIES

Schumpeter consistently argued that the inflation that comes with the primary wave of prosperity and the deflation that comes with recession are normal phases of the business cycle that should not be prevented. Remedies and preventives for the abnormal deflation that comes with depressions had to be based on the recognition that 'depressions are not simply evils . . . but adjustment to previous economic change. Most of what would be effective in remedying a depression would be equally effective in preventing this disturbance' (1951, p. 115). To prevent recessions, as opposed to depressions, would take away the ability of the dynamic capitalist engine to bring economic development that increased the standard of living.

Recovery from depression is 'natural' when it is brought about by the mechanism of the business cycle, and is 'sound' when it does not contain tendencies to reproduce depression problems or produce new problems of inflation (1939, p. 995). But recovery can be 'sound' without being 'natural,' as shown by the case of the National Recovery Administration, which used price codes to raise prices (pp. 995-996). To some extent, Schumpeter thought the deflationary pressures through the first five months of 1931 were not as severe as had been widely inferred (p. 939). But clearly there had been excesses in the large secondary wave of prosperity of the 1920s, and the depression that resulted from those excesses called for preventive and remedial measures on a carefully selective basis that would not interfere with the normal business cycle initiated by innovations.

Monetary Policy

Schumpeter essentially rejected Fisher's 'reflationist' monetary policies as ineffective. In *The Theory of Economic Development*, Schumpeter stated that 'the losses and destruction which accompany the abnormal course of events are *really* meaningless and functionless. Justification of the various proposals for a prophylaxis and therapy of crises chiefly rests with them' (1934, p. 253; Schumpeter's italics). On those grounds, while opposing 'an indiscriminate and general increase in credit facilities' as simply causing inflation, Schumpeter approved of a credit policy that differentiates between the phenomena of the normal process of the depression, which have an economic function, and the abnormal phenomena which simply destroy without serving any function. Such a limited policy would involve providing credit to firms that deserve it while denying it to those firms that have been rendered technically or commercially obsolete by the innovations that initiated the preceding prosperity (1934, pp. 254-255).

But Schumpeter criticized economists who see business cycles as caused by monetary problems stemming from the working of the banking system and see depressions as nothing but 'deflation' that can be turned into prosperity by 'reflationary' creation of bank deposits (1939, p. 643). Because revival due simply to artificial stimulus leaves incomplete the eliminating of 'maladjustments,' which is the work of depression, and adds new 'maladjustments,' more will have to be liquidated in the future. That is particularly true for remedial measures which work through money and credit (1951, p. 117). Schumpeter argued that neither prosperity nor recovery from depression could be initiated by an expansionary monetary policy or by financial innovations. Banking is 'passive' in the sense that bankers cannot force loans on firms or individuals. Nor are the excesses of the secondary wave *induced* by cheap money, although prevention of low interest rates would help to contain them. The judgment exercised by bankers in granting loans is much more important than the interest rate charged and 'reckless banking' does not consist in financing cheaply but in financing irresponsibly, which is fostered by low interest rates. A policy of higher rates would keep bankers acting more responsibly (1939, p. 635).

The extent to which an expansionary monetary policy could be helpful or hurtful was revealed in Schumpeter's assessment of monetary policy during the early 1930s. The monetary easing from just after the 1929 crash through the first part of 1931 led to a revival of new financing (1939, p. 939). At that time the 'vicious spiral' was not unbreakable as business had been 'looking up' for the past five months (ibid., fn). But in the latter part of 1931 and 1932, monetary tightness through five months contributed to 'deflationary pressure,' although Schumpeter asserted that 'this pressure was altogether unequal to the inferences that have been drawn from it' (ibid.).

Endorsement of Financial Regulation

Schumpeter endorsed a number of policies aimed at regulation of banking and the financial sector, particularly those intended to prevent speculation in the stock market. With respect to the latter, he mentioned several times that the speculative boom in stock prices in the 1920s could have been ameliorated by policy actions as had been done in Germany. In 1927, the Reichsbank had shown that it 'really meant business' by energetically exerting its regulating power to administer a 'severe lesson' to speculation. By curbing speculation and preventing its recrudescence for the rest of the period, a crash of the American type was avoided (1939, pp. 881-882). That had been accomplished not by increasing the interest rate but by the Reichsbank forcing banks to stop making the German equivalent to brokers' loans (p. 882, fn). The Federal Reserve's effort at doing the same thing in February 1929 came too late and only precipitated the stock market crash because it was done too late. If that action had been taken in 1927, or even in 1928, the stock market would have been prevented from reaching the point at which the crash became inevitable (p. 900).

Schumpeter noted that the historical tendency to blame individuals for the speculative excesses after the crisis has occurred was being repeated in the early 1930s. He argued that the more rational approach would be to insist on implementing measures for regulating and 'purifying' financial practices. The chief targets of such legislation are the ways of speculation, the responsibilities of promoters and managers, and the methods of banking. Historically, most of the regulations that were imposed after financial disasters had gone too far in some respects and had been ineffective in others. Many of them made immediate recovery more difficult. But on balance, the regulations proved to be justified and effectively accomplished their intended purposes (1951, p. 116)

Schumpeter noted that a 'very comprehensive plan of regulation' could be derived from his analysis of the inability of banks to initiate expansions but it would be primarily (but not entirely) restrictive in nature (1939, p. 643). In particular, the regulations would be aimed at improving banking personnel and at enforcing adherence to standard banking practice. While banks cannot initiate recoveries or prosperities, there are some possibilities for 'corporative initiative by banks' at the end of recessions (p. 642). The problem was that any legislation that enabled some authority to force banks to take initiative action would result, in most cases, in additional maladjustments. Even if such an arrangement could be expected to have remedial or preventive effects, it would still be inferior to a policy of leaving banks free to fill their function and using other policies that directly act on the economic process (p. 643).

Policies That Promote Recovery

Schumpeter argued that recovery in the U.S. economy had started on its own in 1932 but encountered obstacles in 1933 that were partially removed by several policies. Those included the Agricultural Adjustment Act (AAA) and the National Industrial Recovery Act (NIRA) that established the National Recovery Administration (NRA), which Schumpeter described as being 'corrective rather than constructive.' Those measures did not initiate recovery but helped make for a sound and natural recovery by removing the obstacle of general over-indebtedness in the case of the AAA and by breaking the vicious downward spiral of prices in the case of the price codes of the NRA (1939, pp. 988-989, 992, and 995-996).

But Schumpeter was much more ambivalent about the wage policies under the NRA. The NRA codes contained clauses on child labor, hours, minimum wages, and protection for collective bargaining. Schumpeter approved of some of those (which he did not specify) as overdue progress in social legislation. With respect to their effects on recovery, the labor policies overall did not *inhibit* recovery during the period that the NRA was in effect. But persistent efforts to raise the structure of wages would have only the effect of reducing output and employment (1939, p. 994).

Schumpeter remarked that the Agricultural Adjustment Act and the National Industrial Recovery Act were declared unconstitutional at just the right time, their limited ends having been achieved (1939, p. 993). He argued that the strongest remedy to the depression was the 'income-generating expenditure' of the federal government and listed several reasons why government expenditures would reinforce the natural recovery that had started. First, there would be both direct and indirect multiplier effects on income and spending. Second, government spending would provide relief from the 'continuing state of overindebtedness' by helping the public to repay debts and build up depleted savings balances, so that households became 'creditworthy.' Third, there would be 'ulterior effects' on business expectations as the relief from debt, the steadying of prices, and the increased demand in sectors more directly impacted by government spending would tend to create 'the general feeling that a floor is being provided (that) will remove inhibitions and invite advance all around' (pp. 1002-1004). While the size of the multiplier effect (the 'pump-priming' effects) seemed small in 1933-1934, Schumpeter argued that other factors existed that weakened fiscal effectiveness (p. 1004).

On an empirical basis, Schumpeter asserted that three-fourths of the increase in business profits in 1934 were due to government spending and the NRA (1939, p. 1007). He rejected arguments that government budget deficits destroy business confidence (p. 1005) and noted that the economy went into a slump when the budget went into surplus in 1937 (p. 1012). He predicted that with an increase in federal spending budgeted for 1938, recovery would begin but also that it would subsequently weaken as federal spending tapered off (p. 1013). (In a footnote, he observed that as of May 1939, the level of spending was still rising.)

But while government spending was a remedy, Schumpeter warned that it could become an economic narcotic, comparable to such an extensive reliance on morphine in the field of medicine that everyone becomes 'morphinists' (1939, p. 1013). As we will note in the following section, Schumpeter blamed fiscal policies, in part, for the inflationary pressures of the post-World War II economy that were playing a major role in the erosion of capitalism in a trend toward centralized socialism. But, in 1946, he was still addressing 1930s type situations in which government spending responds to emergencies that are not created by government policies (1950, pp. 397-398). When an economic situation exists in which a reduction of output in one sector is leading to repercussions in the form of reductions in related sectors, there is danger of a cumulative downward process. In such cases, deficit-spending by the government will stop the 'vicious cycle,' and thus qualify as an 'efficient remedy' (ibid.).

FOCUS ON INFLATION IN LATER WORKS

As did Veblen, Schumpeter perceived a situation of persistent inflation in his later works. There are several general similarities in their views. Both were analyzing inflationary pressures in post-World War economies but traced the roots of the inflationary conditions to institutional developments that were in progress before the war. Both associated the inflation with democratic government policies resulting from irrational behavior of the mass of voters.

But those similarities were overshadowed by deep fundamental differences in Schumpeter's analysis of the post-World War II inflation and the role of democracy and Veblen's analysis of persistent credit-inflation and the role of democracy in the post-WWI period. As we noted in Chapter 4, Veblen argued that the collusive control of the investment bankers over both the key industries and the financial institutions allowed retardation of production by corporations to keep prices high and a controlled expansion in credit to keep aggregate demand sufficient to absorb the limited output at the higher prices, thus validating the anticipated returns on financial assets. With the approval of the underlying population, the democratically elected government supported the 'one big union of interests.' In the 1940s, Schumpeter presented virtually a polar opposite view of the role of large corporations and banks, and the nature of democratic government policies.

Large Corporations and Banks

In contrast to Veblen, Schumpeter denied that collusive arrangements among large corporations and banks could be effective. There may appear to be a hint of what Veblen perceived in 1923 in Schumpeter's *The Theory of Economic Development*, where he stated that the 'progressive trustification' of the economy was one of the factors making for a weaker business cycle (1934, p. 253). But in *Capitalism, Socialism, and Democracy*, first published in 1942, Schumpeter defended monopolistic pricing as providing profits for financing investment and as a form of insurance or hedging against the uncertainties of the future (1950, pp. 87-88). 'Price rigidity' was a short-run phenomenon that can help avoid the chaos of price declines during depressions. Schumpeter declared that there were 'no major instances of long-run rigidity of prices' (p. 93). While there were cases of raising prices 'in tacit agreement,' those were 'fringe-end cases' and were 'transient by nature' (p. 85), ended by competition from new business developments such as department stores, chain stores, mail-order houses, and supermarkets in retail trade (ibid.). Curiously, that is similar to Veblen's comment in *Absentee Ownership* that the current collusive retardation of production was being threatened by 'such phenomena as the Ford cars and the chain-stores and mail-order houses' (1923, p. 299, fn).

In a curious way, Schumpeter differed from Veblen on the consequences of protective tariffs. Veblen viewed protective tariffs as countering the trend toward deflation and depression but having a negative effect on economic welfare by restricting supply. Schumpeter agreed protective tariffs had 'inflationist' effects, but argued that the main effect had been to speed up the industrial developments that would have come about in any case (1951, p. 168). In apparent reference to Germany, Japan, and Italy in the 1930s, Schumpeter stated that in a 'mercantilist, nationalist, bellicose world dominated by a few great empires,' protectionism may be necessary to assure that the U.S. remained free to determine its own domestic policies (p. 169).

Veblen placed great importance on the control of credit by large bankers, declaring that the 'effectual control of the economic situation, in business, industry, and civil life, rests on the control of credit' (1923, p. 399). In contrast, while credit-creation by banks was a vital part of the capitalist process, Schumpeter argued that banks did not control the economy. At worst, they could only behave irresponsibly in lending too loosely during the secondary wave. As we noted above, in *Business Cycles* he strongly defended the regulatory reforms implemented in banking and financial markets in the 1930s. Perhaps based on his own disastrous personal experience with speculation in Austria in the 1920s, which left him deeply in debt and a failure as a banker, Schumpeter strongly opposed financial speculation and policies of 'reckless finance,' and insisted that credit should be limited to bona fide entrepreneurs by responsible bankers. But he also argued that the U.S. economy needed larger and stronger banks. During World War II, Schumpeter expressed concern that the government was replacing banks as the provider of capital/credit, apparently in reference to the dominant role played by the Reconstruction Finance Corporation in financing capital expansions during the war (1951, p. 180).

While Schumpeter defended the temporary phenomenon of monopolistic profits as being vital to the capitalist process of economic evolution, he perceived the sociological effects of large corporations quite differently. Veblen viewed post-World War II institutional developments as preventing a planned economy managed by engineers and technicians (see, for example, 1923, p. 283). In contrast, Schumpeter interpreted post-World War II institutional developments as one of the factors that were eroding the socio-economic supports for capitalism and leading eventually to centralized socialism. Large corporations with their internal bureaucracies were contributing to the erosion of the institution of private property by separating the sense of ownership from actual ownership and by internalizing and routinizing the entrepreneurial process (1950, pp. 133-134). Schumpeter declared that 'Big business is in fact but a midway house on the road toward socialism' (1951, p. 176). Moreover, as his endorsements of some form of corporatism and self-government of industry suggested (see Cramer and Leathers 1981), Schumpeter viewed the consequences of collusive arrangements quite differently from Veblen.

Government Policies and the New Inflation

In his post-World War II writings, Schumpeter argued that the source of the new inflation was government policies that had started in the New Deal of the 1930s and had been greatly expanded during the war. The bulk of his comments pertained to fiscal policies of taxation and government expenditure, labor policies and their administration, and how the effects of those reinforced. Schumpeter's references to specific legislation were sparse in these writings. It is particularly notable that, in criticizing policies aimed at maintaining high employment, he did not mention the Employment Act of 1946. Similarly, in criticizing policies that he interpreted as aimed at high wages and shifting power from employers to unions, he did not mention the National Labor Relations Act, the National Labor Relations Board, or the Fair Labor Standards Act, which imposed minimum wages. But neither did Schumpeter mention the Taft-Hartley Act of 1947, which curbed the powers of unions.

While both fiscal and labor policies were rooted in the New Deal of the 1930s, Schumpeter's analyses of their effects became much more negative after 1939. In large part, that was due to the huge expansion of government controls over the economy during the war and the changes in social attitudes that were accelerated by the experience of the depression and the wartime economy. A chronological review reveals the extent to which Schumpeter's concerns about inflation intensified as socio-economic changes that had been initiated in response to the 1930s depression were accelerated and transformed during and after World War II.

In his commentaries on New Deal policies in *Business Cycles*, Schumpeter argued that policies which were intended to be inflationary were largely unsuccessful in accomplishing that end. That inflation was a policy goal of the Agricultural Adjustment Act of 1933 was obvious, as it was officially referred to as the Emergency Relief and Inflation Act (1939,

p. 997). But Schumpeter argued that the act also contained ample provisions that could be used to 'defeat any kind of inflation at will' and, in a footnote, he observed that those provisions were extended by other acts, such as giving the Federal Reserve Board the power to change reserve requirement ratios and to set the margin requirement on stocks (ibid.). The existence of underutilized resources and increasing productivity in agriculture were primarily responsible for prices not responding respond more strongly to the price-raising policy of the New Deal administration (p. 1008). The rise in wholesale prices in 1936 did not herald prosperity. Rather, it was inflation caused by an expansionary fiscal policy of public spending and the 'newly created facilities of credit expansion' beginning to 'mesh' (pp. 1018-1019). But Schumpeter argued that the credit expansion could not have gone on indefinitely and the cyclical forces at work would have resulted in falling prices in the absence of the policies (pp. 1020).

What is perhaps most interesting, in light of Schumpeter's post-World War II charges that labor policies and their administration were at least conduits of inflationary pressure, were his assessments of the effects of New Deal labor legislation during the 1930s. In *Business Cycles*, he reported that both nominal and real wages rose from 1934 to 1937, such that real wages in 1937 were 25 percent higher than in 1929 (1939, pp. 1015-1016). His contention that the rise in wages accounted for the unemployment in the sectors where they occurred, in industry and construction, would become a continuing theme in his subsequent writings. Earlier we noted that in commenting on the labor provisions in the National Recovery Act pertaining to minimum wages and protection of collective bargaining, Schumpeter argued that there were no effects during the time under consideration (1939, p. 994). In a footnote, he stated that the mere recognition of the right of collective bargaining and elimination of the yellow-dog contract could not, in themselves, work against recovery since no organized drive had emerged in the two years of the NRA. If such a drive had materialized, the effects could have been non-neutral (ibid.).

Schumpeter's assertion that labor policies under the NRA reduced investment opportunity by forcing up wage rates was immediately qualified by his statement that the negative effect on investment was 'not very great' because rising wages were largely offset by 'labor-saving rationalization' (1939, p. 1042). While observing that under the National Labor Relations Act administrative labor law was used more vigorously than was intended by the provisions of the Act, Schumpeter asserted that

> after the fullest allowance of these and other elements of the case, we shall still be left with the result that labor policies — more precisely, what has actually been done in the field of labor policy — were not, taken by themselves, of decisive importance in shaping the business situations of those years. (1939, pp. 1042-1043)

Writing in 1943, Schumpeter observed that public opinion fear of a postwar slump due to a 'drastic reduction of military expenditure financed by inflationary methods' would give great political support for a continuation of 'the policy of income-generating public expenditure' that had started with the New Deal's economic principles (1951, p. 177). Schumpeter argued that high and progressive taxation would prevent large-scale business from becoming financially able to become independent of government, labor conditions would be set by government legislation, and large business would be strictly regulated (p. 180). The financial role of banks would be one of dependency on government financing and government planning would ultimately control investment (pp. 180-181). This would be 'capitalism in the oxygen tent' (p. 180) or 'Guided Capitalism' (p. 182).

Schumpeter offered no explicit prediction of inflation in the 1943 paper but, in a new chapter to the second (1946) edition of *Capitalism, Socialism, and Democracy*, he presented his views on the state of economic policies of World War II and the immediate aftermath. He saw government policies in 1946 as retarding production and employment and was particularly critical of unemployment benefit policies, which he claimed were keeping money wages high, reducing the incentive to accept employment and raising the cost of labor to the extent that a 'flight from labor' was under way (1950, p. 386). Inflation was still being held down by price controls but the danger of inflation was the most obvious and most serious factor that was preventing the economy from reaching its national output level (p. 391). The great liquidity of the huge public debt and the tax and monetary policies that discouraged holding Treasury securities were playing a minor role. But the real problem was policies that encouraged 'the reckless but universal demand for higher money wage rates' (p. 391). In contrast to Veblen's view of the inflationary results of collusive business, Schumpeter asserted that 'The bureaucracy's persistent hostility, strongly supported as it is by public opinion, to industrial self-government — self-organization, self-regulation, co-operation' was an obstacle to increasing production (p. 387).

In an article published in 1948 entitled 'There Is Still Time To Stop Inflation,' which was written for businessmen, Schumpeter (1948b) spoke as a 'close observer' of the post-World War I inflations in Austria, Germany, France, and Italy. Those inflation were 'simple processes' that were the results of war finance and could have been stopped within a year or two if 'the people who counted politically' had wanted to stop them (1951, p. 236). Where sufficient 'political stamina' emerged (Schumpeter cited Mussolini in Italy as an example), inflation was contained. In 1948, inflation was serious in the U.S. economy only because politicians and 'politically important interests' were refusing to take it seriously (1951, p.

237). Inflation could be easily ended, but would not be because all the effective measures were politically unpopular.

In discussing the new inflationary process, Schumpeter said relatively little about wage policies, although they were clearly in the background. There he explained inflation as occurring when 'means of payment increase more rapidly than the total output of goods and services,' and the source of newly created money was government spending financed by borrowing (1951, p. 237). Schumpeter explained that modern governments indirectly borrow from banks through banks creating deposits when the public buys government securities with bank loans (p. 238).

The effects of government spending on the money supply depend upon the state of the economy. Inflation is 'incipient' if the economy is under-employed. Those receiving the government expenditures use the funds to pay off debts or build up cash positions. Firms may expand production to meet the demand without raising prices, as was the case in the 1930s (1951, p. 238). If the economy is fully employed, the inflation will be 'advanced,' with the primary inflation induced by government spending and a secondary inflation occurring when firms borrow from banks to expand their operations to meet demand under the expectation of rising prices and costs. Since the borrowed funds are promptly spent, the ultimate cause of the inflation is government spending, not credit creation (ibid.). Wages come into the picture because rising wage incomes are spent whereas higher incomes are either saved or taxed away. Because of that spending and the importance of wages in the costs of production, 'the national payroll is by far the most important conductor of inflationary effects' (p. 239).

How to stop inflation depended upon the particular phase. In 1948, the U.S. economy was in the 'advanced inflation' phase, with 'the race between prices and wages in swing' (1951, p. 240). But there is no single remedy and any cure will cause some symptoms of depression. Direct controls never succeed, but in certain individual cases may do more good than harm. For Schumpeter, the natural remedy seemed to be to reduce the means of payment through monetary reform or capital levy, but he argued that structural rigidities in prices and wages worked against that approach (pp. 240-241). Credit restrictions in the form of abandoning the cheap-money policies (the Federal Reserve was still pegging the interest rate on Treasury securities in 1948) should be viewed as the ultimate goal. But Schumpeter argued that the inflation had gone so far that orthodox banking policy could not be expected to be effective and, in an economy with 14,000 banks, additional methods of credit control would be needed. Because consumer and mortgage credit had been increasing too rapidly, credit controls in those areas would minimize the dangers of credit restriction.

The best remedy for inflation was to have aggregate supply increase while restraining aggregate demand by not allowing the volume of credit to increase at the same rate (1951, pp. 243-244). Even though the level of aggregate production was already at 'its practical peak,' it could be increased by longer hours of work and improvements in productivity. But that was politically impossible because workers would resist it even though it would lead to an increase in purchasing power of their wages (p. 244).

A budget surplus was both the most orthodox and the most politically difficult remedy to implement. Schumpeter suggested that elimination of 'war wastes' would produce a surplus. Tax cuts were necessary in the long run but, until inflation was under control, taxes needed to remain high in the short run. It was a matter of which taxes to reduce and which to hold constant or even increase. Tax cuts that funneled funds into investment would be counter-inflationary. Reducing taxes on the higher income groups and eliminating taxes on saving would serve that purpose. But Schumpeter opposed reducing taxes on lower incomes, declaring that: 'Taxation remission in the lower income brackets is, of course, particularly dangerous' (1951, pp. 245-246).

Schumpeter did recognize that the economy was experiencing deflation rather than inflation in 1948 and offered 'a few words on the question of how far the recent fall in individual prices affects the argument of this article' (1951, p. 246). Certain 'individual prices' had risen so high that they had gotten out of line with other prices and were now adjusting downward the general level. Just as Greenspan and others argued that modern price indices overstated the rate of inflation in the 1990s, Schumpeter argued that the effects of the decline in those 'individual prices' on the 'cost of living index' gave the false impression of a general deflation (ibid.). Such decreases were analogous to temporary decreases in stock prices from profit-taking. They occur in 'individual prices' in every inflationary process and are important only because they present momentary opportunities for applying anti-inflation measures before the inflationary pressures can resume (pp. 246-247).

In his 1949 address to the American Economic Association, the incomplete written notes of which were included in the 1950 edition of *Capitalism, Socialism, and Democracy* as 'The March Into Socialism,' Schumpeter asserted that inflation makes for the acceleration of social change. Once again, the source of inflation was identified as government policies that were related to wages. Schumpeter observed that 'At a high level of employment (we seem, at long last, to be abandoning full-employment slogans) whether "natural" or enforced by high-employment policies, wage demands or other demands that increase the money cost of employing labor become both inevitable and inflationary' (1950, p. 422). That is because high employment removes the only reason why wages should not be raised and borrowing from banks and upward revision of prices provide a perfectly easy method of satisfying wage demands when resources are being fully utilized. Now Schumpeter argued that fiscal policies of increased government expenditures and 'hyperprogressive methods of taxation' aggravated but did not create the inflationary situation (ibid.).

Schumpeter again dismissed the significance of the recent fall in prices as measured by standard cost of living indices. Only those economists (whom he did not identify) who pessimistically expect only deflation and depression will interpret the temporary declines in prices that occur in every inflationary period as deflation. But Schumpeter observed that 'it is a compliment . . . to the productive powers of American industry that doubts are possible to whether our society is menaced by inflation or deflation' (ibid.).

Schumpeter was relatively brief in his discussion of how the 'perennial inflationary pressures' could be controlled and was quite pessimistic about the political environment allowing any effective anti-inflation policies. While he thought it necessary to abandon the cheap money policy, the traditional theory of restrictive credit only applied to economies in which everything was flexible and people were not afraid to face the political ramifications of remedial recession. Interest rate increases in those economies were expected to reduce the volume of operations, money wages, and employment. But, in the modern U.S. economy, raising interest rates would only negatively affect businesses, although tighter consumer credit would be beneficial. The political reality was that fiscal policies would raise tax rates primarily on the non-inflation producing higher incomes and corporate profits. The decrease in savings and after-tax profits would result in an increasing resort to inflationary bank credit to finance the replacement investment necessary to keep the high level of production going forward. Price controls would be a surrender of private enterprise to public authority. But at that point Schumpeter stopped writing up his notes, leaving the closing paragraph uncompleted.

The Role of Democracy

The reason why government policies were anti-capitalist and causing inflation in the post-World War II period was explained by the nature of human behavior under democratic political systems. In *Business Cycles*, Schumpeter (1939) stated that 'Experience tends to show . . . that neither capitalism nor the social institutions associated with it, democracy among them, can work efficiently and with comparative smoothness except on a falling trend of prices' (1942, pp. 464-466). But his analysis of democracy in *Capitalism, Socialism, and Democracy* explained why democratic government was creating the opposite of deflation, upon which its efficient functioning was said to depend.

Like Veblen, Schumpeter had a rather contemptuous view of voters in a democratic political system. But, in stark contrast to Veblen, Schumpeter saw politicians and the governments that they formed when successful at the polls as taking self-serving anti-business positions which they easily market to ill-informed voters. Schumpeter developed his theory of democracy within the context of exploring the relationship between democracy and socialism because he argued that misconceptions about democracy obstruct a clear view of the true nature of that relationship. His intent was to both debunk the prevailing delusion that democracy was an ideal in itself and establish an appropriate perspective as to what democracy really means.

In critically evaluating several historical uses of the term 'democracy,' Schumpeter was particularly derisive of the 'Classical' theory. He charged that it was flawed by 'the proposition that "the people" hold a definite and rational opinion about every individual question and that they give effect to this opinion — in a democracy — by choosing "representatives" who will see to it that the opinion is carried out' (1950, p. 269).

Schumpeter argued that the role of the people is not to decide political issues or select representatives from the list of eligible candidates with a perfectly open mind. Rather, the initiative rests in all 'normal cases' with the candidates who bid for office and the role of the people is to 'produce a government' either directly or indirectly through an intermediate body (i.e., a parliamentary system with a prime minister). Their choices are shaped by a process that Schumpeter argued was an essential part of the democratic process: 'Voters confine themselves to accepting this bid (by office seekers) in preference to others or refusing to accept it' (1950, p. 282).

To Schumpeter, democracy was to be regarded as a political method, a certain type of institutional arrangement for reaching political decisions. As such, it was completely incapable of serving as an ideal or end in itself. Moreover, propositions about the workings of democracy were appropriate only to given times, places, and situations; no valid universal, timeless propositions about it were possible. He proposed that democracy, or the 'democratic method,' could best be defined as 'that institutional arrangement for arriving at political decisions in which individuals acquire the power to decide by means of a competitive struggle for the people's vote' (1950, p. 269).

Thus, democracy resolves itself to simple competition for political office, in which only one team or individual attains office by getting more votes than any other (neither majority rule nor proportional representation is required). In making his case for this definition of democracy, Schumpeter drew an analogy between the need to look to the competitive struggle for profits in competitive markets to explain economic activities that lead incidentally to the social ends of the economy (production) and the need to

understand that the competitive struggle for power and office in the political
arena tends to fulfill the higher social purpose in a similarly incidental
manner (1950, p. 282). He remarked that

> our theory is of course no more definite than is the concept of competition for
> leadership. This concept presents similar difficulties as the concept of
> competition in the economic sphere, with which it may be usefully compared. In
> economic life, competition is never completely lacking, but hardly ever is it
> perfect. (1950, p. 271)

Voters function much like consumers. They are easily influenced by
advertising and other devices of salesmanship (1950, pp. 257-258). In
political matters, individuals operate with reduced senses of reality and
responsibility and the lack of 'effective volition' (p. 261). Since 'the typical
citizen drops to a lower level of mental performance as soon as he enters
the political field' (p. 262), he can be easily swayed by the office-seeking
politicians through political salesmanship. Political criticism cannot be
effectively countered by resort to rational arguments (p. 144). Democracy,
which is really the 'rule of the politician,' means only that the people have
the opportunity of accepting or refusing the men who compete freely to rule
them (pp. 284-285). The democratic method produces legislation and
administration as by-products of the struggle for political office by
professional politicians (p. 286).

Schumpeter viewed the candidates for office as similar to firms offering
items for sale. They do so for a purpose (profit for businessmen, power of
office for candidates) and not because they believe what they are offering is
what society needs. Whereas the classical doctrine viewed political parties
as groups of men who intended to promote the public welfare based on
commonly agreed upon principle, Schumpeter simply defined a party as 'a
group whose members propose to act in concert in the competitive struggle
for political power' (1950, p. 283). In drawing an analogy between parties
and department stores, he noted that the planks and principles that each
party stocks 'may be as characteristic of the party . . . and as important to its
success as the brands of goods a department store sells are characteristic of
it and important for its success' (ibid.). Campaigns cannot be defined in
terms of competing principles since different parties often will adopt
exactly or almost exactly the same policies.

The function of the candidates is to put policies before the voters and
attempt to persuade the voters to accept them. Schumpeter stated that 'The
freely voting rational citizen, conscious of his (long-term) interests, and the
representative who acts in obedience to them, the government that
expresses these volitions — is this not the perfect example of a nursery
tale?' (1954, p. 429). Such 'wishful daydreams' are the product of the
natural law system of utilitarianism (pp. 428-429). Parties and machine
politicians are simply responses to the fact that the electoral mass is

incapable of any action other than a stampede. Parties and machines constitute attempts to regulate political competition in a way similar to that of corresponding practices of a trade association. 'The psycho-techniques of party management and party advertising, slogans and marching tunes, are not accessories. They are the essence of politics. So is the political boss' (1950, p. 283).

Using a term strangely reminiscent of Veblen's criticism of voters and democratic governments supporting the rule of the vested interests but with a very different twist, Schumpeter blamed the anti-capitalist, pro-inflationary policies on the 'salesman mentality of the country coupled with the experience of the twenty years preceding the war' (1950, p. 394). A democratic government's focus on the political value of policies and its dealing in votes results in a short-run view that makes it difficult to serve the long-run interests of the country (p. 287). As the successes of capitalism in raising the economic standard of living increase the expectations of the masses, politicians appeal to voters by offering policies that are supposed to prevent the normal recessions. Voters are incapable of seeing the long-run effects of those policies on the viability of capitalism to continue raising the long-run standard of living and, in the short-run, produce the policies responsible for the inflation.

7. Minsky's Financial Instability Hypothesis and Debt-Deflation

Hyman Minsky's contributions to the theories of debt-deflation and financial instability came in the post-World War II period, in articles and books that were published from the late 1950s through 1996. His financial instability hypothesis explains why modern capitalist economies are inherently prone to debt-deflations that start with financial panics that are followed by severe depressions. But an important part of his theoretical and institutional analyses focused on explaining why a debt-deflation/depression (popularly known as 'it') had not occurred since the 1930s, and the inflationary consequences of that avoidance.

Historical experience reveals that debt-deflations occur only between long intervals of time and that they come after financial crises. Why did a sharp decline in stock prices in 1962 not trigger a deflationary process such as that which was triggered by the 1929 stock market crash? Had essential changes occurred in the institutional or behavioral characteristics of the economy so that debt-deflation processes leading to a financial collapse could not now occur? Or was it simply a manner of differences in magnitudes within a financial and economic structure whose essential attributes are essentially unchanged? Each debt-deflation is a unique event, particularly in the details, because financial institutions and practices continuously evolve. But does the modern capitalist system have essentially invariant financial attributes that tend to breed conditions which increase the likelihood of a debt-deflation (Minsky 1982, pp. 3-4)?

Minsky's response to those questions was that processes leading to debt-deflations and depressions triggered by financial panics are endemic to modern capitalist economies with privately owned large, expensive, and long-lived capital assets and highly developed complex financial systems. Capitalism continues to evolve through a variety of forms that are a combination of institutional changes implemented as a result of previous crises and depressions and financial innovations implemented by profit-seeking financial institutions to avoid financial crisis. Minsky's financial instability hypothesis explains how endogenous processes, including financial innovations, transform periods of stability or tranquility into periods of 'euphoria' in which debt structures expand beyond the capability of cash flows to sustain the payment commitments imposed by those structures. Whether the euphoric period ends rather quietly or in a financial panic depends upon the institutional structures and policy actions of the central bank and government. In explaining why the U.S. economy had not experienced another debt-deflation, Minsky integrated theoretical modeling and historical analyses of institutional and policy developments that changed the structure of the financial system and its effects on the real economy since the 1930s.

THEORETICAL TIES WITH OTHER ECONOMISTS

In explicit statements, Minsky acknowledged that his approach builds upon his own interpretation of Keynes' theory and analyses. In his theoretical work, Minsky was in the post-Keynesian tradition, which he defined as one in which 'Keynes provides us with the shoulders of a giant upon which we can stand in order to see far and deep into the essential character of advanced capitalist economies' (1986c, p. xiii). But Minsky also acknowledged Schumpeter's influence on his work, explaining that Schumpeter's essential contribution 'consists of a vision and an analytical framework that reinforce the validity of my prior positions on economic theory' (1990, p. 51). That influence was revealed in Minsky's theoretical and historical analyses of capitalism as an evolving institutional system in which Schumpeter's theory of innovational activities driven by expectations of monopolistic profits was applied to the financial system.

Minsky argued that Keynes and Schumpeter offered somewhat complementary insights into modern capitalism. The Keynesian insights were in recognizing the importance of financing new investments and the subjective nature of the formation of expectations of both businesses and bankers under conditions of uncertainty that result in increases in debt-income ratios that lead to debt-deflation when expectations turn negative. The Schumpeterian insight was that increases in financing available through financial innovations contribute to both the growth and the financial instability of an evolving capitalist economy (Minsky 1990, pp. 112-113).

Like Schumpeter, Minsky explicitly accepted Fisher's depiction of the processes at work in a debt-deflation. He stated that 'The fundamentals of a theory of financial instability can be derived from Keynes' *General Theory*, Irving Fisher's description of a debt deflation, and the writings of Henry Simons' (1986a, p. 172). Minksy argued that Keynes accepted 'the general thrust of Irving Fisher's description in the "Debt-Deflation Theory of Great Depression" of the aftermath of a crisis . . . as a rough-and-ready statement of postcrisis system behavior' (1975, p. 64). But Keynes had never explicitly developed a theory of the boom and financial crisis (p. 106) and

Fisher had never presented a theory of financial crises (p. 64). Similarly, Minsky expressed the view that Schumpeter did not effectively deal with the 1929-1933 crisis (1986c, p. 112), stating that Schumpeter wrote about 'financial catastrophe' without ever explaining it (p. 113).

It seems rather strange that Minsky never acknowledged Veblen's work. Several scholars have noted (Dimand 1998, 2004; and Kelso and Duman 1992) similarities that run through their analyses. Like Veblen, Minsky recognized that capitalism has evolved through a number of stages, becoming increasingly complex and more subject to the influence of the financial sector and focused on business debt as an essential characteristic of modern capitalism. Like Veblen, Minsky focused on the prices of capital assets in developing a theory of financial instability in which endogenous processes lead to debt-deflation and depression. There is relatively little theoretical attention given to deflation in prices of consumer goods and services in either of their analyses. In Minsky's theory, the recognition of 'sticky' output prices in most of the industries in the modern capitalist economy is suggestive of the quasi-monopolistic pricing associated with the credit-inflation phenomena described by Veblen as the 'New Order' in *Absentee Ownership* (1923). Hence, deflation in both Minsky's and Veblen's analyses often appears to be largely in the form of falling stock market prices.

A particularly striking similarity between Minsky and Veblen is the emphasis on the dominance of financial values and conditions in determining aggregate economic activities. The following statement by Minsky is very suggestive of Veblen's theory of the use of industrial technology being subordinated to corporate finance.

> Our world is characterized by heterogeneous capital assets, techniques of production that require extensive financing, and a variety of organizational forms for business and finance. In such a world financial advantages and disadvantages can offset production advantages and disadvantages. The successful can be technological inferior if they have a large enough offsetting financial advantage. (1986, pp. 228-289)

But there are significant differences between Minsky's analyses and those of both Veblen and Schumpeter. Minsky's financial instability hypothesis explains an endogenous cyclical pattern arising from the financial nature of modern capitalism. Where prosperity in Veblen's analysis began with an increase in demand in some sector, usually from government military expenditures, and was initiated by technological or organizational innovations financed with bank-created money in Schumpeter's business cycle, neither is required in Minsky's financial instability hypothesis. Rather, periods of tranquility with stable prices and financial stability are transformed into speculative prosperities through endogenous financial developments.

Unlike Veblen, Minsky neglected the effects of technological innovations on lowering the supply price (as a function of production cost) of capital goods. On the contrary, as will be explained, the supply price tends to rise in Minsky's theory. While Minsky extrapolated from Schumpeter's theory to emphasize the destabilizing role of financial innovations, he neglected the effects of technological innovations. In Veblen's 1904 theory, the secular trend was one of chronic depression. In Schumpeter's theory, recovery from a recession or depression takes the economy to a new equilibrium that is higher than the one existing before the impact of innovations but a swarm of new technological innovations will start another cycle. In Minsky's theory, endogenous financial forces bring to an end periods of debt-deflation and depression and provide for another transformation to prosperity.

Overview

In the following section, we again briefly review developments in the post-World War II economy, but this time from Minsky's perspective. We then begin our examination of his basic theory of prices, profit, and investment, which is the framework for his financial instability hypothesis, under the 'small government' version of his model. That is followed by an examination of the evolutionary changes that gave rise to conditions captured in his 'big government' model, which explains why a debt-deflation did not occur in the post-World War II period. In the last section, we briefly review Wolfson's Minskian modification of Fisher's debt-deflation theory to explain why the stock market crash of 1987 did not lead to a debt-deflation.

HISTORICAL SETTING: THE POST-WORLD WAR II ECONOMY

The historical setting for Minsky's analyses was the post-World War II economy in which monetary and fiscal policies were actively used in attempts to stabilize the economy at high employment levels and maintain a satisfactory growth rate. Dirlam stated that 'the post-World War II era, with its continuous injection of heady drafts of inflation and full employment, bears a remarkable similarity to Veblen's projection of the One Big Union of the Major Interests, which he saw extending into the future from 1923' (1958, p. 214). That was only partially true. Veblen did not project full employment, nor did he consider the role of fiscal policy as a real possibility. However, the extent to which the fiscal stimulus to the economy came from a high level of defense expenditures was perfectly compatible with Veblen's views on both counter-deflationary policies and the role of 'patriotism' in rallying support of the 'common man' for governmental support of the vested interests.

This was the period in which Keynesian macroeconomic theory came to exert a strong influence on policymaking, and continued to do so even when it became politically popular to claim that Keynesian economics was defunct. Important structural changes that had been implemented during the New Deal period strongly supported a high level of aggregate demand. Unemployment compensation, Social Security, and agricultural price supports prevented aggregate spending from falling as it had in the early 1930s. The progressive structure of the income tax provided what became recognized as automatic stabilizing fiscal policy. As Galbraith noted, 'The vast intervention of government and the expenditure and investment that produced the full wartime employment were the ultimate affirmation of Keynes' (1994, p. 136).

The importance of fiscal and monetary policies was recognized with the passage of the Employment Act of 1946. The federal government and the Federal Reserve were given the responsibility to pursue the goals of high employment and stable prices. The Act also created the Council of Economic Advisors to the President and required the President to make an annual economic report to Congress. In 1978, the Humphrey-Hawkins Act was passed to reinforce the goals of the 1946 Act and also address the issue of budget deficits. Steadily over that time period, the level of government expenditures for both defense and social domestic programs grew. The Medicare and Medicaid programs were created in 1965. They have greatly benefited the elderly and the poor, providing medical care to individuals and substantial economic support to a vigorous health care sector of the economy.

The Kennedy-Johnson policies of 1963-1965 demonstrated that fiscal policies could bring the economy to high employment without producing inflationary pressures. But the increase in government spending as the war in Viet Nam was expanded in 1966 produced demand-side inflation. The failure of inflation to respond to monetary and fiscal policies in 1969-1970 led to charges that Keynesian policies had failed. Those who might be termed 'Institutional-Keynesians,' such as Galbraith, argued that the continuing inflation was due to the pricing power of large corporations and that the solution was price controls. The effectiveness of that policy approach was demonstrated by the Nixon price controls from August 1971 until the controls were abandoned in the spring of 1974, after the OPEC oil embargo had resulted in shortages of gasoline at the regulated prices.

The supply-side nature of the new inflation continued to be ignored by those who sought to denigrate Keynesian economics and resuscitate the classical theory of macroeconomics. In particular, monetarism attempted to revive the role of the quantity theory of money while 'supply-side economics' claimed to be a modern form of the classical theory associated with Say's law. Despite the obvious fact that the inflationary pressures of the 1970s were due to OPEC oil price increases and non-competitive behavior of dominant American corporations in consumer goods markets such as automobiles, the monetarists claimed that the inflation was due to the money supply growing too fast and that budget deficits contributed by 'monetarizing' the public debt. Guided by that doctrine, the Federal Reserve under Paul Volcker pursued a highly restrictive monetary policy from 1979 to 1982, which contributed heavily to the deep recession in 1982-1983.

In 1981, the Reagan administration was politically able to implement 'supply side economics' policies of reductions in income tax rates that favored the upper income groups. The result was record budget deficits. In addition to government debt soaring, debt mounted in all other sectors of the economy. Corporate debt increased as leverage buyouts were financed with junk bonds. Consumer debt increased as obtaining credit cards became easier. Foreign debt increased as the U.S. trade deficit rose.

In the 1980s, the inflation did fall, but not because of monetarist or supply-side economics policies. Rather, the driving factors were the recession and increased foreign competition in key markets. Reduced petroleum prices were also a factor, as the OPEC cartel lost its ability to control such oil-producing countries as Saudi Arabia. While inflation in goods and services weakened in the 1980s, it emerged and gained strength in the stock market. A bull market in stocks that began in 1950s and experienced what Malkiel (1999, p. 58) called the 'tronics boom' ended in a market drop in 1962. Stock prices recovered, however, and continued to rise until entering a long bear market in 1969 that lasted through 1981. By the mid-1980s, the stock market was beginning to resemble the boom of the 1920s such that, in January 1987, Galbraith (1987) prophetically warned of a stock market bubble that was destined to burst at some point. On October 19, 1987, the largest single day crash in history occurred, with stock prices falling about 23 percent. Yet, as Galbraith has also predicted, the aftermath of the crash was quite different from the aftermath of the 1929 crash. In only two years, stock had regained their post-crash highs and went on an even larger bull run in the 1990s, before a new bear market began in 2000-2001.

As we noted in Chapter 2, inflation eased in the 1990s to the extent that, in the latter part of the decade, Greenspan was intimating that a new economy had emerged in which productivity increases due to innovations in information technologies and financial innovations such as new derivative instruments were allowing the economy to run at high employment without inflationary pressures. Provided that wages did not start rising, only a

tweaking of monetary restraint in the form of higher federal funds rate
would be required to keep the stable-price prosperity going, with high stock
prices rationally reflecting capitalizing future corporate profits made
possible by continuously increasing productivity.

MINSKY'S FINANCIAL INSTABILITY HYPOTHESIS

Minsky's financial instability hypothesis recognizes two intertwining
features of modern capitalist economies. Those are the importance of large,
expensive, privately-owned capital assets that require financing to acquire
and operate and systems of complex financial institutions and practices that
are constantly evolving. His hypothesis explains why such economies are
subject to endogenous processes that lead from states of financial stability
to financial instability and debt-deflation. Because the focus in such
economies must be on economic processes that go forward in time,
economic theory must focus on investment, the ownership of capital assets
that have productive future lives, and the financial activities that are
involved (1982, p. xii).

The theoretical core of the financial instability hypothesis is rooted in
Minsky's financial theory of investment in an institutional structure that is
subject to evolutionary change stemming from the effects of private sector
innovations and from government policies initiated in reactions to previous
periods of financial crises and debt-deflation. The financial sector plays a
key role in the institutional structure and financial innovations are important
contributors to financial instability. From that emerges an investment theory
of business cycles. We will first review the role of investment in
determining the performance of the economy and Minsky's financial theory
of investment. That will set the stage to examine his financial instability
hypothesis as it applies in a 'small government' economy such as the U.S.
economy in the 1920s. Then we will examine how the tendencies toward
debt-deflation are thwarted in the 'large government' economy that
characterizes the post-World War II U.S. economy, which brings into focus
the importance of monetary and fiscal policies as counters to deflation but
with the consequences of conducing inflation.

Financial Theory of Investment

In its fundamental structure, Minsky's financial theory of investment was
derived not only from his interpretation of what Keynes wrote but also from
his perception of what Keynes neglected to do. With his demand price of
capital assets theory, Keynes explained why the money supply erratically
affected investment. In his discussion of the trade cycle, Keynes hinted at

the various states of the economy that succeed one another in irregular sequence but never explicitly developed a theory of boom and crisis. Minsky argued that was because Keynes never articulated a model that explained how the liability structures of firms, banks, and other financial institutions evolve and the processes by which an endogenous generation of money and money substitutes occurs (Minsky 1975, p. 106). Although Keynes wrote *The General Theory* during a period of debt-deflation and depression that was triggered by the 1929 stock market crash, he offered no explanation or theory of the financial crisis. Without a model of the endogenous generation of booms, crises, and debt deflations, Keynes' theory is incomplete (p. 64).

Minsky's theoretical framework is Keynesian in the sense of aggregate demand determining the level of employment and output. Within that framework, investment is the primary factor that drives the level of income and employment in an economy characterized by a small size of government such as the U.S. economy in the 1920s and early 1930s. Given a stable consumption function, the level of aggregate demand is determined by investment through the multiplier effect. Minsky's financial theory of investment, which links the real economy and conditions in the financial sector, was derived from his interpretations of Keynes' statement in Chapter 17 of *The General Theory* that 'those assets of which the normal supply-price is less than the demand-price will be newly produced; and these will be those assets of which the marginal efficiency would be greater (on basis of their normal supply price) than the rate of interest' (1961, p. 228), and from the *Quarterly Journal of Economics* article in which Keynes (1937) responded to criticism by Viner.

Minsky's theory recognizes that the present state of the economy is linked to past states through inherited assets and liabilities and to the future through expectations formed under conditions of uncertainty. Within that context, Minsky incorporated a 'Wall Street' view of the modern capitalist economy as a complex network of cash flows involving both current economic production and liability structures that necessarily arise because investment has to be financed through 'money now in exchange for money in the future' arrangements. From a 'Wall Street' perspective, the economy is a financial paper world of commitments to pay cash today and in the future. At any given time, the cash flows are legacies of past contracts in which money in hand was exchanged for money in the future. At the same time, new contracts are being written that create commitments to pay money in the future in exchange for money today. The structural viability of this paper world of debt contracts rests upon the cash flows that business, households, and governmental units receive as a result of the income-generating process.

Like Veblen, Minsky focused on business debt because it is an essential characteristic of a capitalist economy. Validation of debt requires that prices and outputs be sufficient for almost all firms to realize surpluses of revenues over costs to either pay the commitments on debt or to merit refinancing based on larger expected future profits (1982, p. 63). Debt comes into the picture because investment, defined as the production of new units of capital assets, has to be financed and internal funds are not sufficient to provide all that financing. A decision to invest is necessarily a decision about how to finance the production of capital assets, which is a decision about the acceptable liability structure. The standard Keynesian theory explains investment in terms of the interest rate and the marginal efficiency of investment as a diminishing function due to diminishing technical productivity. Minsky argued that his alternative approach of explaining investment in terms of the demand price for investment output and the supply price of producing units of investment goods allows the importance of the element of Keynesian uncertainty to be shown more clearly. The standard approach explains changes in the demand price for investment (a downward-sloping investment function) in terms of diminishing technical productivity. In contrast, Minsky explained it in terms of the relative scarcity of capital assets.

Minsky's financial theory of investment integrates the cash-flow and present value characteristics of units of capital assets. The behavior and viability of business firms are affected by developments in financial markets by cash-flow commitments, present value calculations under given states of expectations about future profits and a given interest rate, and liquidity-asset holdings. At any given time, the economy is operating with a given stock of capital assets and a given liability structure inherited from financing investment in previous time. The liability structure imposes cash payment commitments on the firms that borrowed and the financial assets (debt-instruments) provide cash payments to the holders of those assets. At the same time, investment today must be financed, which gives rise to a new liability structure as borrowing firms receive cash today in exchange for commitments to make larger cash payments in the future.

Prices, Profits, and Investment in Minsky's Two-Prices Model
In a modern capitalist economy, profits must be sufficiently high to validate current positions in capital assets, validate the investment decisions made in past periods that gave rise to today's liability structures, and induce new investment in the present period. Prices are important because, along with the strength of aggregate demand conditions, they determine the actual profits that are being realized on existing capital assets, the expected profits on new investment goods (newly produced capital assets), and the conditions that affect the financing of investment. Profits require that prices

be higher than the costs involved in modern business and finance. There are two sets of prices that are determined in different markets and in different ways, but which are intertwined.

First, there are the prices of current output, which consists of the production of consumption goods and services and the production of new units of capital assets or investment goods. Output prices are determined in two different ways, depending on whether the supplying firms have market power. The absence of market power for firms operating in highly competitive markets means variable pricing based on the forced equality of price with marginal cost. But in modern capitalist economies, most markets are oligopolistic in varying degrees, with a relatively few large corporations possessing various degrees of market power. Those firms applying markups to the sum of variable costs, fixed and overhead costs, ancillary costs, and financial commitments determine output prices. When shifts occur in the level of demand for the outputs, these firms adjust the levels of output, not prices. The variable costs are determined by the technical productivity of the inputs and the money wage rates. The ancillary costs are determined by the business style, and the financial commitments are inherited by the liability structures. In sectors of the economy in which firms have market power, the total revenues derived at given output prices depend upon the level aggregate demand, which determines the quantities that can be sold.

Part of current output is in the production of units of capital goods, which may be either the same types as those currently in existence or new types of capital goods. The supply prices of new capital goods are determined by the technical productivity of the capital assets used in their production, the wage costs of labor used, and Keynes' 'user costs.' The latter are the opportunity costs of using owned capital assets to produce goods now rather than in the future (Minsky 1975, p. 83). Profit margins in the production of investment goods (capital goods) are determined by the relative scarcity of specific capital assets, which in turn depend upon the pace of investment. The supply curve of investment goods becomes positively sloped at some point because the specialized capital assets used in the production of investment goods (more capital assets) are relatively fixed in the short run.

The other set of prices is the prices of existing capital assets (capital goods) and financial assets. Prices of capital assets determine the demand price for production of new units of capital assets or investment. Prices of capital assets are functions of the expected yields from their use in future production, q, their liquidity status, l, and the cost of carry, c, which is largely the debt created in financing of the positions (1975, pp. 78-82). The discounted values of cash payments that are committed and their liquidity status determine the prices of financial assets. Money as a financial asset has only one value, that of being perfectly liquid. That value (liquidity preference) is subjective and changes with expectations about future economic conditions.

Determining the Level of Investment

In Minsky's financial theory of investment, three factors together determine the level of investment. Those are (1) the demand prices for investment goods, which are determined by current prices of capital assets; (2) the supply prices of investment goods; and (3) conditions in financial markets (1982, p. 3). Investment occurs when the demand price exceeds the supply price of investment goods. (Minsky also expressed the investment decision in terms of the relationship between the price of capital assets and the price of consumption output. When the former is high relative to the latter, conditions are favorable for investment and, when the price of capital assets is low relative to the price of consumption output, conditions are unfavorable for investment.) The demand price of investment is the sum of the expected yield, q, and the value of the liquidity status of the good, l, minus the cost of carry, c, which includes payment commitments arising from the financing of investment (see 1975, pp. 88-92).

Decisions by firms to finance investment by borrowing are based on their expectations that the future profits will be sufficient to make the committed financial payments on the debt and still leave a sufficient amount for the yield on the capital assets acquired. Bankers' decisions to lend to finance investment are based on expectations that future profits from the investment will be sufficient to cover the financial commitments. Because of uncertainty, both borrowers and lenders must engage in an element of speculation on future cash flows and financial market conditions (1975, pp. 106-111).

Borrowers face the risk that future cash flows will be inadequate to realize the expected yield. Lenders face the risk that the requirement payment commitments may not be met by the borrowers. Both types of risk lead to margins of safety or security. Borrower's risk results in part of the acquisition of capital assets being funded out of internal funds, and a certain amount of liquidity will be maintained to meet failures of future cash flows to meet payment commitments on debt. Borrowers' risk is subjective and does not appear on signed contracts. But lenders' risk does appear in the form of the amount and type of collateral pledged, higher interest rates, shorter maturities, restrictions on paying dividends and further borrowing (1975, p. 110). The two risks will influence investment through their respective effects on demand price and supply price of investment. Demand price will be lowered by borrowers' risk while supply price will be increased by lenders' risk being added to the producers' supply prices of investment goods.

Scarcity of output, capital assets, and the supply of money affect the demand and supply prices of capital assets in different ways. The first two raise the demand price of investment by raising profits. The last reduces the demand price under a given liquidity preference function. If the money supply is held constant, investment increases as long as the demand price is greater than the supply price. But the demand price decreases as the scarcity of capital assets is reduced, while the supply price increases as the existing supply of capital assets used in producing investment goods interacts with rising demand for output.

Money, Financial Markets, and Prices of Capital Assets

Financial markets and banking activities affect investment because current values of capital assets and, thus, demand prices for investment output are determined in financial markets. Financing must be provided if an increase in the demand price for investment goods is to result in an increase in investment, so the amount of investment that will be financed depends upon banking processes. In addition, the supply price of investment depends upon the cost of finance as a component of the total cost of producing investment goods (Minsky 1982, p. 227). Consequently, it is necessary to understand how the banking and financial system works so that an increase in the demand for financing investment leads to an increase in the supply of financing investment, and how an increase in the ability and willingness of banks to acquire assets (loans) leads to an increase in investment.

Keynes denied that the effect of the quantity of money was mainly on the price level of output. Instead, he argued that with a given set of long-run expectations (and with given institutional arrangements and conventions in finance), the supply and demand for money affects the price level of capital assets. Money, along with liability structure preferences, the mix of available capital assets, and the supply of financial assets, determines the prices of capital assets (Minsky 1982, pp. 93-94). That is because each capital asset and each financial asset is a combination of liquidity and future income. Each liability is a commitment to pay cash, either at some specified date (e.g., the maturity date of a bond) or on a contingency basis (a life insurance policy). As a result of the nature of debts and contracts, there will always be a subjective return from holding money to cover expected or unexpected payments. Because the quantity of money determines the amount that *can* be held, it determines the subjective returns from liquidity. Assets that yield cash income streams, but that can be exchanged or pledged for cash only at a cost and with varying degrees of certainty, will have prices that adjust to the standard set by the subjective return on money (p. 94).

Money in the form of bank liabilities endogenously emerges in various forms out of the processes by which investments and positions in the stock of capital assets are financed (Minsky 1986a, p. 227). A level of investment that is sufficient to assure that the economy does well in the present will be forthcoming only if future investment is expected to be sufficient to assure that the economy does well in the future. In order for that to happen, the banking and financial system must not only maintain favorable asset prices and conditions for investment financing now, but they are also expected to do so in the future.

Small Government Economies versus Big Government Economies

An essential feature that links Minsky's theoretical modeling and his evolutionary-institutionalism is his distinction between the 'small government' economy and the 'big government' economy. In the 'small government' model, which captures the essential characteristics of the U.S. economy in the 1920s, aggregate profits of business firms equal investment by business firms. The mark-up on consumption output is equal to the wage bill in investment output. Hence, the profits in consumption output plus the profits in investment output equals investment. In the 'big government' model that captures the essential characteristics of the economy as it has evolved since the 1930s, gross profits equal the sum of investment and the deficit in the government's budget. Large government deficits offset a tendency for the debt-sustaining capacity of business to diminish whenever financial market disturbances induce a decline in consumer and business spending (Minsky 1986a, pp. 13-37).

As we examine Minsky's financial instability hypothesis, the theoretical focus will be on a small government economy. Subsequently, attention will be turned to the institutional evolution of the big government economy that began in the 1930s as a response to the great depression and was greatly expanded during World War II. While large budget deficits and actions by the Federal Reserve have been able to sustain gross business profits and prevent a severe financial panic and debt-deflation, they have introduced a form of financial instability that is biased toward inflation.

The Small Government Model

Minsky explained the debt-deflation process up to the triggering event as an endogenous process. He commented that once the debt-deflation process is triggered, it is easy to describe: 'Irving Fisher did it admirably. But for Fisher and Keynes the initiation of a debt-deflation was basically unexplained' (1982, p. 226). Minsky described the relationship between his financial instability hypothesis and Fisher's 'classic' debt-deflation theory as follows. Fisher did not explain the initial condition of 'over-indebtedness' that results in the debt-deflation processes; Minsky explained it as resulting from the way that financial markets operate (1995, p. 94.) But Minsky actually said relatively little about deflation other than in the prices of capital assets and financial assets. Whereas Fisher spoke of the 'dance of the dollar,' Minsky described the business cycle in terms of a 'dance' between the prices of current output and the prices of capital assets (1986a, p. 143). His attention was largely on the effects of debt-deflation on the levels of aggregate output, profits, employment, and investment in the 'large government' economy in which firms have pricing power.

Integral to Minsky's theory of financial instability are his concepts of business firms as hedge financing units, speculative financing units, or Ponzi financing units. Hedge financing means that the firms and their bankers expect the cash flows from operations to be more than sufficient to cover payment commitments, both in the present and in the future. Hedge financing units do not carry large volumes of debt. They finance their positions in capital assets with internal funds or by issuing new equities. Speculative financing occurs when the firms and their bankers expect that cash flows from operations will be less than cash commitments in the short-run but will be more than sufficient over the long-run. Minsky described this as 'short financing of long positions' (1986a, p. 207). Cash-flows can cover interest payments on debt but will not be sufficient to make payments on the principal. Thus, maturing debts need to be rolled over and it is expected that this can be done. Ponzi financing is similar to speculative financing in that cash payment commitments exceed cash flows. The difference is that cash flows are less than payments of interest on debts, so firms must either borrow more to pay interest as well as to roll over debt, thus increasing total debt, or sell assets that they own.

If the bulk of firms in the economy are hedge-financing, the financial system is robust, and financial stability is achieved. But since both speculative and Ponzi financing units require refinancing, they are vulnerable to adverse developments in financial markets. The financial system is fragile when firms are largely speculative financing and Ponzi financing, making the economy vulnerable to financial crises and debt-deflation.

Minsky summed up his financial instability hypothesis in terms of two postulates (1995, p. 92). The first was that over a period of financial and economic tranquility in which firms are largely hedge financing, changes occur in the financial structure that increase the relative weights of speculative and Ponzi financing. The second was that the increased financial layering and shifting in the structure of payment commitments progressively increase the vulnerability of the financial system to a debt-deflation process that can usher in a deep depression. Earlier, Minsky

(1992) had explained the first theorem of his hypothesis as meaning that 'the economy has financing regimes under which it is stable, and under which it is unstable,' and the second theorem as meaning 'that over periods of prolonged prosperity, the economy transits from financial relations that make for a stable system to financial relations that make for an unstable system.'

In deriving the theoretical aspects of his financial instability hypothesis, Minsky rejected the standard Keynesian model, often called the neo-classical synthesis, which projects full-employment growth. His alternative interpretation of Keynes led 'to propositions that the normal path of a capitalist economy is cyclical; that is, the normal path can be characterized as a succession of system states' (Minsky 1975, p. 131). At times there is tranquility (rather than equilibrium) with general prosperity, but that is transitory. At times there is (assuming no intervening factors) debt-deflation followed by depression, but that also is transitory. The endogenous processes of transition from one state of the economy to another was explained by Minsky's interpretation of Keynes' 1937 *Quarterly Journal of Economics* article in which he responded to Viner's criticism of the general theory. Recognizing that the investment decision drives the aggregate economy, and that decision occurs within the context of capital financial practices, Keynes' main propositions centered on the disequilibrating forces that operate in financial markets. A combination of factors explains why the modern capitalist economy is so subject to fluctuation. Those include intractable uncertainty about the future that gives rise to changes in liquidity preference, debt structures, financing conditions, and stock market valuations of corporations' capital assets. Moreover, evolutionary institutional changes occur in the financial sector through financial innovations that enhance the natural instability (1982, p. 61).

In Minsky's small government model, the level of aggregate demand, which is the sum of consumption by households and investment by business firms, determines the level of employment. The financial instability hypothesis starts with the determinants of each period's effective level of aggregate demand, taking into account how the financial legacy of payment commitments from past financing activities imposes requirements upon the current functioning of the economy and conditions the future behavior of the economy. With a stable consumption function and the financial theory of investment, the financial instability hypothesis leads to an investment theory of the business cycle through endogenous processes. The behavior of the economy depends upon the pace of investment. Investment and financing decisions are made in the face of intractable uncertainty, which implies that views about the future can undergo market changes in short periods of time. In particular, changing views of the future affect the relative prices of various capital assets and financial instruments, as well as the relation between capital asset prices and prices of current output.

The financial attributes of a capitalist economy lead to unstable behavior (1982, p. 62). Money, as the perfectly liquid asset, is held as a defensive portfolio measure against uncertainty. Because of the underlying lack of confidence, events that are not unusual can lead to sharp changes in expectations and liquidity preferences, making present values of future incomes, and market values of assets inherently unstable (1982, pp. 128-129). The valuations of capital assets that determine current investment and the ability to fulfill contractual commitments that determines financing possibilities depend critically upon the levels (actual and expected) of gross profits. In the small government model, those profits are determined by the level of investment spending by firms. Their ability to debt-finance new investment depends upon expectations that future investment spending will be high enough to assure that future cash flows will be large enough to repay or refinance debts that are incurred today. An economy with private debts is especially vulnerable to changes in the pace of investment because both aggregate demand and viability of debt structures are determined by investment. Financial instability follows from the subjective nature of expectations about the future course of investment and the subjective determination by bankers and business firms of the appropriate liability structure for the financing of positions of different types of capital assets. In that way, uncertainty is the major determinant of the path of income and employment (1982, p. 65).

Economic Euphoria: How Stability Leads to Instability

To explain how financial stability during periods of tranquility leads to financial instability and debt-deflation, Minsky started with an economy that has a history of cyclical movements but is currently experiencing high employment and financial stability. The majority of firms are hedge-financing and the financial system is robust. The liability structures, particularly the new liabilities being created, are shaped by high margins of safety as both borrowers' risk and lenders' risk are perceived as relatively high in light of past experiences. But as both firms and bankers become accustomed to stability and prosperity, memories of past events fade and perceptions about the uncertainty of the future undergo change, which affects investment by raising the demand price while lowering the supply price.

The demand price of investment rises for two reasons. First, higher future profits are expected because of a higher expected growth rate and a decrease in expected slack periods, so the present value of those future profits increases at the current discount rate. In Minsky's terms, there is now a scarcity of capital. Second, as firms become more confident about the future they perceive that the borrowers' risk has diminished, which lowers the margin of safety they have required and results in increased amount of debt-financing. The supply price of investment falls because bankers are experiencing the same changes in expectations, perceive less lenders' risk, and perceive that the lenders' risk has diminished. Not only are they now willing to make loans to firms that they previously regarded as too risky, they are also reducing their holdings of safe assets such as Treasury securities.

With the demand price above the supply price, investment increases and the economy moves from a state of tranquility to one that Minsky labeled a state of economic 'euphoria.' When the economy has experienced a high rate of investment for several years, both firms and banks tend to become ruled by expectations of perpetual expansion in the future. In this euphoric new era, an investment boom is combined with a pervasive liquidity-decreasing portfolio transformation to create a highly unstable situation (1982, pp. 121-122). Interest rates rise because the demand for investment is increasing and becoming less elastic with respect to interest rates and contractual terms. In a complex financial system, investment can be financed by portfolio transformations, so that the amount of investment financed can be independent of monetary policy in the short run. The desire by firms to expand by borrowing and the willingness of banks to finance expansion by portfolio changes can become so great that an inflationary explosion becomes likely. The link between financial and real values is shown in the effects on stock market values. The rise in the value of real capital assets that occurs when expectations of recession diminishes is reflected in higher stock prices. The increased ratio of debt financing can also raise expected returns on equities. Portfolio preferences under the new state of expectations shift toward holding stocks, so that a stock market boom both feeds upon and feeds an investment boom (pp. 123-124).

Financial Innovations

In several articles and papers, Minsky (1986b, 1986c, 1990) extended Schumpeter's theory of innovations to the financial sector. Banks and other financial institutions seek the profits available from innovative financial practices and instruments. Minsky recognized that financial innovations have both beneficial and negative effects. They are necessary for the spread of new products and techniques (1986b, p. 347) but they also play an important role in the transformation of a period of tranquility to a euphoric boom. Innovations in financial practices are particularly active when the economy is in a period of expansion. They become important contributors to the transition from tranquility with high employment to a euphoric boom

(Minsky 1982, p. 66). When the demand for financing investment rises because of higher expected future profits based on increasingly optimistic expectations of the future levels of aggregate demand (and memories of past bad experiences have diminishing influence on expectations), lenders seek profits by developing financial products that appear to reduce the lenders' risk of financing high risk positions. A further inducement to new efforts to innovate is provided by the current prosperity seemingly validating past financial innovations.

As profit-seeking financial institutions invent and reinvent 'new' forms of money, substitutes for money in portfolios, and financing techniques for various types of activities, financing of investment becomes easier. Each new financial instrument that is introduced or old one that is used to a greater extent results in the financing of more investment in the form of additional capital and financial assets. That results in higher prices of assets, which, in turn, raises the demand price for current investment and increases the demand for more financing of investment, creating more inducement for financial innovations by lenders.

The financing of investment demand by means of new techniques means the generation of demand in excess of what was being supplied when the economy was at high employment in the tranquil state. The rise in spending for investment leads to an increase in profits, which feeds back and raises the price of capital assets and, thus, the demand price of investment. Thus, any full-employment equilibrium leads to an expansion of debt-financing — weak at first because of the memory of preceding financial difficulties — that moves the economy to expand beyond full employment. Full employment with financial stability is a transitory state because changes in expectations and financial market conditions will lead the economy to an investment boom which leads to inflation and to a financial structure that is conducive to financial crises (1986a, p. 178).

Financial Crises and Debt-Deflations

In the euphoric boom economy, hedge-financing units become speculative-financing units and speculative-financing units become Ponzi-financing units. Such a financial system becomes highly vulnerable to changing conditions in financial markets, which can occur quickly with drastic effects. The financing needs of the investment boom raise interest rates, which has an effect on the stock market by increasing the cost of credit used to finance positions in equities. Initially, the competition for funds among the various financial sectors facilitates the rapid economic expansion, but rising interest rates negatively affect the profits of investing units and increase the costs of carrying equities. The consequent fall in stock prices, combined with the occurrence of local depressions or depressions in particular sectors of the economy, give rise to growing doubts as to whether a 'new era' of prosperity has really emerged, which leads to hedging of portfolios and reconsideration of investment programs. The portfolio commitments created in the euphoric era are fixed in liability structures that must be met out of current cash flows, and those flows are falling as production costs rise due to the short-run aggregate supply curve becoming relatively inelastic at high employment (1982, pp. 122-123).

If the increasingly unfavorable financial positions can be unwound without generating any financial shocks, it becomes easier for the economy to enter another 'new' era. But if euphoric boom ends in a financial crisis, Fisher's debt-deflation process arises out of two situations. In the first, the demand price of capital assets based on the market capitalization of expected future profits remains greater than the supply price, but the borrowers' risk has become so high that investment falls below the level that firms can finance with internal funds. In the second, the demand price of capital assets becomes less than the supply price and investment falls to zero. In that case, all internal funds are used to repay debt as business firms and financial institutions put priority on strengthening their balance sheets (1975, p. 126).

Firms will also be attempting to issue long-term debt to replace short-term debt, which results in long-term interest rates rising while short-term rates are falling. Banks can have the capacity to lend but firms do not want to borrow, nor do the banks want to lend. The economy has now moved into a debt-deflation process that is accompanied by unemployment and depression. The real burden of debt increases and the willingness to finance investment with debt decreases. The velocity of money decreases as speculative capital gains can be realized from holding money as prices fall. The purely financial developments feed back to a reduced level of investment demand, which depresses aggregate demand through the Keynesian multiplier effect.

In the 'small government' economy with competitive labor markets, the situation is made worse by the downward flexibility of wages (1975, pp. 136-142). Because owners of capital goods have reservation prices based on user costs, the employment of capital goods in the production of investment goods will be reserved at some minimum acceptable profit. If there is a surplus of workers in the investment goods sector when that profit has fallen to that level, competitive market forces will lead to falling money wages, which leads to further decreases consumption and, hence, in aggregate demand (ibid.).

AVOIDING DEBT-DEFLATION: THE EVOLUTION OF BIG GOVERNMENT

The foregoing applies to capitalist economies with small government and explains how the 1929 stock market crash was followed by a severe debt-deflation and deep depression. Because capitalism evolves through different forms, the details of the crises and the aftermaths will be different at different historical times. The processes which make for financial instability are an inescapable part of any decentralized capitalist economy, but financial instability does not have to lead to a great depression. Why financial crises have not been followed by debt-deflation since the 1930s was explained by the evolutionary development of big government in the modern capitalist economy.

In Minsky's historical stages of capitalism, 'finance capitalism' replaced 'commercial capitalism' in the early 19th century and reached its peak in the 1920s. 'Finance capitalism' was characterized by financial crises and depressions which effectively undid whatever economic gains many people had achieved during periods of prosperity (1990, p. 67). The 'managerial capitalism' that emerged from the Great Depression and World War II had four distinctive features: (1) a much larger role of government in aggregate demand; (2) a welfare state with substantial income transfers; (3) a financial structure that was initially 'robust;' and (4) broad central bank intervention that prevented collapses in asset values when financial fragility emerged (p. 68). This is Minsky's 'big government' model, in which financial crises can be avoided by fiscal policies providing large budget deficits and by monetary authorities acting as lenders of last resort to prevent financial crises.

Minsky argued that the period of financial and economic tranquility from the mid-1930s until the mid-1960s was the anomalous result of the depression and war finance. A 'robust' financial structure emerged from the war years due to the experiences of the depression and especially to the huge government deficits and direct controls on household and business spending during World War II. During the great economic expansion that occurred from 1941 to 1945, the Reconstruction Finance Corporation had largely replaced commercial and investment banks in providing capital for business investment. All components of the private sector emerged from the war years with a very high degree of liquidity and low debt. Household savings in the form of financial assets increased substantially during the war years while their debts were reduced relative to incomes. Business firms had reduced their debts and became net holders of financial assets. Financial institutions were holding large amounts of government securities and their loans to businesses were relatively small. In the post-war period, the large amount of liquidity did not result in inflationary pressures, in part, because of relatively conservative financial practices stemming from the experiences of the depression and, in part, by monetary and fiscal policy actions that were taken when inflationary pressures seemed to be building. While recessions did occur repeatedly, financial crises and a depression were avoided. During this period, corporations were relatively free of the influence of bankers by relying on internal funds to finance their operations.

But because of the growth of international competition and the sterility of internal corporate bureaucracies, managerial capitalism became increasingly vulnerable to organizational and financial innovations (1990, pp. 68-69). By the mid-1960s, the financial system was again exhibiting the tendency to experience crises, as first revealed with the 'credit crunch' in 1966. While institutional reforms implemented in response to the great depression of the 1930s were largely responsible for the emergence of managerial capitalism, financial innovations by profit-seekers in the financial sector and deregulation legislation were largely responsible for the evolutionary changes that occurred after the 1960s. Minsky asserted that although Schumpeter neglected to develop the financial entrepreneurship aspects of his early theory, his

> vision on the experimenting entrepreneur who innovates need but be extended to financial firms and their clients to explain why portfolios migrate to a brink at which a shortfall of cash flows or a rise in financing terms may lead to a marked revision of asset values and therefore of investment programmes. (1986c, p. 120)

In each of the crises during the post-World War II period, the forces leading to debt-deflation were contained by policy actions, and the financial innovations were validated. Large government deficits sustained both aggregate demand and gross business profits. Special government-sponsored deposit insurance and other 'insurance' funds protected deposits from the failures of savings and loans and large banks. The Federal Reserve actively acted as a lender-of-last resort, expediting increases in liquidity after crises had been contained so that financing terms were improved (1995, p. 87).

An Inflation-Prone Economy

Just as in their later works Veblen and Schumpeter perceived evolutionary changes leading to inflationary rather than deflationary tendencies, Minsky argued that the success of monetary and fiscal policies in preventing a debt-deflation/depression in the post-World War II period had produced an inflation-prone economy. In contrast to Greenspan's perception that rising wages (or the potential for wages to rise) generates inflation, Minsky argued that, in an economy with a complex corporate and government structure, the level of money wages is not what triggers inflation. Rather, inflation is the result of excessive growth in demand for consumer goods stemming from increases in investment, government transfer payments, and consumer debt. In the modern capitalist economy, rising investment or government spending (or both) starts the causal chain that leads to inflation.

Because conventional policies to contain inflation tend to trigger a debt-deflation process, the reluctance to use them allows the inflationary processes to continue. In the 1970s and 1980s, a new development was persistent inflation in times of high unemployment. The stagflation took place as transfer payments increased rapidly, government deficits persisted through business-cycle expansions and increased sharply when unemployment increased, and government wage rates and wage bills increased rapidly. Both business gross profits and consumer prices were sustained and even increased during the recessions of the late 1960s, 1970s, and early 1980s. Government policies that sustained profits enabled businesses and banks to survive the financial traumas of 1966, 1969-1970, 1974-1975, 1979-1982, and 1983-1984. Minsky labeled the result as a 'markup inflation' (1986b, p. 261).

A MINSKIAN MODIFICATION OF FISHER'S DEBT-DEFLATION THEORY

There is a large and growing literature that is expanding and applying Minsky's financial instability hypothesis and his institutionalist analyses to the constantly evolving economy (see, for example, Carter 1989; Isenberg 1988; Mehrling 1999, and Whalen 1999). Kindleberger argued that his historical studies of speculative manias, financial panics, and stock market crashes have generally validated Minsky's model on an international basis and it remains highly relevant to the modern economy (2000, pp. 13-22). Wolfson (1996) demonstrated that relevance by presenting a Minskian modification of Fisher's debt-deflation theory that explains why the modern economy is still prone to debt-deflation processes. Wolfson then used that modified model to explain why the stock market crash of 1987 did not trigger a debt-deflation process such as occurred after the 1929 crash.

Wolfson argued that the bailouts of large banks, the Savings & Loans, and other financial institutions indicate that policymakers have taken Fisher's debt-deflation processes seriously and have moved to prevent those processes from being started. The increased interdependence of the financial institutions and markets makes the system, on an international basis, highly susceptible to a debt-deflation process triggered by a financial crisis, such as the stock market crash of 1987. Minsky's theory and analyses lead to two modifications of Fisher's theory. The first is a recognition that a decline in the rate of inflation has the same effect as a fall in the absolute level of prices in creating cash-flow pressures to meet payment commitments on debt. Since a reduction in the inflation rate was more likely in an economy that had experienced persistence inflation over several decades, that was an important modification. The second is Minsky's recognition that the effects of rising interest rates leading to sales of financial assets (stocks) have effects that are very similar to Fisher's analysis of frustrated efforts to liquidate debts by distress selling.

Wolfson identified several Minskian factors that explain why the stock market crash of October 1987, the largest single-day crash in history, was not followed by a debt-deflation process. In Minsky's analyses, falling stock prices generally lead to a decline in income, which decreases the ability to meet payments on debts. Consumption spending falls because incomes fall, and investment falls because the demand price of capital goods fall as stock prices fall. But, in 1987, a decrease in aggregate demand and pressures to meet payment commitments on debts did not happen because the Federal Reserve acted as a lender of last resort and a large government sector buoyed the level of aggregate demand. Wolfson also noted that the timing of the crash from a business cycle perspective was important. Whereas the 1929 crash came after the economy had gone into recession, the 1987 crash occurred while the economy was in an expansion phase.

8. Deflation Theories and Recent Deflation Concerns

In this final chapter, we present a comparative summation of the common elements and the differences that appeared in the deflation theories of Veblen, Schumpeter, Fisher, and Minsky. The differences in the theories can be placed into two categories. Some reflect the evolutionary changes in the institutional structures of the economy over a period in excess of a century. In *The Theory of Business Enterprise*, Veblen was observing the U.S. economy as it had developed in the closing decades of the 19th century, an era which large corporations and large financial institutions began to dominate and public policies played a minimal role. The gold standard prevailed and there was no Federal Reserve to provide central banking functions. In contrast, Minsky was observing the post-World War II economy into the last decade of the 20th century. Large corporations and financial institutions continued to be the dominant feature of the private sector but the public sector played a much larger role. Aggregate demand was being supported with large government expenditures and was being managed, to some extent, with monetary and fiscal policies. The federal government and the Federal Reserve were actively responding to crises in the financial sector by implementing new policies of assistance. While Fisher's debt-deflation theory was primarily an attempt to explain how the roaring economy of the 1920s could so quickly fall into a deep depression in the early 1930s, Schumpeter observed the same period as Veblen and as Fisher but continued his observations and analyses through the end of 1949.

To a large extent, the historical differences in the structures of the economy were effectively taken into account in Minsky's 'small government' and 'large government' models and in his distinction between competitive market situations in which firms lack pricing power and modern market situations in which firms have pricing power. But the differences in the second category are those that are due to different methodologies and different normative perspectives. In that regard, Veblen and Schumpeter stand as the two extreme cases. Although both dealt with deflation within the frameworks of their evolutionary analyses of the development of modern capitalism in which technological innovations are driving forces, there were deep fundamental differences in their analytical and normative views on the role of business values and institutions. Fisher and Minsky seem to fall somewhere between those two extremes. While Fisher was close to Schumpeter by way of being a somewhat unorthodox mainstream economist, he did not utilize an evolutionary economics approach. But as both Schumpeter and Minsky noted, Fisher's debt-deflation theory of depressions was a descriptive account of the effects on real debt burdens and real interest rates when deflation occurs rather than a genuine theory of the causes of deflation. While Minsky acknowledged a methodological relationship to Schumpeter, his approach and analyses are also suggestive of some aspects of Veblen's earlier work.

When the historical differences are taken into account, the remaining differences in the four theories tend to be more complementary than contradictory. Collectively, they are instrumental in explaining how a modern complex economy can simultaneously experience deflationary and inflationary tendencies of shifting magnitudes. We close out the chapter, and the book, by reflecting on the insights the four theories, individually and collectively, provide into the recent concerns about deflationary forces and the rather sudden evaporation of those concerns.

COMPARATIVE SUMMATION OF THE DEFLATION THEORIES

In considering the common elements and differences in the four theories, we focus on the following: the relationship between debt and prices; which sets of prices and what kinds of debts received the most attention; the contributory roles of technological and financial innovations; the extent to which market power of large corporations is taken into consideration; the 'starters' of periods of debt-funded prosperity that end in financial crises; the socio-economic consequences of deflation; the institutions and policies that counter deflationary forces; and the consequences of containing deflationary forces.

Debt and Deflation

Certain general similarities in the four theories are easily observed. Perhaps the most obvious is general agreement on Fisher's depiction of what transpires when a debt-funded prosperity ends in a financial crisis in the type of economy that existed before the institutional reforms of the 1930s. Within that context, both Schumpeter and Minsky explicitly accepted Fisher's description of the debt-deflation phenomena. While Fisher ignored Veblen's earlier work, the descriptive part of his debt-deflation theory of depressions is very similar to the account of speculative prosperities ending in financial crisis and deflation in *The Theory of Business Enterprise*. In all four theories, debt increases as prices rise during periods of prosperity and, at some point, increases in debt become the driving force that keeps prices rising to unsustainable levels. When the prosperity ends in a financial crisis, all four theories agree that debt becomes a key factor in the severity and length of the ensuing deflation and economic contraction.

There are also easily observed differences. One of those is that while debt-deflation necessarily follows a period of speculative prosperity funded by debt in all four theories, Veblen's theory is unique in that a debt-deflation does not have to be preceded by a speculative prosperity, although that is the usual case. As long as nominal interest rates are above zero and existing firms are carrying debt, chronic deflation/depression can ensue from a period of stability when new firms implement cost-reducing technological innovations. That draws attention to differences in the four theories relating to equilibrium, cycles, and trends, and whether prosperity is endogenously or exogenously initiated.

Working within the general framework of neo-classical economics, Fisher envisioned a relatively unstable equilibrium as being the 'normal' situation. In his theory, there is no endogenous process inherent to the capitalist system that produces periodic episodes of over-indebtedness, nor is evolutionary change integral to his debt-deflation theory of great depressions. At the same time, Schumpeter noted that Fisher's list of 'starters' of periods of prosperity was very compatible with his theory of innovations.

In Minsky's theory, the modern capitalist system is inherently prone to financial instability. There is no true equilibrium and certainly not a full-employment equilibrium to which the real economy and the financial sector gravitate. Rather, financial stability is a transitory phase that becomes transformed through endogenous processes into a euphoric boom with a tremendous increase in debt that ends in a financial crisis, which is followed by another type of financial crises — debt-deflation — and eventually by the same endogenous processes to another transitory period of financial stability. Minsky's theory is evolutionary in the sense that each episode of debt-deflation is unique due to structural changes resulting from financial innovations in the private sector and institutional reforms and policies that were implemented by government as reactions to the last financial crisis. But, in each case, the same inherent processes are at work, giving rise to the same general tendencies, with only the details of events determined by the institutional settings. While Minsky explicitly aligned himself with Schumpeter's theory of innovation, he focused on the role of financial innovations in the transformation from financial stability to euphoria. An endogenous process of technological innovation-driven economic development and change is not an integral factor in Minsky's theory, as it is in both Veblen's and Schumpeter's theories.

While an endogenous process of change driven by technological innovations played an integral role in both Veblen's and Schumpeter's theories, the paths and role of debt were different. In Veblen's theory of capital, debt was an inherent feature of modern business enterprise as every businessman attempts to leverage his capital with the maximum amount of debt. There was no 'normal' equilibrium, except in the mental habits of businessmen to expect that profits are supposed to be high enough to cover debt service costs and assure 'normal' rates of return on funded investments. The combination of funded debt, the expectation of 'normal' returns on investment, the cost-reducing effects of new industrial technology, and competitive pricing results in a secular trend toward chronic deflation and depression. Persistent expansion in the industrial capacity occurs even during the depressions because new firms that do not have the accumulated debts of existing firms can invest in the new industrial technologies and produce profitably at the lower prices. The only relief from the chronic deflationary forces was the temporary prosperity engendered by exogenous increases in sectoral demand. Curiously, Veblen did not recognize that a period of prosperity could be generated by new investments that implement new technologies. Prosperity was due to exogenous factors, primarily government expenditures for war.

In contrast, prosperity in Schumpeter's theory is endogenously generated by debt-financed technological innovations implemented by businessmen — entrepreneurs — that results in both a complete business cycle and long-run economic development and structural change. Deflation is a functional part of the cyclical process in the normal recession and a conspicuous but non-functional feature of the abnormal depression. All phases of the business cycle are transitory, but the long-run trend line in economic development is upward. Theoretically, Schumpeter's recession phase is not equivalent to depression or even to significant levels of unemployment. The depression phase is abnormal to the business cycle proper and is due to the excesses of debt and speculation in the secondary wave of the prosperity. While the economy recovers at some point from depression, Schumpeter also asserted that there is a long-run deflationary trend which is beneficial to both society and the efficient functioning of capitalism that is based on output prices falling as technological innovations result in lower production costs and expansions in supplies.

Types of Debt

In all four theories, business debt receives prominent attention. To a large degree, that reflects the theoretical focus on business investment as the primary link between the financial sector and the performance of the overall economy. To a lesser degree, the primacy of business debt in the earlier three theories reflects the historical structures of the economy. Veblen focused his attention almost exclusively on debt of incorporated firms whose shares were listed on stock exchanges because he was presenting a theory of large corporate business enterprise that had recently evolved (and was still evolving) at the beginning of the 20th century. While he cited conspicuous consumption as a rather ineffective counter to the deflationary conditions, even *Absentee Ownership* was written before the emerging importance of consumer installment debt in the latter half of the 1920s. At two junctures in *The Theory of Business Enterprise*, Veblen briefly mentioned public debt. In discussing the 'wasteful' expenditures that temporarily induce prosperity, he observed that government expenditures are more stimulative if financed by debt rather than by taxes. Government securities 'serve as attractive investment securities for private savings, at the same time that, taken in the aggregate, the savings so invested are purely fictitious savings and therefore do not act to lower profits or prices' (1904, p. 256). But on a much more somber note, when discussing the trends toward increased preparation for war having the short-run effect of stimulating business profits, Veblen warned that the protracted pursuit of war leads to a dynastic state in which business becomes subservient to the state in a way that may end in 'ultimate exhaustion or collapse through the bankruptcy of the state' (1904, p. 300).

While Fisher included debt of all types in rather general statements, his debt-deflation theory clearly focused on business debt. But, in his institutional analyses of the 1920s and the depression of the early 1930s, Fisher noted that the rising stock market led corporations to substitute stocks for debt. While he gave some attention to public debt and consumer debt in the 1920s, Fisher focused primarily on debt that financed speculation in the stock market. While Veblen also related business debt to stock prices (which clearly became speculative), his primary interest was in the higher valuations of firms as going concerns being used as collateral for business loans for the purpose of bidding for more capital goods.

Schumpeter was perhaps the broadest in his coverage of debt in the phenomena of the primary and secondary waves of the prosperity phase of a business cycle. In the primary wave, business debt is necessary for entrepreneurs to implement their innovations. Bankers act responsibly in extending credit only to those entrepreneurs whose projects have real possibilities of being profitable. But in the secondary wave, debt of all types greatly increases, much of which finances highly speculative business ventures and financial activities as bankers irresponsibly engage in 'reckless finance.' In his historical analyses of the 1920s, Schumpeter included consumer debt, mortgage debt, and debt that financed stock market speculation as the 'unproductive' debt that contributed to the ensuing depression. He attributed much of the 'overindebtedness' problem to the increase in mortgage debt under an 'easy money' policy in the late 1920s.

Minsky frequently referred to debt of all types in his general discussions of the structures of liabilities and assets of the various sectors of the economy and the cash-flow commitments involved. But in his theoretical analyses of the relationship between debt and prices, the focus was primarily on business debts. Although he recognized that consumer debt became an increasingly major economic force from the 1950s onward, Minsky gave relatively little attention to it in his theoretical discussions. On the other hand, the role of government debt in the 'large government' economy was a countering factor to deflation but also a contributor in inflation.

'Productive' versus 'Unproductive' Debt

While Fisher spoke of 'overindebtedness,' he admitted that there was no criterion for determining when that point was reached. In criticizing Fisher for failing to adequately define 'overindebtedness,' Schumpeter revised Fisher's terms 'productive' and 'unproductive' debt to give them economic meaning. Debt was 'productive' if used to finance any activity that increased productivity. The most important debt-financed activities were the entrepreneurial ventures that implemented successful technological and organizational innovations. Any debt used to finance activities that did not increase productivity was 'unproductive' debt. Since Veblen assumed that all economic resources, particularly capital goods, were already being put to the most efficient use (in the business sense of efficiency) when businessmen incur debt in seeking strategic advantages, all debt would be classified as 'unproductive.' On that point, however, Veblen's theory was somewhat incomplete. He seemed to imply that during a speculative prosperity, the increase in debt does finance some increase in capital goods, although the main effect is simply to bid up prices of capital goods. Yet, in both *The Theory of Business Enterprise* and *Absentee Ownership*, he explicitly stated that significant investment in new capital goods occurs during depressions, but he did not explain how that investment is financed. Any acquisition of new capital goods financed by credit would imply a 'productive' use of debt since the new industrial equipment would increase technical production efficiency as well as the business concept of cost efficiency.

Which Sets of Prices?

The relative amounts of attention that was given to the several sets of prices also involve differences as well as similarities. Within the framework of his theory of capital as the capitalized value of expected profits, Veblen focused heavily on stock prices, debt, and prices of capital goods during periods of prosperity and on debt payments as fixed costs affecting returns on investment when output prices were falling. But in the deflation/depression periods, Veblen's focus was technological progress in the capital goods industries lowering the prices of new capital goods and subsequently lowering prices of output in general, as long as prices were competitively forced to equality with costs of production.

During the transitory periods of prosperity, rising prices of capital goods due to demand increasing under conditions of a relatively constant supply of those goods led to higher costs of production, which led to rising prices of consumer goods. The failure of money wages to rise as rapidly as prices of output resulted in inadequate increases in consumption spending and, hence, in an inability for the level of effective aggregate demand to support the inflated values of the corporate stocks that served as collateral for the business debts. In addition, money wages eventually do rise during prosperity, which erodes the inflated profits. To a very substantial degree, periods of deflation in Veblen's theory are initially characterized by falling prices of corporate stocks, as the stock market perceives that actual business profits are falling short of the expected levels. In response to the decreasing collateral value of business assets, bankers begin to call in loans, which results in distress selling as indebted firms seek liquidity. But the chronic deflation/depression trend is driven by falling prices of newly produced capital goods, which allows new firms investing in new capital equipment to profitably produce and sell consumer goods at the deflated price levels.

Both Fisher and Minsky put emphasis on the rising prices of financial assets, particularly stock prices, during periods of prosperity. But in relating prices of financial assets and prices of capital goods to inflation and deflation, Minsky was quite close to Veblen. The essential difference was that Veblen dealt with the supply price of new capital goods based on the cost of production as determined by the state of industrial technologies, while Minsky worked with the Keynesian financial concepts of demand price and supply price of capital assets. He emphasized the role of Keynesian uncertainty in the determination of both prices, particularly the demand price.

Schumpeter's theory is more inclusive than the other three with respect to prices. The initial inflation occurs in wages of labor needed by entrepreneurs and in prices of goods being demanded by the entrepreneurs to launch their new ventures. But as the secondary wave of prosperity emerges, there is a general sweep of rising prices in all categories — capital goods, consumer goods, and financial assets — as spending in all categories is financed by easy credit conditions. The deflation in a Schumpeterian business cycle starts with a reduction of demand for labor and supplies by entrepreneurs when their ventures become operational, followed by reductions in product prices that occur for two fundamental reasons. One is that many of the entrepreneurs have implemented cost-reducing technologies; the other is that waves of imitators essentially change the monopolistic positions gained by entrepreneurs into more competitive supply situations. Additional contributors to the general trend of falling prices are the distress selling by indebted speculators (both those who launched speculative business ventures and financial speculators) and the depressing effects of the bankruptcies of firms in industries that become obsolete in the structural transformations that are the natural consequence of successful entrepreneurial ventures.

The Role and Types of Innovations

A very important difference that separates Fisher from Veblen, Schumpeter, and Minsky is the integral role of evolutionary changes in the economy in their theories. While Fisher discussed a number of institutional and technological developments that occurred in the 1920s in applying his debt-deflation theory to the stock market crash of 1929 and the depression of the early 1930s, innovations were not integral to his theory. Minsky's analyses were generally institutionalist-evolutionary, especially in relation to the development of 'big government' and a more actively functioning central bank. The transition from the 'small government' economy to the modern 'big government' economy was largely the product of the institutional reforms in the 1930s and the wartime economy of the 1940s. Minsky recognized that policies of deregulation and globalization have been eroding the institutional protection against deflation since 1980. Innovations in his analyses were largely in the form of new financial institutions, products/instruments, and practices. These played significant roles both in changing a period of financial stability into one of financial instability and making each successive period more prone to instability as those innovations were validated by the avoidance of a debt-deflation, which encourages more innovations in 'creative finance' (Minsky 1995, p. 93).

In their complex evolutionary theories, Veblen and Schumpeter explained deflation as integrally related to both technological progress through innovations and institutional changes. They explained inflation in relation to changes in the institutional system arising from evolutionary developments and government policies. In Veblen's 1923 analysis, organizational developments in business, supported by governmental actions (particularly the creation of the Federal Reserve), changed the natural tendency of the business enterprise system toward chronic deflation and depression to a tendency toward credit-inflation. But, in combination with the institutional factors of heavy reliance on debt and the businessmen's institutionalized expectation of 'normal' returns on investment, the prime factor responsible for protracted deflation and depression in Veblen's theory was the continuous introduction of cost-reducing industrial technology in the capital goods producing sectors.

From the beginning of prosperity to the ending in the normal recession or the abnormal depression, Schumpeter's business cycle was driven by technological and organizational innovations. The impact was not only in the cyclical levels of economic activities but in major structural changes in the economy as new products and production techniques rendered obsolete certain industries and techniques. Minsky asserted that Schumpeter also recognized financial innovations as starters of prosperity. While Leathers and Raines (2004) concluded that prosperity could be initiated by the financial developments in Schumpeter's theory, what happens in the secondary wave of prosperity, in which 'reckless finance' rules, is certainly compatible with Minsky's own theory.

Market Power of Large Corporations

A common element in all four theories is the recognition that when markets are competitive, firms have no pricing power and prices will be fall as costs of production fall. But Veblen, Schumpeter and Minsky recognized the ability of large corporations to create price rigidities on the down side. In *Absentee Ownership*, Veblen argued that the collusive control over the operating corporations in the 'key' industries had made effective one of the remedies to deflation that was identified in *The Theory of Business Enterprise*. Output and employment were reduced to keep prices from falling. In *Capitalism, Socialism, and Democracy*, Schumpeter argued that large corporations had effectively internalized the processes of technological innovation through research and development centers and turned the implementation of those innovations into a continuously routine process. In some respects, the large bureaucratic corporations with market power were the private sector counterpart of the 'big government' economy, as was explained in Galbraith's classic book *The New Industrial State* (see Cramer and Leathers 1988). But Schumpeter argued that price rigidity was not only beneficial to support business profits, but it could only exist in the short run because of dynamic competition from new innovations. In Minsky's theory of output pricing, large firms with market power adjust output to keep prices stable, much in the manner of Veblen's corporations in *Absentee Ownership*. The result is that output prices are largely insulated from deflationary trends. Instead, deflationary pressures affect the level of output, employment, and stock prices. Because of the symbiotic relationships between the large corporations and large government as explained by Galbraith, deflation in the classic sense is highly unlikely to emerge.

The 'Starters' of Debt-Funded Prosperities

While all four theories explain the build-up of debt and the rise of prices as being inevitable features of prosperities, there are differences with respect to whether prosperity is started by exogenous developments or by endogenous processes. While deflation and chronic depression result from endogenous processes in Veblen's theory, prosperity is initiated only by exogenous factors. While one possibility was an increase in the money supply through an increase in the supply of gold, the most likely initiator in the modern business enterprise system was a temporary increase in demand in some sector of the economy, most probably from government spending for military actions. But once the process was started, endogenous factors involving business psychology and institutionalized business behavior took over to drive the prosperity into a speculative boom that ended in financial crisis.

For Schumpeter and Minsky, prosperity is initiated and promulgated through endogenous processes, but in different ways. In Schumpeter's theory, the prosperity begins when entrepreneurs are supplied with new money by banks, which they use to buy the labor and material inputs needed to implement their technological or organizational innovations. In Minsky's theory, the endogenous processes start in the financial sector with reductions in the perceptions of borrowers' risk and lenders' risk, which increases the demand price of investment goods and lowers the supply price. Prosperity is initiated by the resulting increase in debt-funded investment spending which, in the Keynesian framework, has a multiplier effect on total spending and income.

Fisher offered no real explanation of the processes involved, choosing to merely cite a number of factors that initiated prosperity and the expansion of debt in the 1920s. Schumpeter, however, noted that Fisher's list of 'debt-starters' was compatible with his theory of entrepreneurial activities as the starters. It also seems clear that Veblen's increase in sectoral demand from government spending could be one of Fisher's 'starters.'

The Consequences of Deflation

While Veblen claimed that he was expressing no normative values, deflation in his analyses has a negative social impact on the level of employment and real incomes of consumers because of the values and behavior of businessmen. Leaving aside the related Veblenian issue of vendible outputs versus serviceable goods and concentrating only on the macroeconomic aspects, social welfare would be increased if prices were based on the lowest possible costs of production achievable at high levels of output. Veblen made that particularly clear in *Absentee Ownership*, where he noted that high employment of labor would occur because unit costs are inversely a function of output levels under modern scales of industrial production. Continuous technological progress resulted in increases in productivity which lowered costs of production; hence, prices would trend downward over time if they were based on unit costs of production. But, because of debt, businessmen's money illusion, and their expectations of 'normal' rates of return on investment, businessmen reduce output and employment when prices fall and the inability to service debts as revenues fall leads to bankruptcies and, thus, more deflation and unemployment.

Even more than Veblen, Fisher emphasized the consequences of falling prices on real debt burdens and real interest rates turning in a deep depression. A downward spiral unfolds with attempts to reduce nominal debt loads leading to more deflation, which increases real debt burdens, which further depress the business profits situation, which leads to more attempts to reduce nominal debt loans by distress selling of assets and outputs.

While Schumpeter accepted Fisher's account of falling prices raising real debt burdens and real interest rate consequences, he was much more sanguine about the consequences of deflation on social welfare. The deflation of a normal recession and the long-term deflation trend are the ways by which the benefits of capitalist development are spread to the working classes. But deflation in the abnormal depressions that are due to the excessive build-up of debt during the secondary wave of prosperity have the types of negative impacts noted by both Veblen and Fisher and, in Schumpeter's analyses, are both unnecessary and preventable. Minsky accepted Fisher's account of debt-deflation but, since the economy had not experienced a debt-deflation/depression since the 1930s, his attention was more on explaining why weakening aggregate demand in the post-World War II era had resulted in unemployment without deflation.

The Remedies

In some form or other, the two major remedies to deflation that Veblen identified in 1904 — government expenditures and collusive retardation of industrial production by quasi-monopolistic corporations — emerged in fuller form in later time. The possibility of government loans that Veblen briefly mentioned had been used successfully in 1902 would later take the form of the Federal Reserve discount window and open-market operations in the banking sector, the Reconstruction Finance Corporation in the 1930s and during World War II, and a number of special government credit programs in agriculture and housing. In 1923, Veblen thought that collusive retardation of production in key industries, in conjunction with private credit-creation supported by the Federal Reserve, had achieved a degree of permanence. The stock market crash of 1929 and the financial crises that followed showed that was definitely not the case. But the post-World War

II economy, especially in the 1950s and 1960s, was highly suggestive of the situation perceived by Veblen in 1923.

In 1933, the National Industrial Recovery Act (NIRA) attempted to accomplish prices increases through government-sponsored collusive action in the form industry-wide price codes. Fisher opposed the NIRA but one of his 'substantive cures' of debt-deflation was the relaxation of anti-trust laws on the grounds that the result would be lower production costs (achieved by business combinations), thus, raising business profits. Veblen would argue, of course, that the result would be increased power to retard production and raise prices. Schumpeter's take on the NIRA was more ambivalent. He argued that it did have at least the temporary effect of dealing with weak spots within industries, stopping downward spirals in many places, and mending disorganized markets in which demand was inelastic and 'overproduction' had occurred. Moreover, the psychological effects were an important factor at that time. But he also stated that the NIRA was declared unconstitutional at just the right time.

For Fisher and Minsky, monetary policy played a major role in countering the deflationary forces. Fisher wrote the *Econometrica* version of his debt-deflation theory just as the U.S. was leaving the gold standard and before the Federal Reserve Act of 1935 gave the Federal Reserve the set of powers that it exercised in the post-World War II era. But he recommended those powers as well as several others, such as bank deposit insurance. Minsky went beyond just the role of the central bank as a lender of last resort to include institutional reforms to recognize that financial crises may involve solvency problems for banks as well as liquidity problems. An important aspect of Minsky's analysis was that the Federal Reserve was designed to resolve transitory problems of illiquidity, leaving a need for a public institution to make equity infusions into financial institutions suffering negative net worth.

From Minsky comes the ultimate importance of fiscal policy being used routinely for the management of aggregate demand rather than the episodic war expenditures recognized by Veblen. Minsky's theoretical explanation of profits as the sum of investment and the deficit in the federal budget was overly simplified but it points to the need to have fiscal policies that both support confidence in the economic future and aggregate demand in the present. Confidence is necessary to keep business investment forthcoming and aggregate demand helps to maintain profits when investment is weakening.

Schumpeter offered a different perspective in endorsing temporary fiscal policies during a deep depression but opposing fiscal policies on a continuing basis. Deflation was a natural and functional part of the business cycle, and policy attempts to contain the cyclical downturns were only reducing the ability of capitalism to function. What needed to be avoided were the episodes of 'reckless finance' responsible for the unproductive debt build-up in the secondary wave of prosperity that is responsible for normal recessions to turn into abnormal depressions. Banking and financial reforms in the 1930s gained his approval. But he believed that the role of public policy should largely be to provide unemployment compensation to alleviate the economic distress on workers until the next cluster of innovations starts another period of prosperity. Schumpeter could justify credit extension to firms that deserved credit but were being denied it by overly-cautious bankers, who had contributed to the speculative excesses and unproductive debt by being overly easy in their earlier lending standards.

Consequences of the Remedies

In their later works, both Veblen and Schumpeter saw inflation as replacing deflation in the evolutionary development of the economy. In Veblen's 1923 analysis, conditions supporting sustained credit-inflation had been established by collusive control over both financial institutions and the large corporations in the key industries. That control by the investment bankers allowed a continuous expansion in credit/debt and retardation of production to create inflation but government support for that collusive management of credit was provided by the Federal Reserve and the irrationality of the mass of voters assured that government policies of low taxation, trade protection, and limited regulation would support the interests of the large businessmen and financiers. Yet, what Veblen had to say about the increased government spending for armaments in 1904 may have particular relevance to the modern period. Those expenditures increased business profits in the short run but Veblen warned of the economic, financial, and political consequences.

For Schumpeter, the consequence of fiscal policies and labor policies that began in the 1930s was persistent inflation in the post-World War II period. The irrational masses in popular democracies, such as the U.S. and Britain, responded positively to politicians who promised government policies that would limit the power of large corporations, protect the interests of labor, and provide public programs (paid for by taxing the rich and successful and by deficit financing) when seeking their votes for political office. The result was inflation caused by excessive aggregate demand and reduced aggregate supply as the policies reduced the efficiency of the capitalist economic engine.

Minsky's 'large government' model, combined with his recognition of the pricing-power of large corporations, explains that the monetary and fiscal policies that prevent debt-deflations result in an inflationary bias that progressively increases the degree of financial fragility. The false interpretations of reduced borrowers' risk and lenders' risk and the financial innovations that encouraged and facilitate the unsustainable build-up of debt during periods of economic euphoria become validated when monetary and fiscal policies prevent the crisis. The result is that the unstable liability and asset structures are not eliminated but instead remain and are expanded in the next euphoric period. The unstable financial structure continues to require support from more expansionary monetary and fiscal policies to prevent an even larger crisis from occurring.

INSIGHTS INTO RECENT CONCERNS ABOUT DEFLATION

Individually and collectively, the four theories provide a number of insights into the recent concerns about deflationary pressures. Perhaps the most fundamental one is that the developments in 2002-2003 can be explained as a predictable phase in a Schumpeterian business cycle. In his public statements during the late 1990s, Greenspan repeatedly described the 'new economy' in terms of Schumpeter's concept of the 'creative destruction' being wrought by successful innovations, but he never appeared to recognize the full implications of Schumpeter's theory of business cycles. As Leathers and Raines (2004) pointed out, the 'new economy' followed the general contours of a complete Schumpeterian business cycle. In the early 1990s, capital investments (which implemented innovations in information technologies and telecommunications) initiated a primary wave growth spurt. By the late 1990s, a secondary wave of general prosperity was in full swing, with the characteristic features of 'reckless' finance and speculative excesses much in evidence. In 2001-2002, the recession phase was well under way, with the characteristic phenomena of deflation from excess capacity in markets most impacted by the innovations in information technology, plunging stock prices, an excessive tightening of credit by banks, the bankruptcies of a host of 'new economy' corporations, and revelations of financial fraud and manipulations.

Within the general context of the Schumpeterian business cycle, the theories of Veblen and Minsky provide additional insights into several aspects of the analysis of the potential deflation as presented in Greenspan's December 2002 speech acknowledging the Federal Reserve's concern about deflation. Two of those insights were revealed in his statement that 'it seems ironic that a monetary policy that is successful in inducing *stability* may inadvertently be sowing the seeds of instability associated with *asset bubbles*' (2002f, emphasis added). A third was revealed in his admission that deflation in the 'medium run' was unrelated to exogenous changes in the money supply.

Minsky's financial instability hypothesis explains both why and how a situation of financial stability and high employment becomes transformed into economic euphoria, and subsequently to debt-deflation, by the lowering of perceptions of both borrowers' and lenders' risks. That is complemented by Veblen's theory, which explains how a debt-deflation process can develop from a position of stability and low interest rates due to cost-reducing industrial technologies being implemented. Both Minsky's and Veblen's analyses become amplified when the situation is one in which price stability occurs during the prosperity phase of a Schumpeterian cycle driven initially by the implementation of technological innovations. In both theories, as well as in Schumpeter's, the increase in the money supply occurs as an endogenous process, as credit is created by banks to finance business investment spending.

The role of 'reckless finance' and speculative excesses in Schumpeter's secondary wave of prosperity and the attention that both Veblen and Minsky gave to stock prices during both prosperity and deflation have great relevance. In a limited fashion, Greenspan touched upon that in his comment that low inflation and economic stability are most likely to provide tinder for stock market price speculation when new companies are being form to implement technological innovations and in his concern that falling stock prices could precipitate deflation. His concern about the bursting of a stock market bubble as the greatest risk of triggering a deflation draws analytical support from Minsky's explanation of the connection between changes in expectations and liquidity preferences, changes in stock prices, changes in the demand price of capital assets, changes in investment, and contraction in the economy. That also draws support from Veblen's explanation of the false basis for the higher expected future profits that were capitalized in rising stock prices and what happens to stock prices when the stock market perceives that actual profits are going to be lower.

Although there were recognitions by Greenspan and Bernanke that deflation changes real debt burdens, their analyses were seriously flawed by not regarding debt as a contributing factor. In keeping with Minsky's emphasis on the importance of financial innovations accelerating the transformation from financial stability to instability, a new form of debt was involved in the rapid growth of various types of new financial derivatives. While Greenspan consistently defended the unrelated use of derivatives, he acknowledged that many of these instruments are 'complex' and not 'transparent,' and noted that the market 'is still too new to have been tested in a widespread down-cycle for credit' (Greenspan, 2002e). It is clear, however, that the booming stock market and overall euphoric financial sector in the 1990s was assisted by the rapid and large growth of financial derivatives.

Greenspan's admission that consumer and home mortgage debt was critical to the avoidance of a deeper recession and deflation is perfectly consistent with Minsky's explanation as to how deflation has been avoided in the post-World War II economy, as well as with Veblen's analysis of how managed increases in debt in 1923 was keeping deflation 'partial' rather than chronic. The ability of households to increase consumer installment debt to record highs and mortgage debt to generate a boom in the housing market is also consistent with Minsky's theory, which warns that institutional reforms and policy actions that prevent deflation tend to increase the financial fragility of the economy. Consumer debt can continue to rise as long as consumers can gain credit. In the new institutional environment, large financial institutions have been willing to extend that credit because they are confident that the Federal Reserve System, the Fed's power of moral suasion and the federal government will act somehow to prevent a financial collapse. The Federal Reserve's 1998 action to save Long Term Capital Management from a $4.6 billion loss is a case in point. Reducing interest rates in early 2008 to cushion the stock market from the fall out of the sub-prime lending debacle is further evidence of the new institutional environment. The layering of financial institutions made possible by financial innovations has been credited by Greenspan with creating a system in which risk allocation has allowed a great expansion in credit with a high degree of safety but, from a Minskian perspective, the stability of that system ultimately rests on expectations that the Federal Reserve and the federal government will provide the necessary supports when it trembles.

An important insight is provided by Veblen's and Minsky's theories pointing to the difference between deflation possibilities in competitive economies and economies in which large corporations have pricing power. The absence of deflationary tendencies in the U.S. economy before the 1980s was because firms in the key industries possessed considerable pricing power, as Galbraith frequently observed. As long as fiscal and monetary policies were sufficiently expansionary, the oligopolistic firms produced at relatively close to full employment levels with only moderate rates of inflation but, when monetary and fiscal policies became more restrictive, those firms reduced output and employment while keeping the prices constant or rising. Since the 1980s, globalization has increasingly reintroduced competition in a number of key markets, such that lower costs of production and weakening aggregate demand results potentially in deflation of output prices. In a curious development, globalization has recreated a situation in which the private sector exhibits more of the characteristics of what Veblen dealt with in *The Theory of Business Enterprise* and of Minsky's 'small government' model, which makes the role of 'large government' much more important if financial instability and debt-deflation are to be avoided.

Within that context, the role of cost-reducing technological innovations in producing downward trends in prices in Veblen's and Schumpeter's theories becomes very relevant. In those sectors of the economy in which investment was implementing new information technologies, competition would force prices lower as costs of production fell. Particularly relevant is Veblen's focus on the role of technological progress reducing the production costs of capital goods. One of Greenspan's biggest concerns was the downward trend in the production costs of computers and associated equipment, including software. In August 2002, he noted that the capacity in high-tech manufacturing was increasing much faster than demand, so that the high real rates of return on high-tech stock could not be sustained, and that 'similar, though less severe, adjustments were occurring in many other industries' (2002c).

From the perspective of Minsky's 'big government' model, one of the curious aspects of Greenspan's statements about deflation in 2002-2003 was failure to consider the elimination of federal budget deficits in the late 1990s as a contributor to deflation. In Minsky's 'big government' model, a deficit supports business profits while a surplus has a negative effect. Greenspan never directly connected budget deficits with deflation, stating only that 'the conventional wisdom is that reducing budget deficits restrains economic growth for a time' was correct, and that reductions in national defense expenditures had 'cast a shadow over particular industries and regions of the country' (2003c).

Minsky's observation that monetary and fiscal policies had prevented debt-deflation in the post-World War II period easily explains why deflation concerns disappeared in the spring of 2004. Those remedies are, of course, consistent with Veblen's recognition of the need for fiscal policies to support aggregate demand. But Minsky, and in a somewhat different way also Schumpeter, warned that the policies that enable the economy to avoid deflation create conditions for future inflation. That is particularly relevant in two areas of the financial sector that we have already mentioned — a huge increase in mortgage debt through long-term low fixed-rate mortgages and the continued unregulated growth of financial derivatives. Institutions and funds holding the fixed-rate mortgages will suffer portfolio value losses when interest rates rise back to 'normal' levels, which will require more government bailouts to avoid something similar to the S&L crisis of the 1980s. While Greenspan has expressed great confidence in the safety of the financial derivatives, many others are less sanguine.

The evolutionary institutional changes in the economy which help to explain why the deflationary tendencies brought on by cost-reducing technological innovations in competitive markets in Veblen's and Schumpeter's theories also provide some insights into how serious the threat of general deflation really was in 2002-2003. When Veblen and Schumpeter were writing, the structure of the economy was heavily industrial. Falling prices that were due to cost-reducing innovations in industrial technology would thus have very substantial effects on prices in general. But the modern economy has become much more service-oriented. While information technology has certainly had a major impact in service industries, the effect on prices has been much less. Indeed, in the health care field, the results of new technology have been to increase prices. This suggests that the real economy today is structurally much less prone to general deflation tendencies even as the tendencies for financial instability have increased. Weak aggregate demand will result in reduced output and increased unemployment, not in falling prices. Similarly, increases in aggregate supply if not supported by increases in aggregate demand will result in output below the full capacity level and persistent unemployment.

We also observe that developments in 2002-2003 that gave rise to expressions of concern about deflation from monetary policymakers can be explained by Schumpeter's observations about deflation concerns in 1948, especially when those observations are taken in the context of the 'new economy's' complete business cycles. When certain prices fall, as in the case of those in industries most impacted by the heavy investments in new information technologies in the late 1990s, they can have misleading effects on cost of living indices. That is almost the reverse of Greenspan's and Bernanke's concern that the conventional indices were overstating the rate of inflation and, hence, understating the rate of deflation, but the effects are the same. More importantly, the perception that prices in general are falling or about to fall can give rise to false impressions that inflation is over. In Schumpeter's theory, such price declines attended by unemployment occur in every inflationary process, which appears to be validated by the return, in 2004, to concerns about inflation rather than deflation.

As a final observation, Veblen's evolutionary analyses suggest that while globalization has reintroduced competitive market conditions, to some extent, in a number of markets, such that output prices are forced to follow cost reductions, the long-run trend would be for large international corporations to eventually transform world markets into oligopolistic structures similar to those in the U.S. economy in the 1950s and 1960s. That would mean an erosion of any tendencies toward deflation, essentially recreating an international situation suggestive of Veblen's 'credit-inflation' in 1923. In that context, Schumpeter's argument that wage policies were a major factor in the inflationary pressures of the late 1940s now has very different implications. With labor's bargaining power rapidly eroding, inflation cannot be blamed on rising wage costs, which reinforces Minsky's argument on that score. With nominal wages lagging behind labor productivity, the new inflation will be of the type perceived by Veblen in 1923 — prices may actually remain relatively stable but are increasingly above falling costs of output. Weak labor incomes will be insufficient to support aggregate demand, requiring more monetary and fiscal policy action to avoid serious recessions, thus further increasing the financial fragility of the economy.

Bibliography

Allen, R. L. (1993), *Irving Fisher*, Oxford: Blackwell.

Bernanke, B. S. (2002), 'Deflation: Making Sure "It" Doesn't Happen Here,' Washington, D.C.: Federal Reserve Board, 21 November.

Bernanke, B. S. (2003a), 'Balance Sheets and the Recovery,' Washington, D.C.: Federal Reserve Board, 21 February.

Bernanke, B. S. (2003b), 'An Unwelcome Fall in Inflation?' Washington, D.C.: Federal Reserve Board, 23 July.

Boulding, K. E. (1948), 'Price Control in a Subsequent Deflation,' *Review of Economics and Statistics*, February, 15-17.

Brockie, M. D. (1958), 'The Cycle Theories of Veblen and Keynes Today,' in D. F. Dowd (ed.), *Thorstein Veblen: A Critical Appraisal*, Ithaca: Cornell University of Press, pp. 113 –128.

Carter, M. J. (1989), 'Financial Innovation and Financial Fragility,' *Journal of Economic Issues*, September, 779-793.

Cramer, D. and C. G. Leathers (1977), 'Veblen and Schumpeter on Imperialism,' *History of Political Economy*, Summer, 237-255.

Cramer, D. and C. G. Leathers (1981), 'Schumpeter's Corporatist Views: Links Among His Social Theory, *Quadragesimo Anno*, and Moral Reform,' *History of Political Economy*, Winter, 745-771.

Cramer, D. and C. G. Leathers (1988), 'Schumpeter and Galbraith: A Comparative Analysis On the Modern Corporate Economy,' *History of Economics Society Bulletin*, Spring, 47-56.

Degen, R. A. (1987), *The American Monetary System*, Lexington, MA: Lexington Books.

Delong, J. B. (1999), 'Should We Fear Deflation?' *Brookings Papers on Economic Activities*, (1), 225-241.

Dimand, R. W. (1994), 'Irving Fisher's Debt-Deflation Theory of Great Depressions,' *Review of Social Economy*, Spring, 92-107.

Dimand, R. W. (1998), 'Fisher and Veblen: Two Paths for American Economics,' *Journal of the History of Economic Thought*, December, 449-465.

Dimand, R. W. (2004), 'Echoes of Veblen's *Theory of Business Enterprise* in the Later Development of Macroeconomics: Fisher's Debt-Deflation Theory of Great Depressions and the Financial Instability of Minsky and Tobin,' *International Review of Sociology*, 14(3), 461-470.

Dirlam, J. B. (1958), 'The Place of Corporation Finance in Veblen's Economics,' in D. F. Dowd (ed.), *Thorstein Veblen: A Critical Reappraisal*, Ithaca: Cornell University Press, pp. 199-220.

Economist, The (1997), 'Deflation and all that,' 13 November, pp. 77-78.

Economist, The (1998), 'Singing the deflationary blues,' 8 October, pp. 77-78.

Economist, The (1999), 'Could it happen again?' 18 February, pp. 19-22.

Economist, The (2001), 'The new bogey,' 15 November, p. 68.

Economist, The (2002), 'Comparing symptoms,' 7 November, pp. 75-76.

Edwards, G. W. (1938), *The Evolution of Finance Capitalism*, London: Longmans, Green.

Estey, J. A. (1956), *Business Cycles*, Englewood Cliffs, N.J.: Prentice-Hall.

Federal Open Market Committee (2003a), 'Minutes of March 18 Meeting,' Washington, D.C.: Federal Reserve Board, 18 March.

Federal Open Market Committee (2003b), 'Minutes of May 6 Meeting,' Washington, D.C.: Federal Reserve Board, 6 May.

Federal Open Market Committee (2003c), 'Press Release,' Washington, D.C.: Federal Reserve Board, 6 May.

Federal Open Market Committee (2003d), 'Press Release,' Washington, D.C.: Federal Reserve Board, 9 December.

Federal Open Market Committee (2004), 'Press Release,' Washington, D.C.: Federal Reserve Board, 4 May.

Fisher, I. (1909), 'Capital and Interest,' *Political Science Quarterly*, September, 504-516.

Fisher, I. (1922) 'The Business Cycle Largely a "Dance of the Dollar",' *Journal of the American Statistical Association*, December, 1024-1028.

Fisher, I. (1925), 'Our Unstable Dollar and the So-Called Business Cycle,' *Journal of the American Statistical Association*, June, 179-202.

Fisher, I. (1930), *The Stock Market Crash — And After*, New York: MacMillan.

Fisher, I. (1933a), *Booms and Depressions*, London: George Allen and Unwin.

Fisher, I. (1933b), 'The Debt-Deflation Theory of Great Depressions,' *Econometrica*, October, 337-357.

Fisher, I. (1963), *The Purchasing Power of Money*, New York: Augustus M. Kelley (original work published 1911).

Fite, G. C. and J. E. Reese (1965), *An Economic History of the United States, 2nd edn*, Boston: Houghton-Mifflin.

Friedman, M. (1956), 'The Quantity Theory of Money — A Restatement,' in M. Friedman (ed.), *Studies in the Quantity Theory of Money*, Chicago: University of Chicago Press, pp. 3-24.

Galbraith, J. K. (1987), 'The 1929 Parallel,' *Atlantic Monthly*, January, 62-66.

Galbraith, J. K. (1988), *The Great Crash 1929*, Boston: Houghton Mifflin.

Galbraith, J. K. (1994), *A Journal Through Economic Time*, Boston: Houghton Mifflin Company.

Gongloff, M. (2004), 'Greenspan: Deflation Dead,' (online) accessed April 20, 2004 at http://money.cnn.com/2004/04/20.

Greenspan, A. (1997), 'Bias in the Consumer Price Index,' Washington, D.C.: Federal Reserve Board, 4 March.

Greenspan, A. (1998a), 'Problems of Price Measurement,' Washington, D.C.: Federal Reserve Board, 3 January.

Greenspan, A. (1998b), 'Is There A New Economy?' Washington, D.C.: Federal Reserve Board, 4 September.

Greenspan, A. (1999), 'New Challenges for Monetary Policy,' Washington, D.C.: Federal Reserve Board, 27 August.

Greenspan, A. (2002a), 'The State of the Economy,' Washington, D.C.: Federal Reserve Board, 29 January.

Greenspan, A. (2002b), 'Federal Reserve Board's Semiannual Monetary Policy Report to Congress,' Washington, D.C.: Federal Reserve Board, 16 July.

Greenspan, A. (2002c), 'Economic Volatility,' Washington, D.C.: Federal Reserve Board, 30 August.

Greenspan, A. (2002d), 'The Economic Outlook,' Washington, D.C.: Federal Reserve Board, 13 November.

Greenspan, A. (2002e), 'International Financial Risk Management,' Washington, D.C.: Federal Reserve Board, 19 November.

Greenspan, A. (2002f), 'Issues for Monetary Policy,' Washington, D.C.: Federal Reserve Board, 19 December.

Greenspan, A. (2003a), 'Federal Reserve Board's Semiannual Monetary Policy Report to Congress,' Washington, D.C.: Federal Reserve Board, 11 February.

Greenspan, A. (2003b), 'Follow-up to the Federal Reserve Board's Semiannual Monetary Policy Report to Congress,' Washington, D.C.: Federal Reserve Board, 30 April.

Greenspan, A. (2003c), 'Economic Outlook,' Washington, D.C.: Federal Reserve Board, 21 May.

Greenspan, A. (2003d), 'Federal Reserve Board's Semiannual Monetary Policy Report to Congress,' Washington, D.C.: Federal Reserve Board, 15 July.

Greenspan, A. (2003e), 'Remarks,' Washington, D.C.: Federal Reserve Board, 6 November.

Greenspan, A. (2004a), 'Risk and Uncertainty in Monetary Policy,' Washington, D.C.: Federal Reserve Board, 3 January.

Greenspan, A. (2004b), 'Testimony of Chairman Alan Greenspan Before the Joint Economic Committee, U.S. Senate,' Washington, D.C.: Federal Reserve Board, 21 April.

Greenspan, A. (2004c), 'Follow-up to the Federal Reserve Board's Semiannual Monetary Policy Report to Congress,' Washington, D.C.: Federal Reserve Board, 30 April.

Hawtrey, R. G. (1927), 'The Monetary Theory of the Trade Cycle and Its Statistical Test,' *Quarterly Journal of Economics*, May, 471-486.

Hegeland, H. (1969), *The Quantity Theory of Money*, New York: Augustus M. Kelley.

Humphrey, T. M. (2004), 'Classical Deflation Theory,' Federal Reserve of Richmond *Economic Quarterly*, Winter, 11-32.

Isenberg, D. L. (1988), 'Is There a Case for Minsky's Financial Fragility Hypothesis in the 1920s?' *Journal of Economic Issues*, December, 1045-1069.

Kelso, P. R. and B. L. Duman (1992), 'A Veblenian View of Minsky's Financial Crisis Theory,' *International Journal of Social Economics*, 19(10/11/12), 222-234.

Keynes, J. M. (1937), 'The General Theory of Employment,' *Quarterly Journal of Economics*, February, 209-223.

Keynes, J. M. (1961), *The General Theory of Employment, Interest, and Money*, London: Macmillan (original work published 1936).

Kindleberger, C. P. (2000), *Manias, Panics, and Crashes, 4th edn*, New York: John Wiley and Sons.

Kumar, M. O., T. Baig, J. Decressin, C. Faulkner-Mac-Donagh, and T. Feyziogulu (2003), *Deflation: Determinants, Risks, and Policy Options*, Washington, D.C.: International Monetary Fund.

Laidler, D. (1991), *The Golden Age of the Quantity Theory*, Princeton: Princeton University Press.

Leathers, C. and J. P. Raines (2004), 'The Schumpeterian Role of Financial Innovations in the New Economy's Business Cycle,' *Cambridge Journal of Economics*, September, 667-681.

Malkiel, B. G. (1999), *A Random Walk Down Wall Street*, New York: W. W. Norton.

Mandel, M. J. and P. Engardio (1997), 'The Threat of Deflation,' *Business Week*, 11 November, pp. 54-59.

Mehrling, P. (1999), 'The Vision of Hyman P. Minsky,' *Journal of Economic Behavior & Organization*, June, 129-158.

Mill, J. S. (1961), *Principles of Political Economy*, New York: Augustus M. Kelley.

Miller, R. (2003). 'Greenspan Is Keeping His Scissors Sharp,' *BusinessWeek/Online*, www.businessweek.com, 4 June.

Minsky, H. (1975), *John Maynard Keynes*, New York: Columbia University Press.

Minsky, H. (1982), *Can 'It' Happen Again?* Armonk, New York: M. E. Sharpe, Inc.

Minsky, H. (1986a), *Stabilizing an Unstable Economy*, New Haven: Yale University Press.

Minsky, H. (1986b), 'The Evolution of Financial Institutions and the Performance of the Economy,' *Journal of Economic Issues*, June, 345-354.

Minsky, H. (1986c), 'Money and Crisis in Schumpeter and Keynes,' in H. J. Wagener and J. W. Drukker (eds), *The Economic Law of Motion in Modern Society*, Cambridge: Cambridge University Press, pp. 112-122.

Minsky, H. (1990), 'Schumpeter: Finance and Evolution,' in A. Heertje and M. Perlman (eds), *Evolving Technology and Market Structure*, Ann Arbor: University of Michigan Press, pp. 51-74.

Minsky, H. (1992), 'E-mail on Debt-Deflation,' (online) accessed (23 Oct. 2004) at http://csf.colorado.edu/pkt/pktauthors/Minsky.Hyman/debt-deflation, 23 October.

Minsky, H. (1995), 'Longer Waves in Financial Relations in the More Severe Depressions II,' *Journal of Economic Issues*, March, 83-95.

Minsky, H. (1996), 'Uncertainty and the Institutional Structure of Capitalist Economies,' *Journal of Economic Issues*, June, 357-368.

Papadimitriou, D. B. and L. R. Wray (1998), 'The Economic Contributions of Hyman Minsky: Varieties of Capitalism and Institutional Reform,' *Review of Political Economy*, April, 199-225.

Papadimitriou, D. B., A. M. Shaikh, C. H. Dos Santos, and G. Zezza (2002), 'Is Personal Debt Sustainable?' Annandale-on-Hudson, N.Y.: The Levy Economics Institute.

Raines, J. P. and C. G. Leathers (2000), *Economists and the Stock Market*, Cheltenham, UK and Northampton, MA, USA: Edward Elgar.

Rist, C. (1966), *History of Monetary and Credit Theory*, New York: Augustus Kelley (original work published 1938).

Schumpeter, J. A. (1934), *The Theory of Economic Development*, Oxford: Oxford University Press (original work published 1912).

Schumpeter, J. A. (1939), *Business Cycles*, New York: McGraw Hill.

Schumpeter, J. A. (1948a), 'Irving Fisher's Econometrics,' *Econometrica*, July, 219-231.

Schumpeter, J. A. (1948b), 'There is Still Time to Stop Inflation,' *Nation's Business,* June, 33-39.

Schumpeter, J.A. (1950), *Capitalism, Socialism, and Democracy*, 3rd edn, New York: Harper (original work published 1942).

Schumpeter, J. A. (1951), *Essays*, Cambridge, MA: Addison-Wesley Press.

Schumpeter, J. A. (1954), *History of Economic Analysis*, New York: Oxford University Press.

Smith, A. (1976), *The Wealth of Nations*, Indianapolis: Liberty Press (original work published 1776).

Stolper, W. (1994), *Joseph Alois Schumpeter*, Princeton, N.J., Princeton University Press.

Taus, E. R. (1943), *Central Banking Functions of the U.S. Treasury*, New York: Columbia University Press.

Veblen, T. (1904), *The Theory of Business Enterprise*, New York: Viking.

Veblen, T. (1908), 'Fisher's Capital and Income,' *Political Science Quarterly*, March, 112-128.

Veblen, T. (1919), *The Vested Interests and the Common Man*, New York: B.W. Huebsch.

Veblen, T. (1921), *The Engineers and the Price System*, New York: Viking Press.

Veblen, T. (1923), *Absentee Ownership*, New York: Viking Press.

Whalen, C. J. (1999), *Hyman Minsky's Theory of Capitalist Development*, Annandale-on-Hudson, NY: The Levy Economics Institute.

Williams, R. M. (1994), *The Politics of Boom and Bust in Twentieth-Century America*, Minneapolis/St. Paul: West Publishing Company.

Wolfson, M. H. (1996), 'Irving Fisher's Debt-Deflation Theory: Its Relevance to Current Conditions,' *Cambridge Journal of Economics*, May, 315-334.

Wray, L. R. and D. B. Papadimitriou (2003), *Understanding Deflation*, Annandale-on-Hudson, N.Y.: The Levy Economics Institute.

Index